The Windham papers : the life and correspondence of William Windham, 1750-1810, a member of Pitt's first cabinet and the ministry of "all the talents", including hitherto unpublished letters from George III, the dukes of York and Gloucester, Pitt, Fox, Bu

William Windham

THE WINDHAM PAPERS

THE LIFE AND CORRESPONDENCE OF THE
RT. HON. WILLIAM WINDHAM 1750-1810
A MEMBER OF PITT'S FIRST CABINET AND
THE MINISTRY OF "ALL THE TALENTS"
INCLUDING HITHERTO UNPUBLISHED
LETTERS FROM GEORGE III THE DUKES
OF YORK AND GLOUCESTER PITT FOX
BURKE CANNING LORDS GRENVILLE MINTO
CASTLEREAGH AND NELSON MALONE
COBBETT DR. JOHNSON DR. BURNEY ETC.

WITH

AN INTRODUCTION BY THE RT. HON.

THE EARL OF ROSEBERY

K.G. K.T.

IN TWO VOLUMES
VOLUME ONE

❀ HERBERT JENKINS LIMITED ❀
ARUNDEL PLACE HAYMARKET LONDON SW
MCMXIII

THE BALLANTYNE PRESS TAVISTOCK STREET COVENT GARDEN LONDON

INTRODUCTION

BY THE RT. HON.
THE EARL OF ROSEBERY, K.G., K.T.

WILLIAM WINDHAM was the finest English gentleman of his or perhaps of all time. Had he lived in the great days of Elizabeth, he would have been one of the heroes of her reign ; indeed he almost seemed out of place in the times of George III. As a country gentleman no doubt he was not the equal of his friend and neighbour Coke, whom genius and fortune made the greatest of benefactors to agriculture ; but Coke as a politician was narrow and fanatical. And with devotion to rural life and manly sport Windham combined much more. He was a statesman, an orator, a mathematician, a scholar, and the most fascinating talker of his day. He was brilliant in that galaxy which comprised Johnson and Burke, Pitt, Fox, and Sheridan, though their memory will survive his. For, by the irony of events, he is now best remembered as the successful advocate of bull-baiting. So that it is worth while to revive his real character and repute.

As a statesman he was proud of his independence, a rare and intrepid quality in political life. It was indeed reproached against him that he was so enamoured with this virtue that he sought out occasions of being on the unpopular side. This, indeed, if it were true of him, is not likely to be a contagious quality. It could only exist so far as parliamentary life is concerned in the House of Lords or in close boroughs, and Windham was at last driven to this last refuge. He was more than once invited to join the House of Lords, but he greatly preferred Higham Ferrers or St. Mawes.

This aloofness, mainly due to the paramount influence of Burke, is shown by the fact that Windham in domestic politics could be found arrayed with both the great political parties. He was the enthusiastic advocate of Roman Catholic emancipation, and the unflinching opponent of parliamentary reform. He had a foot therefore firmly planted in each of the two camps. He was, however, in reality by temperament a Tory. No disciple of Burke could be other than a supporter of Catholic emancipation. But where Windham was left to himself his attitude to politics was strongly conservative. He was not indeed often left to himself. For it is strange to find of a man who piqued himself on independence that no one was so susceptible to personal influence. It is this circumstance which gives a strange and fickle appearance to his political career. He was called by turns a Foxite, a Pittite, a Grenvillite, and a Greyite, but was always and supremely a Burkite. Burke influenced many minds, but none so much as Windham's. It was his essential fidelity to the creed of Burke which made him apparently variable. No man indeed under an appearance of change was so truly faithful to his principles and himself. But as Burke was charged with inconsistency, so, as a necessary consequence, was Windham. He seemed to wish always to know what Burke thought or would have thought on any subject, and when he knew, to feel no doubt or misgiving. In the great agony of the Whig party, when every Whig felt the anguish of a separation from Fox, Windham hesitated for a moment. He was under the charm of Fox, whose tastes he shared ; but as soon as the voice of the master was heard, clear and imperative, Windham came to his side, without further question or doubt.

When the storm of the French Revolution broke, it swept all minor issues away ; you were either a " Jacobin " or an " anti-Jacobin " ; you either thought that good might come out of the convulsion while deploring its excesses ; or you saw in it the root of all evil, you descried its poison in all sorts of unexpected forms and developments, and you proclaimed that the Revolution was the monster to be destroyed at all costs. The reader indeed becomes a little weary of the monotonous denunciation of " Jacobinism " and " Jacobins " in the speeches of Windham and the writings of Burke.

No consideration of means or proportion weighed with either for one moment. The dragon must be utterly exterminated, even should it devour all the available St. Georges in the process. Then and then only should we have done our duty. Then and then only would the world know peace.

This violence of conviction kept Windham both uncompromising and independent. Though he joined Pitt he regarded Pitt as little less than a necessary evil, as a minister who had parliamentary power and so was able to carry on the war with France, but who fell sadly short of grace. They were only colleagues in a war, as to the methods and objects of which they fundamentally differed.

To Pitt the war was a disagreeable necessity forced on him by circumstance, but from which he hoped that circumstance would relieve him and his country. To Windham it was a high and holy crusade to be carried on to extermination. The object with him was to replace on the throne of France the sacred race of Bourbon. Pitt cared less than nothing for the Bourbons, his object was the preservation of his country, and of some sort of balance of power. Windham looked on him therefore as a Peter the Hermit may have looked on a soldier of fortune. When Pitt retired Windham felt relief, he was no longer linked to an uncongenial colleague, and was free to pummel the luckless Addington and Addington's peace.

He thundered against this truce with the evil one, but some years afterwards acknowledged his error manfully enough to Addington. For he saw in 1809, what Pitt had seen in 1801, that a pause was necessary to recruit the exhausted energies of Great Britain. When Pitt returned to office, Windham thundered against Pitt; Pitt was inadequate, all that he did was insufficient. But Windham had yet to give a further and final proof of independence. For, when Pitt died, he joined Grenville's cabinet, and when that ministry came to an end in the ensuing year, was fierce against Grenville and on the brink of an individual resignation.

All these changes, though they were nominal and not real, put him in the bad books of both political parties. He obtained the nickname of the " Weather-cock " ; the virulent and pedantic Parr called him the " Apostate." But the independent man in politics must accustom himself to harder knocks than nicknames. Windham was indeed the most consistent of politicians. He was neither Whig nor Tory, but always an anti-Jacobin, and always, as has been already said, a Burkite.

His oratory must have been remarkable ; though his voice was ineffective. But he had presence and charm. He was not indeed handsome, yet his deportment was manly and dignified. "A tall, thin, meagre, sallow, black-

eyed, penetrating, keen-looking figure." We have
three volumes of his speeches, but reporting
in those days does not seem vivid or exact, and
latterly Windham rushing, as his way was, to
join an unpopular cause, quarrelled with the press,
and henceforth went unreported. But he revised
and published several of his orations from which
a fair idea of his powers may be obtained. One
of these, that in which as Secretary for War he
developed his military proposals in 1806, was
pronounced by Fox to be one of the most eloquent
ever delivered. Fox's nephew, Lord Holland,
who did not like Windham, gave him the highest
praise as an orator. In fancy and imagery, in
taste and above all in delivery, says Holland, he
was far superior to the great god of his idolatry
Mr. Burke. In variety of illustration, in acuteness
of logic, he scarcely yielded to Fox. In felicity of
language he approached Pitt. In true wit and
ingenuity he more than rivalled Sheridan. Testimony of this kind from a man who had heard
Windham is worth a ton of criticism from the
student who can only read him. What a reader
would say of his recorded efforts is that they are
characterised by closely-knit and even philosophical
argument, couched in the lofty style of those days.
But their distinctive charm was originality,
a felicitous agility and unexpectedness of mind,
a raciness of expression and sudden bursts of
pleasantry which probably drew to him fully as

great a House as even Pitt or Fox could command.
Of his quaint humour the best sustained example
is the speech on the Repeal of the Additional
Force Act in May 1806; its fun is still brisk
and vivid. His most famous flash of fun was
on the intention to take Antwerp by a *coup
de main.* "Good God, Sir, talk of a *coup de
main* with forty thousand men and thirty-
three sail of the line! Gentlemen might as
well talk of a *coup de main* in the Court of
Chancery." This drollery convulsed the House,
and made, it is said, that grave and illustrious
judge, Sir William Grant, roll from his seat with
laughter. So happy a jest survives superior
arguments on forgotten bills. Another sally, still
more memorable, was that with which he slew a
Reform Bill, as with a smooth stone from the
brook. "No one," he said, "would select the
hurricane season in which to begin repairing his
house"; a happy metaphor containing sound
political truth. There is no doubt that Windham
at his death was the finest speaker in parliament; ⟨S⟩
the other giants had gone; Sheridan was extinct, ⟨P⟩
and Canning had not reached his full development.

What is most remarkable is the rapidity with
which he reached a high parliamentary position.
He delivered his maiden speech in the House of
Commons in February 1785, and in 1787 he was
considered of sufficient weight to be entrusted
with one of the charges, and nominated one of the

managers of the impeachment of Warren Hastings. Nine years after his first speech he was admitted to the Cabinet, a far greater and more limited distinction then than now, besides being in virtue of a minor office which had never before been associated with Cabinet rank. He was, moreover, the only Cabinet Minister in the Commons with Pitt and Dundas. So rapid a rise is seldom recorded, and proves a command of parliament by eloquence and character such as few men of his standing can have achieved.

As a minister there is less to be said. He was always connected with the War Office, a territory which it is perilous for a civilian even in narrative to tread. It must be admitted that the few pebbles which he left on the shore of military history scarcely constitute a memorial cairn. But it must be remembered that during the first seven years of his administration he was not the Secretary of State, but a nominally subordinate minister, though with all the influence of Cabinet office; and that he was only Secretary of State for a year. Still it was notorious that, though ardent and vigorous, he was a bad man of business. In his first office he was responsible for the disaster of Quiberon, which represented his personal policy of carrying on the war by supporting the French Royalists on the soil of France. During his second short tenure he countenanced the amazing scheme of despatching an inadequate army for vague purposes of conquest in South America, when we needed every man and every musket in Europe to grapple with Napoleon. This is no captivating record. On the other hand it stands to his credit that he shortened the term of service in spite of the formidable resistance of George III. To the volunteers he was stoutly opposed, though he had a private but eccentric corps at Felbrigg in which he was the only officer. But few and rare are the British ministers of War who have earned distinction, for the conditions of their office render success hardly possible. The nation which furnishes superb military material is absorbed in the primary interest of the fleet, and though it passively votes vast sums for its army never gives that active interest and support which strengthens the arm of the minister. The one great exception is Chatham. But Chatham, like Napoleon, wielded the whole strength of the Empire, political, financial, naval and military, and was backed by the confident enthusiasm of his country.

The real reputation of Windham, apart from his oratory, lay in the charm of his conversation. In that vanished realm he was a prince. Testimony on the point is unanimous. It is safe to say that no one has recorded a meeting with Windham who is not a witness to his fascination. Miss Burney gives a lively account of her talks with him during the Hastings trial which enables us to realise in a measure how it was that he won, if not all hearts, at least sympathetic admiration. His expression was various and vivid. He was earnest, playful, and eloquent. He had the faculty, which is perhaps the most attractive of all, of appearing to give his very best to the person with whom he was conversing. Talk may be recorded, but its spell cannot. And so, though we rejoice in Miss Burney's record, we feel that we must rely on tradition, which, in so controversial a matter, must be held, when unanimous, to be an authority beyond dispute. The supreme judgment, from which there is no appeal, is that of Johnson. Windham had been elected to the famous Club when he was a country gentleman of twenty-eight, a sufficient tribute to his precocious repute. But in 1784, when the great man was near his end, Windham went far out of his way to spend a day and a half with him at Ashbourne. "Such conversation," writes the dying sage, "I shall not have again till I come back to the regions of literature ; and there Windham is *inter stellas Luna minores.*" Such a testimony from such a man is almost unique, but it is in truth confirmed by every witness.

Conversational fascination is apt to be a snare, and we are bound to hazard an opinion that Windham was a flirt. And yet there was no character that he condemned so strongly. Before going up in a balloon he addressed a testamentary

letter to Cholmondeley, his closest friend, re-
monstrating strongly on Cholmondeley's conduct
to a certain Miss Cecilia Forrest.　Cholmondeley,
he declared, had ruined the girl's life, by inspiring
her with a fatal affection of which he was unworthy.　Thirteen years afterwards, with singular
secrecy, Windham married the lady himself.　He
was then forty-eight and she past forty.　And he
completed this unusual transaction by making
Cholmondeley one of his reversionary heirs.　This
is Windham all over.　And we also learn that he
had fallen, perhaps unconsciously, into the same
error with which he had reproached his friend.
He had engaged the affections of a daughter of
Sir Philip Francis, and a lady endeavouring to
console the unhappy girl told her that Windham
had long hesitated between Miss Forrest and a
devoted widow.　In this one letter, therefore, we
are confronted with three ladies whose hearts were
captured by Windham.　He had, moreover, come
under the magic charm of Mrs. Crewe.　To Mrs.
Crewe, and Mrs. Crewe alone, he confided the
secret of his marriage, and he records his agitation at meeting her immediately after the event.
But perhaps the most authentic basis for conviction
as regards Windham's attraction for the other sex
is Lady Minto's remark on his resignation in 1801:
"I suppose he will return to his old line of
gallantry."　There let us leave the matter.　It is
worthy of observation as an essential part of a

whimsical character. We may be sure that Windham's flirtations were unconscious, honourable, and innocent.

Unhappily, he was fated to be something of a suicide, for he dealt an almost mortal blow to his own reputation. For we cannot doubt that it would have stood much higher but for his Diary. And yet he himself set store by it, as if, one would think, he regarded it as a sure base for his future fame. He left the fourteen quarto volumes of which it was composed as an heirloom to pass with the entailed estates, and yet any judicious friend would have put it without hesitation behind the fire. Extracts of this strange record were published by Mrs. Baring in 1866, after the estates and entail had all disappeared in the hands of a hapless and irresponsible spendthrift. As so much has been afforded, it is regrettable that more should not be given. Lord Holland and Charles Greville intimate that parts could not be made public. But it seems clear that we have not all the decorous portions of the fourteen quarto volumes, and these we should possess to complete a veracious and candid, though damaging, auto-biography.

In the Diary, which is almost valueless as a record of historical fact from the extreme vagueness of date and expression, we have an exact, though painful, picture of Windham's character, and an explanation of why it was that he did not achieve more in public life. It is full of vacillation on the smallest points of conduct, full of morbid self-reproach on every subject, and in a minor degree disfigured by a lavish use of the distressing substantive "feel," almost if not quite peculiar to himself. Windham, indeed, though in public life he held firmly to his main convictions, in private life and in smaller matters was singularly variable. On the all-important question of marriage, as we have seen, he seems to have hesitated long. That may have been wise, but he records endless agitations about a ride, a walk, or a speech. Conscientious diaries are apt to make men morbid, and this one is certainly an instance in point. He seemed to worry himself with his pen. One passage indeed redeems the whole book: it is the pathetic description of his last interview with Dr. Johnson. That is classic. But it is counterbalanced by a denunciation of a literary 'gem of purest ray serene,' the delightful "Vicar of Wakefield." We may surmise that this outburst may have been elicited by Windham's having heard it excessively praised, which would certainly drive him into extravagant reaction. Countless are the caprices of these strange journals. It had been better for his fame had this heirloom disappeared with the others.

Still, with all deductions, he remains a noble figure. The influence of Johnson and Burke, grafted on to the stock of a fine and cultivated nature, could not but produce goodly fruit. His prime quality was independence, at once the choicest and the least serviceable of all qualities in political life. He was on the other hand excessive, like his great master, Burke; excessive in enthusiasm, excessive in resentment. To him, for example, when a manager of the great impeachment, Warren Hastings was the vilest of criminals. But to him also, though their relations were not always easy, Burke was among the gods. There was in truth a want of balance in this rare character, which marred its great qualities. It was this, from a fanciful fear of deterioration in the British character, that made him preach bull-baiting. It was this which made him deem it necessary, in the midst of the national grief for Pitt, to stand up and oppose the funeral honours proposed; a course which brought him many enemies and which seemed in execrable taste. But the mere fact of isolation was the same temptation to him that the company of an over-whelming majority is to meaner minds. His argument, weak enough at best, for "'tis not in mortals to command success," was that Pitt's policy had not triumphed, and that distinctions denied to Burke should not be given to failure. Most men who felt the same would at that tragic moment have held their peace. But such a decent compliance seemed cowardice to Windham; so he wound his melancholy horn. This same irritable conscience made him an uncomfortable colleague, and it is noteworthy to observe how strenuously the idea of relegating him to the House of Lords was pressed by Grenville, as it had occurred to Pitt. It was strange, as Windham himself remarked, that Grenville should be so anxious to move the best speaker that his ministry possessed in the House of Commons out of that chamber into the House of Lords. Promotion for another Grenville was no doubt the urgent cause, but, as that could be managed, and was managed in other ways, there were probably reasons connected with Windham himself. Independence in a public man is, we think, a quality as splendid as it is rare. But it is apt to produce and develop acute angles. Now a colleague with angles is a superfluous discomfort. And independence in a great orator on the Treasury bench is a rocket of which one cannot predict the course.

His independence then, admirable in itself, was a conspicuous bar to his success in politics. He was not indeed formed by nature for a politician in a country where party rules the roast. We will go a step further, and hazard the opinion that his heart was never really in politics at all. He loved mathematics, he loved the classics, he loved reading, he loved country life; but for parliament he had no natural propensity. From his first contact with politics in Ireland he instinctively shrank. His self-conscious, self-tormenting nature was indeed wholly unsuited for public life. But he loved oratory. From the moment when he found that he wielded that rare power over his fellow men he delighted in exercising it. And he was imbued with one burning enthusiasm, the crusade against Jacobinism. He conceived himself to be the bearer of the sacred torch handed to him by Burke. This was his single purpose; oratory and the French Revolution kept him in political life. Fox said cynically that Windham owed his fame to having been much frightened. But those who were apprehensive in that dark period were wiser than those children of light who, like Fox, were content to watch the Revolution with blind and heedless favour.

Such then was Windham. A noble gentleman in the highest sense of the word, full of light, intellect, and dignity, loved and lamented. His best qualities, no doubt, as is often the case, he carried almost to excess; for his cherished independence led to a morbid craving for isolation. But to the charge of vacillation in public affairs he was not obnoxious; he was always true to his faith. He was indeed vitally influenced by two men. But he chose his masters well, Johnson and Burke; the one gave him his religious, the other his political creed. In life he was brilliant and successful. In oratory, in parliament, in society, he was almost supreme. But he can scarcely be said to survive. He left no stamp, no school, no work. To those, however, who care to disinter his memory he displays character and qualities of excellence, rare at all times, rarest in these.

ROSEBERY

OPINIONS OF CONTEMPORARIES

" The first gentleman of his age, the ingenuous, the chivalrous, the high-souled Windham."—*Macaulay*.

" He is just as he should be ! If I were Windham this minute, I should not wish to be thinner, nor fatter, nor taller, nor shorter, nor any way, nor in any thing, altered."—*Edmund Burke*.

" Poor Mr Windham is, I fear, dying He will be a sad loss to society : I never knew a man so felt for as he is."—*Lady Sarah Spencer*, in a letter dated, May 31, 1810. " Correspondence of Sarah Spencer, Lady Lyttelton," p. 107.

" Mr. Windham was there, whose conversation I could live upon any length of time ; it is quite perfection ; but he staid only one night." —*The Dowager Lady Spencer*, in a letter dated December 16, 1807. " Correspondence of Sarah Spencer, Lady Lyttelton," p. 5.

" Good breeding, in England, among the men, is ordinarily stiff, reserved, or cold. Among the exceptions to this stricture, how high stood Mr. Windham ! . . . He is one of the most agreeable, spirited, well-bred, and brilliant conversers I have ever spoken with. He is . . . a man of family and fortune, with a very pleasing, though not handsome face, a very elegant figure, and an air of fashion and vivacity."—*Fanny Burney*.

" His person was graceful, elegant, and accomplished ; slender ; but not meagre. The lineaments of his countenance, though they displayed the ravages of the small-pox, were pleasing, and retained a character of animation, blended with spirit and intelligence. Over his whole figure, nature had thrown an air of mind. His manners corresponded with his external appearance ; and his conversation displayed the treasures of a highly cultivated understanding."—*Sir Nathaniel William Wraxall*.

PREFACE

IT is strange that though more than a hundred years
have passed since William Windham died, no full
biography of him has hitherto been composed.
This is the more astonishing because he has been
the subject of more panegyrics than any man of his
time. Friends and foes alike loved and honoured him,
and his foes were not less eager than his friends to sing
his praises. He was the intimate of Johnson and Burke
and Fox, the political associate of Pitt, the Duke of Portland, and Lord Grenville. He was a favourite with
George III., he was beloved by Malone ; Jeffrey had a
good word for him, Brougham could not speak too highly
of him, Fanny Burney exhausted her superlatives in
describing him. Years later Macaulay summed up the
general opinion of the statesman's contemporaries and
of succeeding generations by dubbing him " high-souled
Windham."

Windham died on June 4, 1810, and to the next issue
of the *Gentleman's Magazine* Malone contributed an
appreciative obituary notice. Thomas Amyot desired
to write the biography of the man whose private secretary he had been for many years, and in February
1811 he applied to the executors, Heneage Legge and
Mr. Palmer, to be entrusted with the Diaries and other
papers. The executors, however, induced George Ellis,
now best remembered as a contributor to the *Rolliad*
and the *Anti-Jacobin*, to undertake the task. Amyot,
however, was determined to pay tribute to his old master

and friend, and this he did in an admirable but brief memoir which he appended to a collection of Windham's speeches, published in three volumes in 1812. George Ellis, in the meantime, made little or no progress with the official biography, and he was, he admitted, overwhelmed by the vast mass of papers to be examined. So late as January 1814 he wrote to Heneage Legge: "Every information that can be collected respecting his early life would be very acceptable but how are they to be procured?—Alas! I know not."[1] When Ellis died in 1815 he had finished only an introductory note to the Diaries. This was published in 1866 by Mr. Henry Baring, as a Preface to a volume of Selections from the Diaries.

The author of a biography of Windham is fortunately not dependent upon printed sources for his material, for there are at his disposal some ninety-four volumes of the Windham Papers, acquired by purchase in 1909 by the British Museum. This collection is of extraordinary value, for it is not only a mine of information concerning Windham, but it throws light upon the secret political and military history of the time. The correspondence covers the period from 1783, when Windham entered public life, until his death seven-and-twenty years later. The roll of Windham's correspondents include, besides the members of his family and his private secretary, George III.; the Dukes of York and Gloucester, Fox, Pitt, Burke, Addington, Canning, Nelson, the Grenvilles, Dundas, the Duke of Portland, Cobbett, Sir Arthur Wellesley, Sir Gilbert Elliot, Sir Sidney Smith, Sir John Coxe Hippisley, Lord Grey, Mrs. Siddons, Mrs. Crewe, Hoppner, Sir Thomas Lawrence, Sheridan, Johnson, Malone, Hazlitt, Dr. Burney, and Dr. Parr. All these papers are unpublished, except the Burke-Windham correspondence, which, admirably edited by Mr.

[1] Add. MSS. 37907 f. 175.

J. P. Gilson, Keeper of Manuscripts at the British
Museum, was, at the instance of the Right Hon.
Arthur James Balfour, privately printed two years ago
for the Roxburghe Club. The text of the letters has
been closely followed, except that, for the convenience
of the reader, abbreviations have been printed in full,
and, as a rule, the spelling of proper names and places
has been standardised.

The value of the Windham Papers is considerable.
Windham it was who had the courage to put into writing
what others only dared to whisper about the utter incompetence of the Duke of York as commander-in-chief of the
army in Flanders. His correspondence with Pitt on this
subject, marked " Most Private," here printed for the
first time, is a genuine contribution to the history of the
war. It was through these letters that George III. first
learnt the feeling of his ministers and of the country on
this matter, and it must be placed to the credit of the
King that the incident in no degree lessened the respect
and admiration in which he held his Secretary-at-War.
It was to Windham that the Duke of Gloucester wrote,
marking his letter " Most Secret," regarding the defences of the country and the inefficiency of the junior
officers of the army and militia. In this same interesting
letter he urged the desirability of a treaty between
that Republic and Great Britain, whereby the maritime
defence of the United States should be undertaken by
Great Britain lest the States themselves should set
up a powerful navy. Other correspondence relates to
secret ministerial negotiations between the political
parties at home, and the arrangements between the
British Government and the French Royalists. A very
interesting letter is that written by a French *émigré*
in 1793 from Philadelphia.

There are gaps in the Windham Papers, but the information contained therein can be supplemented from many sources. The Pelham Papers include letters hitherto unpublished, exchanged between Windham and Lord Northington and the Hon. Thomas Pelham, and the privately printed "Miscellanies" of the Philobiblon Society contain a series of letters addressed to Mrs. Crewe. In the Ketton MSS. (published by the Historical MSS. Commission) will be found interesting extracts from a Diary kept by Windham in 1773; while in the Fortescue MSS. (issued under the same auspices) is a voluminous correspondence with Lord Grenville. Other sources that can be studied with advantage are Boswell's "Life of Johnson," Fanny Burney's Diaries, Wraxall's "Posthumous Memoirs," Stanhope's "Life of Pitt," Russell's "Life of Fox;" Prior's memoirs of Burke and Malone; the biographies of Sidmouth, Minto, Charlemont, Sheridan and Reynolds; the recollections of Lord Albemarle, Lord Malmesbury, and Lord Holland; the correspondence of Johnson and Burke; the "Memoires du Comte Joseph de Puisaye"; and Mrs. Stirling's "Coke of Norfolk." There is also an interesting character study of Windham by Brougham in "Statesmen of the Reign of George III."

"Why may not the Life of Windham be written by his letters?" asked a friend of the statesman, who disguised his identity as "An Old Member of Parliament."[1] The suggestion is sound, and this plan has been followed by the present writer. In the absence of any considerable number of letters written by or to Windham during the first thirty-two years of his life, the Editor has told the story of this period in a brief narrative.

The Editor's thanks are due to the Right Hon. the Marquis of Crewe, K.G., who has kindly allowed him to print the letters from Windham to Mrs. Crewe, which were contributed by the late Lord Houghton to the privately printed "Miscellanies" of the Philobiblon

---

[1] *New Monthly Magazine*, December 1831, vol. xxxii, p. 561.

Society ; to Earl Nelson, who has permitted the publication of letters of Horatio, Lord Nelson ; and to the Controller of his Majesty's Stationery Office, who has sanctioned the insertion of some correspondence between Windham and Lord Grenville from the Fortescue MSS. (Historical MSS. Commission's Reports). The Editor wishes further to thank Messrs. J. P. Collins, C. E. Lawrence, A. Francis Steuart, Thomas H. B. Vade-Walpole, and A. Winterbotham, who have kindly read the proofs of this work, and have made many valuable suggestions. The Rev. T. South Jagg, Rector of Felbrigge-cum-Melton, has been so good as to supply information concerning Windham at Felbrigg.

CONTENTS

SECTION I

EARLY LIFE. 1750–1782

SECTION II

CHIEF SECRETARY TO THE LORD-LIEUTENANT OF IRELAND. 1783

SECTION III

FIRST YEARS IN PARLIAMENT. 1784-1793

CHAPTER I

CHAPTER II

1784-1792

CHAPTER III

1793

CONTENTS xxxi

SECTION IV

SECRETARY-AT-WAR IN THE PITT ADMINISTRATION, 1794–1801

CHAPTER I

1794

CONTENTS

CHAPTER II

1795

LIST OF ILLUSTRATIONS

CHRONOLOGICAL TABLE OF EVENTS, 1778–1810

1778

February 6.	Treaty of Paris between France and America, recognising the independence of the United States.
February 17.	Appointment of British Commissioners to treat with the Americans.
May 11.	Death of the Earl of Chatham.
June 18.	British troops evacuate Philadelphia.

1779

June 16.	Spain declares war against England.
August	Gibraltar besieged.

1780

January 16.	Rodney relieves Gibraltar.
May 12	Charleston taken by the British.
June 2.	Gordon riots
August 15	Cornwallis defeats General Gates.
	Projected French invasion of England.
	Formation of " The Armed Neutrality " against the British claim of right of maritime search.

1781

	Prussia joins the Armed Neutrality.
August 5	Naval battle between the British and Dutch off the Dogger Bank.
October.	Cornwallis capitulates at Yorktown.

1782

February 27	Resignation of Lord North's ministry.
March 30.	Formation of Lord Rockingham's administration.
April.	Grattan's Declaration of Right.
April 12.	Rodney's victory in the West Indies.
July 1.	Death of the Marquis of Rockingham.
July 10.	Formation of the Shelburne Administration.
September.	Howe relieves Gibraltar.
November 30.	Preliminaries of Peace accepted by Great Britain and America
December 5.	George III. acknowledges the Independence of the United States.

1783

February.	Siege of Gibraltar raised.
April 5.	Formation of the Coalition Ministry
November 30.	Peace of Versailles.
December 17.	Fox's East India Bill rejected by the Lords.
	Downfall of the Coalition Ministry.
December 22.	Formation of the Pitt Administration.

1784

	Convention of Constantinople.
March 25.	General Election in Great Britain.

1785

February.	Return of Warren Hastings to England.
June 1.	Adams, the first United States Minister, received at St James's.

1786

February 17.	Articles of Impeachment against Hastings exhibited by Burke.
August 17.	Death of Frederick the Great. Accession of Frederick William II.
September.	Commercial Treaty between England and France.

1787

February 7.	Impeachment of Hastings agreed to by the House of Commons.
	Prince of Wales's debts paid by Parliament.
May 13.	First convict fleet sails from England for Botany Bay.

1788

February 13	Impeachment of Hastings before the House of Lords.
April 15	Treaty between England and Holland.
November.	The King's illness announced.
December.	Regency debates in the House of Commons

1789

February 5.	Pitt's plan for a restricted regency.
February 19.	Regency Bill abandoned owing to King's recovery
April 30.	Washington elected first President of the United States.
June 17.	The States-General proclaims itself the National Assembly.
July 14.	Destruction of the Bastille.

1790

February.	Burke and " the Alarmists " attack the French Revolution in the House of Commons.
November.	Burke publishes " Reflections on the French Revolution "

1791

March.	Paine publishes " The Rights of Man "
September 3	French Constitution voted
October 1	The Legislative Assembly sits at Paris.

1792

May.	Grey's measure of Parliamentary Reform introduced
May 21.	Proclamation against seditious writings and irregular meetings.
August 10.	Louis XVI. taken prisoner.
September 20	The battle of Valmy

1793

January 21	Louis XVI executed.
February 11.	Great Britain declares war against France.
March 11.	Revolutionary Tribunal established at Paris
March 14	Revolt in La Vendée.
March 18	Dumouriez defeated at Neerwinden.
April 5	Dumouriez deserts to the Austrians.
July 13.	Assassination of Marat
August 8	Valenciennes captured by the Allies
August 28.	Hood occupies Toulon.
October 16.	Marie Antoinette executed.
November 12.	Philippe Egalité executed.
November 22.	Commercial Treaty with the United States.
December 18.	Toulon evacuated by the Allies.
December 26	Wurmser defeated at Weissenburg.

1794

April 5.	Danton executed.
July	The Duke of Portland, Lord Spencer, Lord Fitzwilliam, and Windham join the Pitt Administration.
July 28.	Robespierre, St. Just, and others executed
August 30.	Valenciennes and Condé recaptured by the French.
December.	The Duke of York removed from the command of the British Forces in Flanders.
December 27	Pichegru invades Holland.

1795

February.	Surrender of Ceylon by the Dutch to Great Britain.
April 14	British Army evacuates Holland.
April 23	Acquittal of Warren Hastings.
May 16	Holland makes terms with the French
June 27.	Royalist expedition to Quiberon.
July 22.	France makes peace with Spain.
September	British occupation of Cape Colony
October.	Convention dissolved.
October 29.	Clerfait victorious on the Rhine.
November 3	Directory installed.
November	The Treasonable Practices Bill

1796

April.	Napoleon invades Italy.
	La Hoche's expedition to Ireland.
August 19.	Treaty of San Ildefonso.
October 11.	Great Britain declares war against France.
October 22.	Lord Malmesbury's peace mission to Paris
December.	Return of Lord Malmesbury.

1797

February 14.	Battle of Cape St. Vincent.
April 16.	Mutiny at Spithead.
May 2.	Mutiny at the Nore.
July 9.	Death of Edmund Burke.
October 11.	Battle of Camperdown
October 17.	Peace of Campo-Formio.

1798

February 10.	Berthier enters Rome.
March 5.	Battle of Berne.
March 29.	Helvetic Republic proclaimed.
May.	Napoleon's expedition to Egypt.
May.	Irish rebellion.
June 12.	Malta surrenders to the French.
July 21.	Battle of the Pyramids.
August 1.	Battle of the Nile.
August 22.	French land in Ireland.
September 8.	French in Ireland surrender.

1799

March 7.	Jaffa occupied by the French.
March 19.	Acre besieged by the French.
May 20.	The siege of Acre raised.
July 25.	Battle of Aboukir.
August.	Duke of York's expedition to Holland.
August 22.	Napoleon leaves Egypt.
September 19.	Battle of Bergen.
December 13.	Napoleon chosen First Consul.

1800

January 24.	Treaty of El Arish.
June 14.	Battle of Marengo.
July 2.	Act of Union with Ireland passed.
September 5.	Malta surrenders to the English.
December 3.	Battle of Hohenlinden
December 14.	Battle of Salzburg.

1801

January 1.	Act of Union between England and Ireland comes into force.
February 16	Pitt resigns office.

March 17.   Addington becomes Prime Minister.
March 21.   Battle of Alexandria.
March 28.   Treaty of Naples.
April 2.   Battle of Copenhagen.
August   French Army in Egypt capitulates.
October 1.   Preliminaries of Peace between France and England signed.

1802

March.   Peace of Amiens.
May.   Napoleon appointed First Consul for life.

1803

May 16.   War declared between England and France.
June 5.   French occupy Hanover
July 23.   Emmett's insurrection in Ireland.

1804

March 16.   Execution of the Duc d'Enghein.
May.   Addington resigns office.
May 12.   Pitt becomes Prime Minister.
May 18.   Napoleon proclaimed Emperor of the French.
December 2.   The Pope crowns Napoleon at Nôtre Dame.
   Spain declares war against Great Britain.

1805

April.   Treaty of St. Petersburg (Great Britain and Russia).
May 26.   Napoleon crowned King of Italy at Milan
July.   Battle of Cape Finisterre.
October 8.   Treaty of Naples.
October 17.   Capitulation of Ulm.
October 21.   Battle of Trafalgar.
November.   Napoleon enters Vienna.
December 2.   Battle of Austerlitz.
December 15.   Treaty of Vienna (France and Prussia).
December 26.   Peace of Pressburg (France and Austria).

1806

January 9.   Public funeral of Nelson.
January 12.   Vienna evacuated by the French
January 23.   Death of Pitt.
February 5.   Grenville-Fox Administration (" All the Talents ") formed.
February 15.   Joseph Bonaparte proclaimed King of Naples and Sicily.
July.   Battle of Maida.
July.   Confederation of the Rhine constituted.
August 18   Jerome Bonaparte proclaimed King of Westphalia.
September 13.   Death of Charles James Fox.
October 14.   Battles of Jena and Auerstadt.
October 25.   Napoleon enters Berlin.

November 8	Capitulation of Magdeburg.
November 20	Napoleon's Berlin Decrees.
November 28.	The French enter Warsaw
December 26.	Battle of Pultusk.

1807.

January 7.	British " Orders in Council."
February 7.	Battle of Eylau.
March.	Formation of the Portland administration.
March 25.	Slavery abolished in the British dominions.
April.	Convention of Bastenstein (Russia, Prussia, and Sweden).
June 10.	Battle of Heilsburg.
June 14.	Battle of Friedland.
July 7.	Treaty of Tilsit (France and Russia).
September 5.	Danish Fleet at Copenhagen surrenders to the British
October.	Treaty of Fontainebleau (France and Spain).

1808

May.	Joseph Bonaparte becomes King of Spain.
June 15.	Siege of Saragossa.
August 17.	Battle of Rolica
August 21.	Battle of Vimiera.
August 30.	Convention of Cintra.
September.	Convention of Paris.
October.	Convention of Erfurt.

1809

January.	Treaty of the Dardanelles (England and Turkey).
January 16.	Battle of Coruña.
February 21.	Capitulation of Saragossa.
April 20.	Battle of Abensberg.
May 12.	Napoleon enters Vienna.
May 21.	Battle of Aspern.
July 12.	Battle of Wagram.
July 28.	Battle of Talavera.
July to November.	Walcheren expedition.
October 24.	Peace of Schönnbrunn (France and Austria)
October 30.	Death of the Duke of Portland.
November.	Perceval forms an Administration.

1810

January.	Treaty of Paris (France and Sweden).
July.	Napoleon annexes Holland.
September 27.	Battle of Busaco.
October 29.	Wellington secures the lines in Torres Vedras.

SECTION I
EARLY LIFE. 1750–1782

SECTION I

EARLY LIFE. 1750–1782

Family history : Birth of William Windham : Windham at
Eton : Fond of books and sports : Nicknamed " Fighting
Windham " : His interest in the King : The death of his father :
His guardians : Withdrawn from Eton : The reason for this
step : At Glasgow University : His love of mathematics :
At University College, Oxford : His reputation there and
academic career : In early life uninterested in public affairs :
Sets out on a voyage of exploration in the Polar Seas : Pre-
vented by sea-sickness from proceeding : He is landed at
Bergen : Extracts from his Diary concerning his sojourn in
Norway : Scanty records of early life : His occupations :
First plunge into political life : A letter to Sheridan : His
maiden speech : He quells a Militia mutiny : A serious illness :
He goes abroad to recover strength : Invited to contest
Norwich as a supporter of the Rockingham party : Defeated
at the election of 1780 : Invited to stand for Westminster :
The formation of the Rockingham Administration : Corre-
spondence : The death of Lord Rockingham : Lord Shelburne
becomes Prime Minister : An extract from Windham's Diary.

THE Right Hon. William Windham came of an
old Norfolk family, which had acquired
from William Halcs in 1436 the manor of
Crownethorpe, in the parish of Wymond-
ham. From this parish (pronounced " Wind′-am ") the
family derived its surname. In 1460 John Wymondham
purchased from Sir John Felbrigg the manor of Felbrigg,
near Cromer, and this became the chief seat of the
family. John was knighted in 1487 on the battlefield
of Stoke. Sixteen years later, for being associated
with the Earl of Suffolk in a conspiracy against Henry
VII., he was tried for high treason, found guilty, and

3

beheaded on Tower Hill. Sir John married Margaret, fourth daughter of John Howard, Duke of Norfolk, and by her had a son (afterwards Sir) Thomas, who entered the Navy and attained the rank of Vice-Admiral. Sir Thomas married Eleanor, daughter of Sir Richard Scrope, of Upsal, Wiltshire, who bore him a large family. Of his eldest son and successor, Sir Edmund, it is recorded that being condemned by James I. to lose his right hand for striking a Mr. Cleer in the royal tennis court, he prayed that he might rather lose his left hand, for with the right, he said, " I may do ye King gode service," whereupon he was pardoned. Edmund's eldest son Francis died without issue, and the estate then passed to the second son, Sir John, who had married Elizabeth, daughter of John Sydenham, of Orchard, in Somersetshire, in which county he had settled. During the Civil War, his sons fought for the King, and after the battle of Worcester, Colonel Francis Windham, Sir John's fourth son, conducted Charles II. to his seat at Trent. The eldest son, Thomas, came into possession of the property on his father's death, and survived until 1653, when he had reached the patriarchal age of fourscore years and two. Thomas, who married a daughter of Sir John Lytton of Knebworth, was succeeded by his second son William, whose history is thus recorded on a monumental brass in the parish church of Felbrigg :

In a vault near to this monument lieth the Body of
WILLIAM WINDHAM, Esqr., second son of Thomas Windham of Felbrigg in the County of Norfolk Esqr. by Elizabeth his second wife. He married Katharine, Eldest d^r. of Sr Joseph Ashe of Twittenham, in the C^y of Middlesex Bart. with whom he lived twenty years, and had issue

eight sons; Ashe, William, Thomas, John, Thomas, John, Joseph and James, and three daughters Katharine; Mary and Elizabeth. The eldest Thomas and two Johns dyed Infants. All the rest survived him. He departed this life the ninth of June 1689 in the 42nd year of his age.

In the same vault lieth ye Body of Katharine Windham Relict of Willm. Windham Esqr. who departed this life the 24th day of Decr. 1729, In the 78th year of her Age.

M^{rs}. Mary Windham died June 29th 1747, aged 71, and was buried at St. Edmund's Bury, in Suffolk.

Ashe Windham, who was born in 1672 and survived until 1749, married Elizabeth, daughter of William Dobyns, of Lincoln's Inn. By her in 1717 he had an only son, William, who early in life quarrelled with his father, and thereafter spent many years abroad. He lived for some years in Spain, and in 1741 travelled with Richard Pocock in Switzerland, subsequently writing one of the first published accounts of Chamonix and Mont Blanc. Later he went to Hungary, where he served as an officer in one of Queen Maria Theresa's hussar regiments. At his father's request he eventually returned to England, where he devoted himself to the study of military subjects. After Pitt had passed the National Militia Act of 1757, he, in conjunction with Lord Townshend,[1] formed a corps in his own county, of which, in recognition of his services, he was appointed Lieutenant-Colonel. He interested himself in his duties, and drew up a " Plan of Discipline composed for the use of the Militia of the County of Norfolk," which was highly praised by the authorities and generally adopted throughout the country. He was a patron of all manly exercises, and to the end of his days

---

[1] Charles Townshend, third Viscount Townshend (1700–1764).

followed the hounds. He was a good classical scholar, a fine linguist, and that he had agreeable social qualities is proved by the fact that he was intimate with David Garrick and many of the London wits, who visited him frequently at Felbrigg. He married a noted beauty, Sarah Hicks, widow of Robert Lukin, of Dunmow, Essex, by whom he had a son, William, the subject of this memoir.

William Windham was born on May 3, 1750, at No. 6 Golden Square, Soho, London. At seven years of age he was sent to Eton, where, among his contemporaries was Charles James Fox. Dr. Barnard, the Headmaster, stated, when the lads had become distinguished men, that they were the last two boys he flogged. Their offence was rank : they had gone into Windsor without leave and attended a performance at the theatre. All accounts concur in declaring that at school Windham was con- spicuous for vivacity and brilliance and for the ease with which he acquired knowledge. Not only in scholastic attainments was he successful beyond most of his fellows, but he was as prominent in sport as in the class-room. A sound cricketer, a skilful oarsman, and so useful, too, with his fists that he was known at Eton as " Fighting Windham."

This nickname long clung to Windham, for he dearly loved a fight. On one occasion he was grateful that he had learnt the use of his fists. After his re-election at Norwich in July 1794, he was being chaired,[1] when a ruffian in the crowd threw a stone at his head. Like

---

[1] " The chairing in Norfolk differed from that of other counties. A chair of state, gaudily decorated, placed on a platform and sup- ported by poles, was borne on the shoulders of four-and-twenty stalwart men. By the side of this chair the member elect took his stand, and in this manner was carried through the principal streets of

the Admirable Crichton he was, he caught the missile in his hand, jumped off his moving platform, and thrashed the coward within an inch of his life.   In a few minutes he was again hoisted and continued his triumphal progress, bowing on all sides as if nothing had happened. When Windham could no longer fight it pleased him to watch others, and to the end of his days he was a patron of the Ring.   In his Diary he noted some of the combats he witnessed —

May 2, 1786.   The circumstances of the fight, which was the object of our excursion (to Newmarket), need not be recorded.   The winner's name was Humphries (Richard, I think) ; and the butcher's Sam Martin. . . . The spectacle was upon the whole very interesting, by the qualities, both of mind and body, which it exhibited. Nothing could afford a finer display of character than the conduct and demeanour of Humphries, and the skill discovered far exceeded what I had conceived the art to possess.   The mischief done could not have affected the most tender humanity.

June 9, 1788.   I had been that morning with Fullerton and Palmer to Croydon, to a boxing match. . . . The boxing match was, in consequence of a purse collected by subscription, under the direction of H[ervey] Aston, G[eorge] Hanger,[1] &c.   The combatants, Fewtrill and Jackson, both of them large ; one of them, Jackson, a man of uncommon strength and activity, but neither of them of any skill, or likely, so far as appeared upon that occasion, ever to become distinguished.   The fight, which

Norwich   At intervals, the bearers made a halt, and by a simultaneous action tossed their burden so high as to give him occasional peeps into garret windows.   When William Windham, the statesman . . was elected for Norwich he underwent a like ordeal "—Albemarle, " Fifty Years of my Life," 11. 296

[1] George Hanger (1751–1824), an intimate friend of the Prince of Wales, succeeded his brother as (fourth) Baron Coleraine, 1814.

lasted an hour and ten minutes, was wholly uninteresting, it being evident from the beginning which was to prevail, and no powers or qualities being displayed to make the prevalence of one or the other a matter of anxiety. The fight which succeeded this between Crabbe, a Jew, and Watson, a butcher, from Bristol, under 21, was of a different character; so much skill, activity, and fine make, my experience in these matters has not shown me. After a most active fight of forty minutes the Jew was very fairly beat. There was also another fight, between a butcher and a spring maker, neither of them large, but one of them, the butcher, a muscular man, which though smart enough for the time, ended soon by what seemed a shabby surrender on the part of the spring maker; his plea was having sprained both his thumbs, or, as he called it, but not truly, according to their appearance to me afterwards, put them out.

In February 1789 Windham went with Crewe,[1] Fitzpatrick,[2] Grey,[3] and George Cholmondeley [4] to Rickmansworth to see a contest between Johnson and Ryan, and on July 6 of the same year drove to Wimbledon to watch matches between Darch and Gainer, James and Tucker,

---

[1] John Crewe (1742–1829), afterwards Baron Crewe of Crewe, who had married in 1766 the beautiful Frances Anne Greville.

[2] Richard Fitzpatrick (1747–1813), second son of John, Earl of Upper Ossory; the friend of Fox; Colonel, 1778; General, 1793; Secretary-at-War in the Coalition and All the Talents Ministries.

[3] Charles Grey (1764–1845), afterwards second Earl Grey, Prime Minister, 1831–4.

[4] George James Cholmondeley (1752–1830) was the son of the Hon. and Rev. Robert Cholmondeley, Rector of St Andrews, Hertford (the second son of George, third Earl of Cholmondeley), by his wife Mary Woffington, the sister of the famous actress. He married three times: 1st, 1790, Maria, daughter of John Pitt, who died 1808; 2nd, 1814, Catherine, daughter of Sir Philip Francis, who died 1823; and, 3rd, 1825, the Hon Mary Elizabeth, daughter of John Thomas, Viscount Sydney, who survived him. Cholmondeley became Receiver-General of Excise.

Hooper and Tyne. The last battles he witnessed were at Moulsey in October 1808 between Gregson and Tom Cribb; the champion; Cropley and Tom Belcher; and Powell and Dogherty. He believed in prize fights, and on August 6, 1788, hurried to London to write an article, " to take off, as far as one could, the effect of the accident at Brighton, of the death of a man in a boxing match," which had resulted in the Prince of Wales, who was present, announcing that he would never again attend any pugilistic encounter.

In 1761 Colonel Windham died, and left his son in the guardianship of Benjamin Stillingfleet,[1] Dr. Dampier,[2] David Garrick, and a Mr. Price of Hereford.[3] For five years after his bereavement the boy remained at Eton; and then was suddenly withdrawn.

Dr. Dampier *to* Mrs. Windham

March 7, 1766

There have been great disturbances amongst the boys here, and I am sorry that your son is accused of having a large concern in them. In order therefore to cover his retreat and to prevent a publick expulsion, which would probably be the consequence of his longer stay, I shall *see* him home to you tomorrow morning. When I am in town, about a fortnight hence, we must meet and consider how to dispose of him. If I may advise I would not have you mention to any one the cause of his coming home so soon before the holidays.[4]

---

[1] Benjamin Stillingfleet (1702–1771), naturalist. One account says Stillingfleet did not act as a guardian, but the writer of the article on Stillingfleet in the "Dictionary of National Biography" does not accept this statement.

[2] Dr. Dampier, an under-master at Eton, and from 1774 Dean of Durham, the father of Dr. Thomas Dampier, Bishop of Ely. The elder Dampier had been Colonel Windham's tutor.

[3] (?) Robert Price, the friend of Stillingfleet, who died in 1761.

[4] Ketton MSS.

In the summer of 1766 Windham was sent to Glasgow to attend the classes at the University. There he studied under Dr. Anderson, the Professor of Natural Philosophy, and Robert Simson, the mathematician. It was Simson who imbued him with a taste for this science, one which fascinated him then and continued to do so through his life. In his Diaries are numerous references to the work he did and the books he read on the subject. At his death he left three treatises on mathematical themes; which his will directed should be placed in the hands of Dr. Horsley,[1] Bishop of St. Asaph, with the suggestion that if they were of any value they should be published. Horsley, however, predeceased Windham, and the works passed into the hands of George Ellis, who contented himself with extracting certain Notes from them.[2] It may therefore be presumed that, at least in his opinion, the treatises were not worthy of being presented to the public.

From Glasgow Windham went to Oxford, where he was entered in September 1767 as a gentleman-commoner at University College. His tutor was Robert Chambers, and Malone has put it on record that during the young man's academic career " he was highly distinguished for his application to various studies, for his love of enterprise, for that frank and graceful address, and that honourable deportment, which gave a lustre to his character through every period of his life." More direct evidence is forthcoming in a letter, dated September 2, 1770, to Mrs. Windham from Dr. Dampier, who says he has seen her son at Oxford and has heard the best reports of him. " He is, indeed," he added, " a very extra-

[1] Samuel Horsley, F.R.S. (1733–1806), afterwards Bishop of St. Asaph, the author of several mathematical works.
[2] These Notes were published in Windham's " Diary " (1866)

ordinary young gentleman, and if please God, he enjoys his health, he cannot fail of making a very considerable figure in the world." [1] Though, according to all accounts, very studious, Windham did not win any academic distinctions. He took his B.A. degree in 1771, in which year he left the University. He proceeded to the degree of M.A., October 7, 1782; and eleven years later, at the installation of the Duke of Portland as Chancellor, he was made D.C.L.

While at Oxford Windham interested himself not at all in public affairs. Indeed, so little attention did he pay to current events that one of his friends, as it amused the statesman in later days sometimes to recall, remarked, "Windham would never know who was Prime Minister." Proof that his attitude of indifference was sincere is to be found in his refusal of the offer made to him, while he was still at Oxford, by his father's old friend, Lord Townshend,[2] then Lord-Lieutenant of Ireland, to go to Dublin as His Excellency's secretary. That the offer should have been made, however, may be accepted as evidence that even at this early age Windham was recognised as possessing unusual ability.

Windham was fond of outdoor sports ; he loved books, and was never happier than when engaged in the composition of his mathematical treatises. When he was twenty-three years of age, in 1773, a thirst for adventure led him to join his friend, Commodore Phipps,[3] who, in the *Racehorse*, set out, in company with the *Carcass*, to attempt the discovery of the northern route to India. He suffered so severely from sea-sickness, however, that he had to abandon the expedition. He was landed, on June 29,

[1] Ketton MSS.
[2] George, fourth Viscount and first Marquis Townshend (1724–1807).
[3] Constantine John Phipps (1744–1792) succeeded his father as second) Baron Mulgrave in 1775.

at Bergen, in Norway, where, Amyot mentions; though
unhappily without giving any particulars, he passed
through "a series of adventures and 'hair-breadth
'scapes' in which his courage and humanity were conspicuous."[1] Some extracts from a diary Windham
kept at this time have been preserved, the first part of
that printed here having probably been written shortly
after he left England.

SECRET AND SEPARATE. This is my confidential book ;
in this will be contained all those thoughts, memo-
randums, notes, reflexions, &c., which no eye must see
but my own. To thee, my ever-adorable friend, do I
dedicate it, with whose name it will chiefly be filled.
May God grant that we may meet again, and enjoy
together the recollection of the times when these were
written !

How have I fulfilled my resolution ? The time since
the writing of the above, indeed since my getting on
board at Sheerness, has been a chasm in the history of
one's mind ; instead of exerting myself to preserve a
lively recollection of things past or absent ; instead of
thought and vigilance and exertion, which I fancied
would be excited by the newness of the situation, my
mind has been occupied only with melancholy reflexions
on the business I had undertaken, and a comparison of
my present state with the enjoyments of Ickleford
parlour. Not one purpose which I proposed in the voyage
has been answered : on the contrary my powers of
reflexion have been weakened, and my thoughts been less
active and my perceptions less lively than they would
have been at Felbrigg or Oxford. I could form no strong
conception of the condition in which I stood, nor feel
myself excited by the recollection of my own sensations
at other times. Let me learn from this, what I might

---

[1] Amyot, "Memoir of Windham," p. 6.

have known indeed by former experience, and from the nature of the thing itself, that the state of a person's mind is not materially altered by change of place ; *cælum non animum mutant qui trans mare currunt.*

The interval from my coming to Sheerness to my quitting the Hamburgh vessel I will set aside by itself, and either leave it wholly to memory, or take some notes of it at some future time : my diary commencing from that time and now instant, I will endeavour to keep with some regularity.

After getting clear of the ship, we set off very pleasantly for Bergen, the schipper and I being in the pilot's boat; and his boat with his own people attending us. The sight of land, and the prospect of being shortly in a town, and among people who could speak English made me feel at first very comfortably : but it soon began to occur to me that I had conducted affairs with my usual mismanagement. By bringing this man to the town with me, I was publishing the bargain I had made with him, and all for no purpose but to procure money for a fellow, without any occasion, who had already fleeced me most unmercifully. At any rate I was discovering that which I wished to have concealed ; and a thought now came into my head which had never occurred before, that the particularity of such a bargain might suggest an idea, which idea might travel a great way, of the agreement having been made in some fright, taken at an appearance of danger. The landlord was likely to mention the circumstance of an English gentleman, of such a name, having come in such a manner, in his letters to Scotland : there might be several Scotch and Irish masters of ships in the place ; as improbable stories had risen from as little beginnings and been circulated by less direct means. These reflexions made me very uneasy, and threw me into a fit of rage and despair at my own folly, in which state I with some difficulty got to sleep. . . .

At about 4 o'clock, then, on Tuesday morning, being

the 29th of June and the day before yesterday. I landed at Bergen. The appearance of the place at coming in was very fine and romantick, but the mortification I felt about this affair had depressed my spirits and I was foolish enough to be quite melancholy at the idea of being alone in a strange country, or, what was less remarkable, at the prospect of a journey of 600 miles through such a tract of mountains. The hospitality however, and civility of my landlord have made my stay here very comfortable. . . .

The Consul here is Alexander Wallace, Esqre., whose sons, in his absence, I went on Tuesday to wait upon, and found as completely Scotch as if they had lived in Edinburgh all their lives. The youngest asked me in token of his sentiments, whether Mr. Wilkes was hanged yet, but it is to be observed that he is a little disordered in his head, which prevented my giving such a reply as I should otherwise. . . .

The town of Bergen contains no very striking edifices, nor has it any very regular or spacious streets, but the whole appearance of it is clean and lively, the houses being built of wood and painted, and the roofs covered in general with red tiles. At the water's edge on one side are warehouses raised on piles and projecting over for the convenience of receiving and shipping timber, and on the opposite side is a broad wooden quay which is set apart entirely to the fish traders. . . .

Till within these few years, there were I believe no stone buildings, but they have now got a Dutch church, and a sort of castle and some houses built by a Scotch mason, who came over with his people, after the last fire; and what is very remarkable, the stone was obliged to be fetched from Scotland likewise. . . .

July 3*rd*. I have just had a visit from the Consul who came very civilly to wait upon me immediately on his return to town. He seems a brisk intelligent man, and to be of much pleasanter manners than his sons. I dined yesterday at his house, before his return. The dinner and what belonged to it, was certainly ordinary . . . it consisted of three dishes . . . sent up one by one according to the Bergen fashion, to which the company were helped in order after the master of the family or his wife had taken off a sufficient number of portions. . . .

No liquor was given at dinner, that I saw, besides wine, to which we were helped from time to time by Mr. Wallace or his brother, and at each glass some toast was given, such as, Friends in Norfolk, in Scotland, &c. . . .

11th, Sunday. This morning at a little before seven, after rising at three in order to finish my letters to Cholmondeley and Mrs. Byng [1] I set off from Bergen. . . . 'Tis now near 7 in the evening, and we have passed the 5th Gastschever's house or the 5th Norse mile. The weather has been very pleasant, and I am much refreshed by my dinner and some sleep I got between 12 and 4, yet I am far from being in spirits, and the reflexions that for three months I shall have known nothing of those I love, and that no age is insured from the common fatality of nature, makes me very unhappy.

12th. After continuing upon the water all last night, and to-day, and thus much of this night I am just arrived, two o'clock in the morning at Ardalsare [? Aardal]. . . .

The town very small, consisting of about 50 buildings, most of which I understood were used only as warehouses. . . . Tuesday about three o'clock, after much chattering between Gron and the people, we left Landal [? Laerdalsören] : I had been detained some time by my letter to my dearest friend . . . at the end of the two mile we were forced to ascend part of a steep mountain

[1] Mrs. Byng was the wife of the Hon. John Byng, afterwards fifth Viscount Torrington. She was a daughter of Commodore Arthur Forrest, who, with the *Dreadnought, Edinburgh,* and *Augusta,* beat five sail-of-the-line and three French frigates off Cape François. He died on May 26, 1770, while Commander-in-Chief at Jamaica. His second daughter was Augusta ; the third Cecilia, who in 1798 married William Windham. Forrest had married a daughter of Colonel Lynch, of Jamaica. She died in 1804, aged eighty-two.

to meet the river on the other side. The passage during this ascent and our descending the river again was the wildest I had ever seen. I was admiring a fine fall of waters that descended on the opposite side, when my guide chose to entertain me, by way of anecdote of the place, with the story of a man who had been robbed and murdered there. . . . I think this scene was adequate to all my hopes of a mountainous country. After getting through a road infinitely abrupt and rugged, we crossed the river again on a bridge about 40 feet in length and twenty in height, thrown over without any support in the middle, so that, as my guide told me, it was customary to let only one horse pass at a time.

. . . At last we met with a house where the woman regaled us very comfortably with eggs and loaf-bread and some cheese that was very eatable. I gave her 4 or 5 stivers and she expressed her thankfulness in the same manner as the girl at Landal by taking me by the hand.

.   .   .   .   .   .

Arrived at Elsinore on Saturday the 31st of July between 11 and 12 at night. . . . My first care on coming thither was to enquire about the post, and put in a letter to my dearest friend. The next day dined with Mr. Godwin and made the necessary enquiries about a ship, and in the evening went over to Copenhagen. . . .

GOTTENBERG. Almost all the women that I saw in the streets of Gottenberg of the appearance of gentlewomen were covered with black veils. The women in Sweden were much more comely than those in Norway, owing chiefly I believe to their taking some pains to protect their faces from the weather.

For the first part of my journey from Bergen, the women I think went entirely without covering on their heads, and were the most disgustful objects I ever saw, which undoubtedly was owing very much to that cause, though I don't think entirely. A great change was to be observed in their countenances as we came nearer to Christiania, where the use of a large covering of linen began.

Friederickshald was the first place where I observed any oak.[1]

The records for the next few years are extremely scanty, as George Ellis complained a century ago when he sat down to write the biography of his friend. Windham divided his time between Felbrigg, where he hunted and read, and London, where he went into society. He became a member of Brooks's; and vastly extended the circle of his friends. He made the acquaintance of Horsley and Francis Maseres,[2] and corresponded with them on mathematical subjects. He wrote occasional verses, and a specimen of his pedestrian efforts in this direction has been preserved.

VERSES SENT BY MR. WINDHAM TO A YOUNG LADY WITH A COPY OF DR. JOHNSON'S WORKS, 1785

As Adam, by the great Archangel led,
Saw life's great plan, in destined order spread ;
So in these leaves to thee, fair nymph, is shown,
Th' instructive image of a world unknown ;
There thou mayst learn, by trial yet untaught,
How never happiness by wealth was bought ;
There see what ills assail the rich and great,
Nor scorn the blessings of an humble fate.
Still to this fate with equal hand are given
The choicest bounties of indulgent heaven ;
Untainted joys, the sunshine of the breast,
Love's purest flame by mutual ardour blest ;

---

[1] Ketton MSS. 211–214.
[2] Francis Maseres (1731–1824), mathematician, subsequently Cursitor Baron of the Exchequer.

To the fair charmer be fuch joys decreed,
Of worth and beauty fuch the precious meed !
Blefs with thy charms fome fond admiring fwain,
Some fwain be found, worthy thofe charms to gain ! [1]

It was not until the beginning of the year 1778 that Windham first stepped into the political arena; and he did so then only because of the interest he took in the momentous affair of the American War of Independence. Though entirely unpractised in public speaking, he; under the stress of the strong views he held, nerved himself to take the field at Norwich against those who supported the continuance of what to him, as to so many clear-sighted men, appeared an altogether hopeless and unjust campaign. An early intimation of his attitude is given in a letter to Sheridan; whose acquaintance he had made earlier at Bath.

WILLIAM WINDHAM *to* RICHARD BRINSLEY SHERIDAN

Felbrigg (?). *January* 5, 1778

I fear my letter will greatly disappoint your hopes. I have no account to send you of my answering Lord Townshend—of hard-fought contests—spirited resolves —ballads, mobs, cockades, and Lord North burnt in effigy. We have had a bloodless campaign; but not from backwardness in our troops, but for the most creditable reason that can be—want of resolution in the enemy to encounter us. When I got down here early this morning, expecting to find a room prepared, a chair set for the president, and nothing wanting but that the orators should begin, I was surprised to learn that no advertisement had appeared on the other part ; but that Lord Townshend having dined at a meeting where the

---

[1] Crewe Papers: Windham Section, p. 12 ("Miscellanies" of the Philobiblon Society, vol. viii.). *See* also Add. MSS. 37934 f. 66.

FELBRIGG HALL (1779)

From a print in the Norwich Public Library

proposal [to raise a War Fund at Norwich] was received very coldly, had taken fright, and for the time at least had dropped the proposal.   It had appeared, therefore, to those whom I applied to (and I think very rightly) that till an advertisement was inserted by them; or was known for certain to be intended, it would not be proper for anything to be done by us.   In this state, therefore; it rests.   The advertisement which we agreed upon is left at the printers, ready to be inserted upon the appearance of one from them.   We lie upon our arms, and shall begin to act upon any motion of the enemy.   I am very sorry that things have taken this turn, as I came down in full confidence of being able to accomplish something distinguished.   I had drawn up, as I came along, a tolerably good paper, to be distributed to-morrow in the streets, and settled pretty well in my head the terms of a protest—besides some pretty smart pieces of oratory, delivered upon Newmarket-Heath.   I never felt so much disposition to exert myself before—I hope from my never having before so fair a prospect of doing it with success.   When the coach comes in, I hope I shall receive a packet from you, which shall not be lost, though it may not be used immediately.

I must leave off writing, for I have got some other letters to send by to-night's post.   Writing in this ink is like speaking with respect to the utter annihilation of what is past ,—by the time it gets to you, perhaps, it may have become legible, but I have no chance of reading over my letter myself.

I shall not suffer this occasion to pass over entirely without benefit.

[P.S.] Tell Mrs. Sheridan that I hope she will have a closet ready, where I may remain till the heat of the pursuit is over.   My friends in France have promised to have a vessel ready upon the coast.[1]

---

[1] Moore, " Life of Sheridan " (fifth edition), i. 290–292.

Windham delivered his maiden speech at a public meeting convened at Norwich on January 28, when he spoke against the war and also opposed Lord Townshend's proposal for a subscription to defray its cost. A few days later he drew up a remonstrance against the war, which was signed by about five thousand people, and presented to the House of Commons.[1] Once Windham had taken the plunge, and found it to his liking, it is probable that he might at once have embraced a political career, had he not soon after been prostrated by illness.

It was early in the year that the Militia was called out; and Windham, who was a Major in the Norfolk regiment, had to take up his military duties. It happened that an opportunity at once offered for the display of his courage. It was customary to pay the men a " marching guinea " before they started; but the Colonel on this occasion, for some reason best known to himself, gave instructions that it was not to be paid until the regiment had left the county. The men assembled near the Castle at Norwich; but when Windham gave the word to march; they grounded their arms and refused to move until they received the guinea apiece. When the command was repeated; some of the men wavered, and, seeing this; one of the ring-leaders left his place, and told the waverers to be firm. Him Windham seized, and in spite of the threatening attitude of the soldiers, hauled to the Guard-House. When the comrades of the imprisoned man demanded his release, Windham stood at the door of the Guard-House, drawn sword in hand, and swore that while he lived the man should not go free. Eventually Windham was rescued from this precarious position by some men of his own; the Western; battalion. Shortly after

[1] Walpole, " Last Journals " (ed. Steuart), ii. 119.

this exciting episode his life was in even greater danger. Marching with the regiment, he, with two brother-officers, rode, " for the fun of the thing," through a deep rivulet. He had to remain for hours in wet clothes, with the result that he contracted a high fever, and was brought within an ace of death. It is said that from the effect of this illness his constitution never entirely recovered. When he was well enough to travel he went abroad, and remained in Switzerland and Italy for nearly two years.

The speech that Windham had made on the war impressed his hearers, and some of them invited him to stand at the next election as a Coalition candidate at Norwich. To this offer he returned an acceptance. A good speaker, a rich man, and belonging to an old family well-known in the county, he was an excellent selection, and offers of support poured in upon him while he was still abroad.

Viscount Townshend *to* William Windham

March 22, 1779

The reason of my giving you this trouble is, that I have thought it fair to assuer you, that I shall endevur to serve you, with all the little interest I may pretend too in Norfolk, heareing you intend to stand at our next Election for that County, and fiending that Sir J[ohn] H[olland] hath bine so warmly receved, I iudge it may not be long before there will be another Election, and therefore that teime is not to be lost in preparing our friends, upon which I desier to heare a word or two from you, for I know as these Knights are very free, and open in declaring their intentions of standing again, so they are by friends in the Country soliciting all mankind, and I looke upon this affaire as of great importance to all our reputations, upon which I desier no advantage may be gained in point of conduct.

I wish you would let Sir John Holland and as many more as conveniently as you can, know your mind early in this matter, otherwise some will pretend engagement.

I know all news you have from better hands and abler to write at large than I am ; and the truth is of myselfe never I desierd to have a long letter from such one as mien is, wherefore remembering the old rule of doeing as I would be done by, I conclud, in great ernest both to you, my sister, and all yours, that I am as related and obliged with all affexions and reall humble service.[1]

WILLIAM WINDHAM *to* VISCOUNT TOWNSHEND

March 26, 1779

The Assurance your Lordship is pleased to give me of your countenance and Assistance at the next Election, will incourage me to declare I am willing to serve the Countie, if they think me worthy of the Imployment. And I am so sensible of the Influence, the success of this affair will have upon this County, that I have lost no time towards the setting up of the old English Interest, which I hope to see once more flourish among us.[2]

At the election in September 1780 William was nominated with Sir Harbord Harbord,[3] who had represented the constituency for twenty years, against Bacon, one of the Lords of Trade, and John Thurlow.[4] Windham was on his way home, all unconscious of what had happened, when the election began, and he arrived at Norwich only three days before the polling commenced, too late to take any effective part on his own behalf. Sir Harbord Harbord and Bacon were returned.

[1] Add. MSS. 37911 f. 1.   [2] Add. MSS. 37911 f. 8.
[3] Sir Harbord Harbord, afterwards Lord Suffield
[4] John, a brother of Edward (afterwards Lord Chancellor) Thurlow, died March 11, 1782.

Windham was much in London after his return from abroad. As a member of Brooks's he became more and more drawn into the vortex of political affairs. His intimacy with Fox and Burke not unnaturally induced him to be enrolled, more or less officially, as a supporter of the party of which the Marquis of Rockingham was the nominal head, and he was urged to stand for the first vacancy for the Parliamentary representation of Westminster, an offer he declined in favour of Norwich. He was, of course, keenly interested in the fall of Lord North and the composition of the Administration that followed.

WILLIAM WINDHAM *to* BARTLETT GURNEY, NORWICH

March 25, 1782

After every expression of dislike and reluctance, the bitter draught is at length swallowed, and His Majesty has submitted to the hard necessity of taking for his Ministers the most virtuous set perhaps of public men that ever appeared in this country. About four o'clock to-day Mr. Dunning announced to the House of Commons, in the room of Lord North, who did not choose to come down, that the arrangement known to have been proposed the evening before, was accepted, and that it would be signified in form to the House on Wednesday next. The arrangement is as follows :—First Lord of the Treasury, Lord Rockingham ; Chancellor of the Exchequer, Lord John Cavendish ; President of the Council, Lord Camden ; Privy Seal, Duke of Grafton ; Commander in-Chief, General Conway [1] ; Ordnance, Duke of Richmond ; Admiralty, Admiral Keppel ; Secretaries of State, Lord Shelburne, Mr. Fox. Other appointments are left for further consideration. Every art of evasion and negotiation was put in practice to the last, and it was hardly

[1] General Henry Seymour Conway (1721-1795).

known what was determined upon till the moment Mr. Dunning came to the House, his message coming to him, as I understood, from Shelburne, to whom it was signified by the King. Lord Rockingham's conduct has been as great in the latter part of this negotiation as in the former. He refused absolutely to abate one jot of his first declaration ; at the same time he was willing to sacrifice every private punctilio by which the King hoped to have created a jealousy between him and Lord Shelburne. The first-fruits of this administration will be an exclusion from Parliament of all those who have fattened on the ruins of the country by jobs and contracts, and the destruction of one source of undue influence without doors in the exclusion of the votes of revenue officers. Secondly, the great articles of reform proposed in Mr. Burke's life, will go on with all despatch. With what face will people oppose the appointment of a Ministry, composed of men who have uniformly supported the cause of the country for near twenty years, and who make it the condition of their entering into office, that they should deprive themselves of the means of corrupt influences ?

Those who declare themselves enemies to this administration must declare themselves the friends of corruption and enemies of reform.[1]

WILLIAM WINDHAM *to* E. NORGATE [2]

Queen Anne Street

June 5, 1782

You have heard, no doubt, from the papers, as well as from a letter or two of mine sent to Norwich, a general account of my transactions, with respect to becoming a candidate for Westminster. In the whole business, from

---

[1] Windham's " Diary," p. 37.

[2] A gentleman at Norwich who was an active supporter of Windham's parliamentary interests there.

the first mention of it soon after the general election, to the present occasion, I had remained nearly passive ; not thinking a seat for Westminster an offer to be declined, if attainable upon easy terms, nor considering it an object to be pursued through the medium of much difficulty or expence. This intention of leaving matters to their own operation, produced at first by the considerations above mentioned, was confirmed afterwards by another feeling, when, by the management of some particular persons, a resolution was carried at one of the general meetings for putting up Mr. Pitt, in case of a vacancy. After that, propriety required that a renewal of our correspondence should come as a formal invitation from them ; and partly in that form it was about to come, that is, as a resolution of the Westminster Committee, without any sort of application from me ; when, upon inquiry into the general sentiments of the people on the question of Parliamentary Reform, by which, though my election could not have been prevented, my situation, upon the whole, would have been rendered unpleasant ; and from the reflection that, on a vacancy happening in the meanwhile at Norwich, a person might be chosen who could not afterwards be set aside, I determined not to wait till a resolution of the committee might make refusal more difficult, but to forestal their deliberations by a letter declining the honour that might be intended me. The reasons assigned in my letter were, the difference of opinion that prevailed in some of the independent interest with respect to myself, destroying that unanimity of choice, without which I should not be ambitious of a seat at Westminster ; and my disagreements, signified in pretty explicit terms, with many of the opinions that seemed then to be popular. I should flatter myself, that no part of this transaction can have prejudiced my interest at Norwich, and that the conclusion ought rather to have promoted it.[1]

[1] Amyot, " Memoir of Windham," p. 14.

'Lord Rockingham died on July 1, 1782, and, after much negotiation and many intrigues, Lord Shelburne became Prime Minister, whereupon Fox, Burke, and others of the Rockingham party withdrew from the Ministry.

WILLIAM WINDHAM *to* E. NORGATE

Queen Anne Street
July 4, 1782

You feel no doubt at Norwich, as at every other place, a share of the general consternation into which all good men are thrown by the death of Lord Rockingham. There could be no time in which the loss of such a character as his, must not have been severely felt ; but now it falls with a weight that *crushes*. The every existence of that interest which has maintained the cause of the country since the Revolution, is in danger of terminating in his person. The only hope and endeavour must be, in my humble opinion, to keep the troops [in America] together, by withdrawing them from action for a time, and leaving the enemy to pursue his operations, till they can have recovered their spirits, and retrieved their losses, sufficiently to make a new attack. Some of the most considerable amongst them are strongly of that opinion, and urge the immediate resignation of their places, if Lord Shelburne is to be at the head of affairs. Others are of opinion that they should still continue in, in order to complete the good they have begun, and not quit the public service till his conduct shall have driven them from it. The advocates for either opinion are actuated by perfectly honest motives. I am, for my own part, clearly for the sentiments of the former, and think there can be neither credit nor safety to themselves, nor consequently final advantage to the country, in their continuing in office. The danger of continuing is, that they will miss an opportunity of breaking off with credit and effect, and never find another.[1]

EXTRACT FROM WINDHAM'S DIARY

October 3, 1782

This day at one o'clock after an interval of ten years, I arrived at Oxford, not having been here, except for one night, since I quitted it in the year 1772. It happens particularly that I am in the very same rooms, in which I was placed, just fourteen years ago, at my first entrance into the University. At the latter end of August, or beginning of September of the year 1768, did I enter a member of the University of Oxford, and make my first trial of academical life in these rooms. The recollection which this circumstance revives, and the reflections it gives rise to, are not such as dispose one to cheerfulness. Has the intermediate time been passed in a way, that I can look back upon it with pleasure or approbation ? Has the effect of fourteen years been such as expectation represented it ? Am I, comparatively with what I was, in knowledge, habits and powers, what I looked forward to be, and what I might have been ? If I look back to the performances of that time, one might be led to think that the difference of power was inconsiderable ; in powers merely natural, it may be doubtful whether there is any. The chief difference is in habits, and in powers dependent on habit (meaning by the former, rather practices, habits of life ; and by the latter, habits more properly) and in short may be called methods. In all these, and particularly perhaps, in the last, something has been done ; but it is a melancholy truth that the greatest part of what has been done, has been the work of a little more than three years, and was, in its nature, equally capable of being done ten years ago.

[1] Amyot, "Memoir of Windham," p. 16.

SECTION II

CHIEF SECRETARY TO THE LORD-LIEUTENANT OF IRELAND.   1783

SECTION II

CHIEF SECRETARY TO THE LORD-LIEUTENANT OF IRELAND. 1783

Lord Northington appointed Lord-Lieutenant of Ireland in the Portland Administration : Windham accepts office of Chief Secretary to the Lord-Lieutenant : His misgivings as to his qualifications : Dr. Johnson's encouragement : Windham accorded a hearty welcome in Dublin : His reputation in 1783 : He retires in August : The reasons for his retirement discussed : His letter notifying Northington of his resignation of the post : His correspondence with the Lord-Lieutenant and the Hon. Thomas Pelham.

WHEN, on the retirement of Lord Shelburne in 1783, the Duke of Portland [1] formed a ministry, he appointed Lord Northington [2] to the office of Lord-Lieutenant of Ireland, and Lord Northington, in his turn, offered Windham the post of Chief Secretary. This Windham accepted, but with misgivings. He confided to Dr. Johnson his doubts as to whether he was possessed of the necessary diplomatic qualifications. " Don't be afraid, Sir," said the great man; with a pleasant smile, " you will soon make a very pretty rascal." [3] It is not surprising that Windham accepted reluctantly, for affairs in Ireland were in a state that might well try the nerves of a man versed in

[1] William Henry Cavendish Bentinck, third Duke of Portland (1738–1809).
[2] Robert Henley, second Earl of Northington (1747–1786).
[3] Boswell, " Life of Dr. Johnson " (ed. Hill), iv. 200.

31

political matters, and were likely to prove remarkably difficult for an unfledged statesman. Grattan and his party were flying in the face of the viceregal policy, and making strenuous efforts to secure the independence of the Irish party—this within little more than a decade of the Union—and to obtain a measure of Catholic Emancipation, a concession which, it was an open secret, the King bitterly opposed.

In Dublin Windham was accorded a hearty welcome, for he was already known as a distinguished scholar, and looked upon as one who would probably become a power in the political world. " He had the fire and the dignity of genius," wrote Francis Hardy, the friend and associate of Grattan in the Irish Parliament.[1]

Some months later Windham wrote to Lord Northington : " I am in no danger of losing the recollection of it [Dublin Castle] altogether—it would be ungrateful in me to forget such a scene of joy. I shall long retain the idea of myself, placed in my chair of audience, or traversing with my box in my hand, that ' region, dark and dolorous ' that divided our respective habitations. The whole period, so short in its duration; so unlike the way of life from which I emerged, and to which I am returned, appears like a dream."

Windham resigned his post in August, after a tenure of only four months. The reason of his retirement has been much discussed. There were those who declared that it arose out of a disagreement between him and his chief, and this view found support in a letter; dated Dublin; August 26, 1782, which somehow found its way into the newspapers. " Some assert," so runs a passage; " that his resignation was chiefly owing to a coolness

[1] Life of the Earl of Charlemont (2nd ed.), ii. 82.

between him and a certain great personage.—Mr. Windham is a person of deep science, and of great penetration
and abilities ;—the great personage likes a deep bottle—
to penetrate a cork—and has strong abilities of bearing
wine.   The one was an enemy to thinking ;—the other to
drinking, and so they parted."[1]   That this-was not the
case is proved by the correspondence between Lord
Northington and Windham, now printed for the first
time.   The writer of the letter already quoted went on to
say that the resignation was occasioned partly by a want
of " due requisites in Mr. Windham to become a supple
and venal courtier "—precisely the deficiency that Windham feared would unfit him for the office.   " The Story of
Windham's resignation, as I heard it at Brighthelmstone,"
Pitt wrote to W. W. Grenville,[2] August 23, 1783, " supposed him to have got into some scrape in Borough
transactions, which made him afraid to shew his face in
the House of Commons.   It did not come from the best ·
authority, but the letter I recollect hearing of at Stowe
made me think it not improbable."[3]   Francis Hardy
declared that it was the result of the Lord-Lieutenant's
patronage being distributed in favour of the old Court
party.   Yet another account gives the reason that
Windham believed in Ireland for the Irish; and gives in
support of this contention that when a clergyman came
to Windham with a letter from Burke, the Chief Secretary
" assured the gentleman he should be happy to present
a person so strongly recommended by Mr. Burke with a
much greater piece of preferment than that requested ;

[1] Quoted by Amyot, " Memoir of Windham," p. 18.
[2] William Wyndham Grenville (1759–1834), Chief Secretary for
Ireland, 1782–3 ; created Baron Grenville, 1790 ; held high ministerial
offices, and was chief of the " All the Talents " ministry.
[3] Fortescue MSS , i. 218.

but that it was his fixed determination . . . to give every place in his power to Irishmen ; as he had long been persuaded that the natives had the best right to the bread of their own land."[1]   Burke's letter,[2] however; was to ask Windham to secure for the Rev. Richard Marlay, Dean of Ferns, the post of second chaplain to the Lord-Lieutenant.   Windham's reasons for resigning are set out at length in the following correspondence, in which it will be seen that an attack of fever gave him the excuse to retire from a position where he was worried to death by the numerous applications for the exercise of patronage. The fact that a dissolution was imminent and that he desired to enter Parliament was not without weight, too, in determining his action.   He did not, however, as his letters show, definitely make up his mind to retire until he was on a visit to London in July.

WILLIAM WINDHAM *to* THE EARL OF NORTHINGTON
London, July 16, 1783

It seems odd to say that in the whole circle of my correspondence as Secretary I have had no letter so unpleasant to write as that which I am now addressing to you.   I could better have undertaken to acquaint the Provost that his peerage had failed than I can state to you what I am now about to communicate.   The subject will undoubtedly surprise you ; I cannot wish it should please you ; but I hope and trust it will create no other uneasiness than that of temporary regret.   Before I explain a matter introduced with this exordium, let me acquit myself of the levity of having acted from any momentary impulse, or of the disingenuity of having concealed from you what I had long determined in my own mind.   With respect to the first I can assure you

---

[1] Quoted by Amyot, " Memoir of Windham," p. 19
[2] Dated May 5, 1783. *See* Add. MSS. 37843 f. 2

that the matter has been a subject of frequent and anxious thought, and if I have hitherto said nothing, the reason has been, not a want of openness towards you, but a disposition to wait the issue of further trial and to defer the decision to the last moment. The present measure of the dissolution of Parliament forces an immediate determination, and upon the fullest deliberation, and the utmost trial that the case will admit, I must decide against continuing in my present situation.   .

Of this decision the first circumstance which I am anxious to explain is, that it is not the result of that general dislike and impatience with the extent of which you are well acquainted, and the force of which you feel equally with myself. These feelings, though very good reasons for not accepting, are more for relinquishing such a situation. It does not proceed either in any great degree from an objection to that which must be considered however, as sufficiently objectionable, the sed[entary] work that makes the greater part of a secretary's employment, so much worse than what used to be the business of Mr. Robinson,[1] as an Irish House of Commons is worse than an English one. The real ground of my determination is my conviction that the bodily infirmity, brought on by the life I must lead, and the business I must go through, will for the time so oppress and incapacitate me, as to render me totally incapable of discharging the duties of the situation either with credit to myself or advantage to the Government. People of different degrees of strength will be differently affected by the same situations ; and of persons equally affected in body some will find their minds more disturbed by such indisposition and their faculties more impaired than others. Of this latter species of infirmity few persons I believe have so much as myself ; and from my experience of the effects of this in the last five weeks, I am persuaded

---

[1] John Robinson (1727–1802), the confidential agent of the King and Lord North, was Secretary of the Treasury, 1770- 1782

that my state during a parliament winter must be such as I have described. A life of close confinement, constant application, anxious thought, and late hours in hot rooms, is what I am satisfied I cannot stand, by which expression I do not refer to such illness as is to endanger life, or ruin constitution. If the evil were of that sort only, it would be one's duty perhaps to take one's chance for it ; but the apprehension is of that equivocal and intermediate state, which in a situation where every exertion is wanted, would deprive me at once of the powers of health and of the excuse of sickness.

If there ever was a person in any situation who needed to have all his faculties about him, it is myself in the situation I am in ; first, from the difficulty of the undertaking itself, then, from my own entire want of preparation ; and, finally, from the foolish expectation of some people, of the figure I am to make. Under these circumstances it behoves me well to consider in what state I shall be to contend with these difficulties, supply these deficiencies, and satisfy these expectations. I am far from thinking that my prospects in these respects would be very good, supposing me even to possess all the advantages of perfect health : but what can it then be considered, when even the state in which I have been for some time past must probably exceed so far what I am to look to in future ? You may have been witness in some measure of the fits of languor and debility which I frequently experience : but no one but myself can judge of the effect they have on any exercise of the understanding. They have at various times rendered me incapable of the business, such even as it has been hitherto. What then is to become of me, when my powers are likely to fail in the same proportion as the business increases ? This is not the language of momentary despondency, nor the consequence, as you may be apt to suspect, of the attack mentioned in my former letter —quite the contrary. I argue to the effect of my situation on the other side of the water from the difference of my feelings for some days past. After the sickness of the passage; the journey through Wales and a dose or two of physick I am a different being from what I was ten days ago, or shall be probably ten days hence. The idea of Flood's[1] oratory has at this moment no terrors, but I know to what state a fortnight of the business and confinement of the Castle will infallibly reduce me. Do not consider these, therefore, as idle apprehensions founded on such inequalities as every one experiences in himself, and the mere effect of the moment. They are the result of frequent observation of myself at various times ; and upon these, as well as more recent experience, and after weighing the difficulty of the business, my own comparative strength, when at its best, and the impaired state in which it is likely to be at the time of trial, I am settled in opinion that the best thing I can do, either in prudence to myself, or in justice to those with whom I am connected, is to withdraw in time from the situation.

Though I can believe from your friendship, and from the footing on which we have been, that you will feel concerned at this, yet you have, possibly before this, so far come over to my opinion about myself as to regret the loss of a pleasant associate rather than of an able assistant. My uneasiness at present at the thought of creating to you any new distress prevails so much over my own vanity that I feel great comfort in that assurance. The reality of the fact convinces me that you must by this time feel that, for the office of Secretary, there are within the land five hundred as good as me. To one person, who might be thought of this number, but whom I know you would not include in it, namely, Townshend, I have already mentioned your objections to the Duke of Portland

---

[1] Henry Flood (1732–1791), the Irish statesman, at that time in opposition to the Government, and in league with Grattan to secure the independence of the Irish Parliament.

—the Duke of Portland, by the way, is the only person whatever to whom I have yet communicated the purport of this letter, with a request of secrecy, till he should hear from you or me. He said what you may suppose, from his sentiments before, and which nothing but strong previous determination and experience of former weakness, enabled me to resist. I have great confidence in the belief that you think of me with respect to my present situation so much as I do of myself, that this letter will not communicate to you any part of the pain which it has occasioned to me. I shall of course return to you, and the moment I have executed the few things I had to do, which I think will be on Saturday next.[1]

WILLIAM WINDHAM *to* THE EARL OF NORTHINGTON

Brooks's : July 17, 1783

My letter last night, sent by the messenger, left me so unpleasant that I could not bring myself to write on any other subject, or to send you, as I had intended, the amount of my proceedings and inquiries, since my letter of Monday night. With respect to the main article, the continuance of the ministry, I find no person,—not having as yet talked with either of the persons whose intelligence was sent to us from Conway—that seems to have any doubt of their continuing till the next sessions. As is said of Filch in " The Beggar's Opera," they will stand till another sessions. The chief reasons in support of this opinion are that the King wants money too much to promise himself much success in the creation of a new parliament, and that the power of the Crown in general, for those purposes, has been so abridged by Crewe's bill [2] that the same hopes cannot be entertained from that measure as formerly. His determination, however, not

---

[1] Add. MSS. 33100 f. 198.
[2] The Bill introduced by John, afterwards Baron, Crewe (1742–1829) for disfranchising excise officers, 1782.

to contribute to their strength or render them at all independent, is manifested without much reserve ; for he absolutely refuses to make any English peers. Whether Lord North [1] is to be an exception I did not think to inquire ; but Welbore Ellis's [2] is refused ; so you may imagine no one else has much chance. Fox's [3] opinion I do not know, not having seen him as yet to talk upon that subject, but the Duke of Portland is what I have told you ; and other speculators such as Hamilton, [4] and people of that sort, concur in the same notion. Let me mention now all the other matters necessary to be taken notice of as they come into my head.—Lord Carhampton's [5] step was positively refused, not however in a manner harsh or angry, but by a dextrous turn of putting the refusal on your not having recommended any steps in the peerage. Lord North's opinion is that it would have been equally refused, had you recommended that alone ; but would have passed in company with any other.

The business of the Staff, &c., I have talked over with Burgoyne, [6] who was not aware of the circumstance of the message from Lord Townshend, nor seemed to have thought before of the necessity of confining the numbers precisely to those limited on that occasion : but he agrees to the necessity of both, now they are stated ; indeed his proposal for the staff was of itself perfectly conformable to the message. I am to desire also my Lord North to take the King's pleasure on the immediate reduction of the staff, except as to his own pay, about which, though the exception sounds ridiculous, his wishes and opinions are, as

[1] Lord North (1732–1792), Prime Minister, 1770–1782 ; succeeded his father as (second) Earl of Guilford, 1790

[2] Welbore Ellis (1713–1802), created Baron Mendip of Mendip, 1794.

[3] Charles James Fox (1749–1806), at this time Secretary of State for Foreign Affairs.

[4] William Gerard Hamilton, " Single-speech Hamilton " (1729–1796).

[5] Simon Luttrell, Viscount Carhampton, subsequently created Earl Carhampton (died 1787).

[6] General John Burgoyne (1722–1792), at this time Commander-in-Chief of the forces of Ireland.

upon every other occasion, perfectly fair and liberal. The circumstance which you mention (for I have received your letter) of the troops being in Ireland before the meeting of Parliament, has been already mentioned to Conway, but must be enforced again by me, as I find he shows a disposition to be careless about it. Clinton,[1] when I last saw Lord North, was understood to have refused his peerage, not being able to succeed as to being a viscount, which the King refused on the old grounds of not granting two steps at once. They have acted rather scurvily in sending over so many as they have done when you had recommended only five.

The same post as brought me your letter has brought me one from Ogle,[2] written with civility, but with much discontent. He begins with *Dear Sir*, but ends with having the *honour* to be. The footing on which he puts [it] is of having been *struck out* of the Duke of Portland's list, which he feels as a marked slight. This is the best ground one would wish him to put it upon ; because it is such as one [can] take away ; by stating that any former recommendation of the Duke's was not only out of the question, but not even known. I conceive one shall be able to set him right again ; though it is a queer thing that almost the only fair and honourable man should be so troublesome to deal with. The Duke of Portland, when I talked to him the other day, seems of opinion that there would have been [no] difficulty about including him, or very many others as you had a mind, His Majesty seeming perfectly disposed to consent to anything in Ireland, while he can keep his ministry low at home. I should tell you that the King affects to speak of you with great cordiality.

This letter is written from Brooks's, where I am going to sup for the first time. My situation here begins to have as little repose as in Dublin. I have had

---

[1] General Sir Henry Clinton (1738 ?–1795).
[2] (?) George Ogle (1742–1814), Irish politician, who opposed Catholic Emancipation, and after the Union represented Dublin at Westminster.

N. Dance, pinxt.   *T. Burke, sculpt.*

FREDERICK NORTH, SECOND EARL OF GUILFORD

Clermont[1] with me half the day about the riband : and finding I am to sup here, he cannot refrain from the *satisfaction* of being of the party. I wish you were here too, and the whole business over.[2]

The Earl of Northington *to* William Windham

Dublin : July, 1783

As your letters from London gave me reason to think that your departure from thence was to take place before any letter from me could possibly reach you, I had deferred, of course in expectation of your return, to take any notice of the subject of these. The bad accounts of you from Oxford, and the variety of complaints which at present you suffer under, and the slow progress made in your case, leave me little hope of seeing you soon; even if I could be so uncharitable to wish you to undertake such a journey at the moment of your re-establishment from such severe attacks.

The subject of your letter of the 16th Inst., you may readily suppose, afforded me no less surprise than mortification. That a measure of that moment in which, next to yourself, I was by far the most seriously concerned, should have been so long decided upon without any communication to me of the resolution which you had taken, did, I must confess, appear to me a sort of conduct which my frankness of behaviour and constant friendly Intercourse with you did not lead me to expect from your hands. Notwithstanding, however, this apparent slight of me (hurting me in my private feelings, and affecting me very seriously in all publick points of consideration) I am willing to believe, because I wish it, that notions of delicacy alone, and a strong feeling at the time of the difficulties and embarrassments the step you was about to take would create to me; were alone the

---

[1] William Henry Fortescue, Earl of Clermont (died 1806), Postmaster-General, and M P for the County of Louth.

[2] Add MSS. 33100 f. 204.

notions which led to the concealment of your purpose at our last parting. My anxious and earnest wishes attend you for the speedy recovery of your Health, and as the most likely means of restoration, I desire you will divest your thoughts of a Subject which I am sure has contributed most to your present unpleasant state.

Let me, therefore, advise you to drop all thoughts of a Return to Ireland. Your Return has been doubted ever since your departure, your disinclination to the Business of your Department had not escaped the Eagle-Eyed observers of the Castle. Their conjectures spread—gained ground upon your non-Arrival, and became to a certain degree confirmed by a whisper—Intelligence from General Lutterell.[1] To what purpose then would your Return serve ? If only to fulfill an engagement of a point of Honor to me, and to keep your word, I cannot be so devoid of feeling as to wish you in your present state to attend to such an engagement, since I think it might be productive of much unpleasantness and mortification to you, and could be no further of service to me, than the giving me a Detail of the Conversations you have had with the Duke of Portland and Fox upon many interesting subjects during your stay in Town.

This communication may, however, be given me nearly as well, if I draw out a short account of what you have already sent me, and desire you to add to it what upon further recollection may suggest itself to you. This I will either send at the same time this letter goes or just after.

I have not been well myself for these last three or four days—and I am now without even Hamilton, who has been with the Bishop of Clogher upon his Election. You may be sure from your knowledge of the Enemy, that without any of these advance Guards to intercept, the Castle and the Lodge have had a continual Assail.—I am vexed therefore, tired and continually importuned ; but

---

[1] Henry Lawes Luttrell (1743–1821); Major-General 1782 ; succeeded his father as (second) Earl Carhampton 1787.

none of these distress and disturb me equally with the silly sort of conduct of our worthy friend in Downing Street [the Duke of Portland] with regard to his Irish connections. What does he mean ? Is it to disgust me with my Situation ? God knows it is not so very desireable but what a man would be happy to find an honorable Cause of retirement ! If he wishes me to continue by a mistaken partiality to a Post he is marring the Harvest of my Government which is to be reaped by the whole of his friends. But such, I find, if an explanation does not ensue, at least I am to expect, such sort of Attempts will be made to carry points in the teeth of Government here, which if they prove successful must overturn the Power of any Government here.[1]

WILLIAM WINDHAM *to* THE EARL OF NORTHINGTON

July 22, 1783

. . . The Duke of Portland sent for me last night and informed me that all the Ponsonby's were in arms. By his desire I called this morning on William Ponsonby,[2] and found him in a state of agitation hardly less than that of Clements,[3] and of a sort much more ferocious. In the course of conversation, however, I thought I had rather subdued him ; but on coming home this evening I find a letter, in which he says that on reflection he cannot help seeing the transaction in the same light as at first; and that the only reparation for the marked slight put upon all his family (by not recommending O'Callaghan)[4] would be immediately to make good the omission. Without this atonement he and all his people are to go into opposition. In his conversation with the Duke he had

---

[1] Add. MSS. 33100 f. 533.

[2] William Brabazon Ponsonby (1744–1806), member of the Irish Parliament from 1764 ; appointed joint Postmaster-General of Ireland ; created Baron Ponsonby 1806.

[3] Robert Clements (1732–1804), afterwards first Earl of Leitrim

[4] Cornelius O'Callaghan (1742–1797), afterwards first Baron Lismore. He married Frances, the sister of William, Lord Ponsonby.

extricated a regular list of charges against you and me, either jointly or separately. One was of general neglect of the Ponsonby's ; another of my having on the day of my going declined to see old Ponsonby,[1] and having neglected afterwards to send him any excuse (the same may be said by every one who called that day) ; the third, the difficulty about the Deanery ; and the fourth, last and heaviest; the refusal of O'Callaghan's peerage   On all these charges I met him, I think, with sufficient success, and upon the whole seemed to have silenced his battery : but he has mounted his guns anew, and the engagement recommences with the menace I have just stated.   My answer will be that I can give no answer in your absence, but that, in my own opinion; no injury is proved requiring such reparation.   George Ponsonby,[2] as he says, has sent over his resignation. It would have been more in course if he had given it to you. He complained heavily of the bargain attempted to be made for the Deanery of Ossory, which I defended ; though I rather believe the matter had better be yielded at once ; as I meant to have observed previous to this conversation ; but it may now be matter of consideration whether this threat held out should not be required first to be withdrawn.

The terms insisted on by Mrs. Grenville I don't understand.   Nothing passed between her and me but what is known to Cooke,[3] viz. : that there must be no return for her borough of a person not to continue there, and that she rather expected 2000*l* English, but should take the

[1] John Ponsonby (1713–1789), father of William (afterwards Baron) Ponsonby ; Speaker of the Irish House of Commons (1756–1771)

[2] George Ponsonby (1757–1817), third son of John Ponsonby, was Irish Chancellor of the Exchequer during the vice-royalty of the Duke of Portland, 1782.   In 1806, under the Fox-Grenville administration, he was Lord Chancellor of Ireland

[3] Edward Cooke (1755–1820) went to Ireland in 1778 as private secretary to Sir Richard Heron, Chief Secretary to the Lord Lieutenant At this time he held some minor official post in Ireland.   In later years he returned to England, was in 1807 Under-Secretary for War, and 1812–1817 Under-Secretary for Foreign Affairs.

best I could get for her, provided it was not less than the estabished market price.

The stocks fall very much, without any reason assigned except the great scarcity of money, owing very much to the high price of gold in Holland, which has occasioned great quantities of coin to be carried out of the kingdom. Much has been smuggled from the coast of Norfolk.[1]

WILLIAM WINDHAM *to* THE HON. THOMAS PELHAM [2]

Salt Hill: August 11, 1783

I came hither last night from Oxford . . . not without some hopes, though unknown possibly to you, of your coming at the same time. . . . Should it be inconvenient to you to meet me here, I will, if you wish it, take the very first opportunity of coming to London : in the mean while, any information which you may wish from me shall be communicated as fully as can be done by letter ; and, without waiting your inquiries, I will myself suggest anything which may occur to me as useful for you to know. Under this head, I may immediately mention some articles, of small consequence in themselves; yet equally trying and vexatious with things of greater importance. I mean all that relates to Household establishment. Of these the articles are not numerous; though some of them expensive—Plate, Chariot, Coach-horses and Liveries. Plate is not absolutely necessary; but is upon the whole more eligible, and as you need not be sollicitous about the fashion, but may buy it at second hand, will, I understand, answer better in point of economy. For a chariot, any decent Town-chariot, a little vamped up, will, I apprehend, do perfectly well; particularly as you will have had such short notice. Coach-horses you had better buy here, ready broke and

---

[1] Add. MSS 33100 f. 215.
[2] The Hon. Thomas Pelham, afterwards second Earl of Chichester (1756–1826), succeeded Windham as Chief Secretary to the Lord-Lieutenant of Ireland.

seasoned from the Job men : and these, if good, will, I find, at any time sell without loss in the country : you must have a set.   Of the livery you will order the lace and buttons here, and take the cloth there.   There must be frock liveries and state, each of them such as you would make, under the same description, here.   With respect to horses, should you not be able to get a set easily and to your mind before you go, you may take the same method as was recommended to me, and was followed by me, for the time I staid, namely, to hire jobs, which, under the plea of want of time for preparation, you may probably continue, without notice being taken of it, during the whole time.   Of servants you will want four immediately in livery, including the porter, who remains under all changes.   These you must take from England, unless you have a mind to take one or two of mine, and they are willing to stay.   A Coachman and postillion you will find there also, but I would advise you by no means to take them, but at wages vastly less than they received from me, and if you have any coachman of whom you have a good opinion, to take him at once.

One of the most material concerns is a good maître d'Hotel ; and in this article I am happy to be able to assist you, at least for the present, should you not otherwise be provided, by leaving with you for some time my servant, who was recommended to me by Sir Richard Heron,[1] and whom I found so far as I had experience of him, a most diligent, trustworthy and intelligent servant. If he can be of any use, he shall remain with you as long as you wish.—All other articles of establishment you will either find upon the spot, or can easily provide.   There is a set of desert china, which was bought for me at a sale just before I came away, and which they tell me are very handsome.   These you may have, if you please, at the same price they cost me, or, if you think that some

---

[1] Sir Richard Heron (1726-1805), Chief-Secretary to the Lord-Lieutenant, John, Earl of Buckinghamshire, 1776-1779.

abatement should be made, at such a price as shall be deemed reasonable. Other odd matters, which you will wish probably to take from me, will go by appraisement : but these are of small amount.

Having run through these few things, which, though least in consequence, are perhaps first in order, I will neither detain you nor delay my letter any longer, than to say that, being persuaded you will not feel those objections to the office, either from health, temper or peculiarity of habit that I do, I most sincerely rejoice at your acceptance of it, principally because it relieves me from all apprehension of inconvenience that might be occasioned by my retirement. Without any affected modesty about myself, or insincere compliment to you, I assure you I think the interests of the present administration, to which I am happy to think we are now united in wishing well, will not only suffer no prejudice but gain considerably by the exchange. Consider that I really think my constitution not sufficiently good ; no one does well what he does with an ill will.[1]

WILLIAM WINDHAM *to* THE EARL OF NORTHINGTON

Oxford :[2] *August* 15, 1783

After the receipt of your most friendly letter, I shall feel every hour long till this letter reaches you, not only to say how much your kindness affects me, but to acquit myself of a charge, of all others most painful to me, and which is rendered doubly sensible by your very gentle and tender manner of urging it. Let me be suspected of anything rather than of having been intentionally wanting in candour and attention towards you. Whatever may be my faults, reserve and duplicity are not of the number ; or if any such qualities had place in my composition, this would have been the last occasion on which they would

[1] Add. MSS. 33100 f. 252.
[2] After his illness Windham resided for some time at Oxford

have shewn themselves. Nobody could be more sensible that your conduct to me called for every possible return of confidence and attention : nor has anything given me more pain than the appearance, which I felt I incurred, of acting in a way not conformable to those sentiments.

Two ideas might naturally strike your mind, each of them making a very reasonable ground of complaint : either that I had secretly resolved on what I should do; at the time I took my leave of you, and had concurred in the proposal of going to England, as a convenient opportunity of declaring it : or that I deferred finally to make up my mind upon the subject till I should have consulted the Duke of Portland. I do assure you that neither of these was the fact. I neither knew, at the moment I parted from you, what I should do : nor had I an idea, should the resolution be taken, of communicating it except to yourself at my return. That I should forbear to say anything, till the matter was absolutely decided, can easily be conceived. The question was of a sort which I *must* determine for myself ; the task of intimating such an intention was not so pleasant as that one would wish to undergo it unnecessarily : and I was too well acquainted with my own weakness in resisting the arguments of those for whom I had a regard, to hazard the mention of such a purpose, till I could resolve that it must at all events take place. I had nothing to do; therefore, but to endeavour by a careful estimate of all circumstances of health, liking and ability—considering the two former chiefly as they affected the latter—to make up my own mind upon the subject : to accomplish which was no easy task : one's sentiments varying almost every twelve hours, according as a night passed at the Phœnix Park gave one a feel of strength and confidence; or the confinement of a day in the Castle brought on such languor, weariness and disgust as sunk one into absolute despair.

In this state of uncertainty I took my leave of you;

thinking that a fortnight was yet left me for deliberation, while in the meantime the journey would afford me opportunities of discussing the question more coolly and connectedly than was possible in Dublin, and at the same time furnish me with a new datum, by ascertaining the chance of release, by a dissolution of the ministry. The idea of the letter I afterwards wrote to you, on the mention of the matter to the Duke of Portland, had never entered my mind. As to the person to whom such a communication was first due, it would never have been a question with me, not only in point of what may be called official propriety, but because the effect which it was too likely to have in embarrassing you, was the circumstance so much uppermost in my thoughts. To confess the truth, it was the only circumstance that very materially distressed me : for though I have the greatest esteem, regard and attachment to the Duke of Portland, and that I could never disappoint his wishes without pain, yet the circumstances attending my acceptance of this office had been so peculiar, my disinclination had been so strongly marked, and the importunity by which that was overcome was so near what might be called unfair; that I by no means felt the same obligation to consult his inclinations, as I should upon any other occasion. A conversation had accordingly passed with him, without my uttering a word upon the subject ; as indeed it would have done, independent of that consideration, unless I had resolved on writing to you.

What brought on the measure so suddenly, and compelled an immediate decision, was the reflexion which from strange inadvertence I had not before made, that my option of a seat in the new Parliament would not stand over till the return of the writs but must determine the instant of my election ; that the resolution therefore must be taken immediately or not at all. When I had settled to write to you, I then thought it best to mention it to the Duke of Portland for the sake of saving time, requesting, however, that till he should hear from you, it might remain an entire secret, and not intending that he should speak of it, even to Fox. Possibly in that restriction I might have been wrong, as the same purpose that induced the mention of it to the Duke of Portland made it desirable that Fox also should be acquainted with it.

This is a faithful representation of the progress of the business as it passed in my mind. The measure itself has been sufficiently distressing to me, without the aggravation of having added to it an appearance of contrivance and stratagem. What struck me most and could least be got over, was the idea of leaving you, as it were, in the lurch, of deserting you in the midst of difficulties on which we had entered together, and effecting my own escape, without regarding those I left behind. My only consolation was that by consulting my own ease and comfort, I hoped I should not make your condition worse ; and that my sharing your plagues and vexations could contribute little to relieve them, but this reflexion would lose much of its efficacy, if I had not the satisfaction of seeing my place supplied by such a man as Pelham. I know but very few men who are so fit for the situation, and I know none with whom I conceive and hope you will find yourself so much at your ease. I have upon this occasion great pleasure in thinking that you will never feel a moment's regret of me. I must make haste now and finish my letter, having been delayed by some visitors this morning till I am in danger of being too late for the cross post. By an unfortunate combination of circumstances, I did not receive yours till last night. I had gone for a night to Salt Hill, in order to meet Pelham, but by a delay in the receipt of letters, was detained there too, and have come back not quite so well as I went. I am to meet him however if I can next Monday in London ; when, if I get your letter with the Queries you mention, I may answer them more completely by further conversation with the Duke of Portland and Fox.

As Pelham purposes to set off within a fortnight, to which both for his own sake as well as yours I shall urge him strongly, I will without further hesitation follow the advice which you so kindly urge, and drop all thoughts of returning to Ireland : I should have had some satisfaction, as far as a trifling motive goes, in returning there, if it were only to mar the self-complacency of those who will now pretend to have foreseen that I never meant to return ; but this is not much worth thinking on. I wish I could as easily follow your advice in divesting myself of all other anxieties in that quarter ; which I shall not do till I hear things are more settled and in a prosperous train ; I might say, till you are out of the country. I shall have an interest in your success, not less personal than if I had still continued a party ; for every difficulty in which you are involved, I shall feel as reproaching me for leaving you. It is well for me that matters were so settled before I got your letter ; for otherwise the very kind and handsome manner in which you there express yourself would infallibly have brought me back to the situation, whatever miseries it might have cost me. I will now take my leave of you for the present, by observing that for the whole of this business, anxious as it has been, I shall think myself well repaid by the privilege which I derive from thence, of assuring you that I am, with the greatest truth, my dear Lord,

most sincerely and affectionately yours,

W. WINDHAM.[1]

WILLIAM WINDHAM *to* THE EARL OF NORTHINGTON

Oxford : August 26, 1783

I cannot depart my official life, without charging Pelham, as my heir and executor, to be the bearer of

[1] Add MSS 33100 f. 262.

my last farewell to you. I meant to have had a number of letters ready against his arrival ; but by the same indolent procrastination that in Lord North ruined an empire, and in me, had I continued where I was, would have been productive of a thousand distresses, I have left them all undone, and can only write these few lines to you, to be sent to him before I am up. I don't know anything I have to say, till I shall receive your queries to the Duke of Portland.

The more I see of Pelham, the more I am satisfied with his being my successor. He seems to set about his business in a composed, methodical manner, to apply his mind readily to the work, to form very good judgments and to be perfectly vigilant and discreet.[1] . . .

WILLIAM WINDHAM *to* JOHN COXE HIPPISLEY [2]

Oxford : September 16, 1783

It seems a strange time to begin a letter to India, when the post is within half an hour of setting out : but I must write now, or I shall miss the opportunity they tell me of the next packet. How shall I comprize in so short a compass an account even of my own history ? Let me tell you at once, that in the course of five little months since I wrote last, I have been in the responsible office of Secretary to the Lord-Lieutenant of Ireland ; and that I am now returned again to the condition of a private man. This, perhaps, need not surprise you in one respect, as we have seen whole Ministries change in as short a period : but happily that has not been the case in the present instance   The abstract of my history is, that I undertook the office much against my will, having been formerly in the country, and being well acquainted with the unpleasant nature of the business ; and finding,

---

[1] Add. MSS. 33100 f. 290.
[2] John Coxe Hippisley (1748–1825), Agent of the British Government in Italy, 1779–80 ; afterwards in the East India Company's service ; created baronet, 1796.

upon trial; that the liking did not increase; and that
my health suffered, I took the opportunity of a fever;
that attacked me during an absence on some business in
England; and before I was elected into the new Parliament, and while my resignation could not be attended
with much embarrassment to Government, withdrew
from a situation, which was too little suited either to
my talents or temper, to admit a hope of my filling it
with credit. I am now, therefore, returned to my privacy,
with a greater enjoyment of it than ever, though possibly
not so rooted in it as formerly : the transition to public
life having been once made, will be more easy on any
future occasion ; just as going abroad is to a person who
has once crossed the Channel. At present, however, I
have no prospect of such an occasion, nor any wish for
one. When a vacancy happens at Norwich I shall
probably come into Parliament, and my attachment to a
particular set of Men will then probably lead me; by
degrees, to take an active part in business; but my
genius lies to employment of a different kind, and however
I may embark for a while *civilibus undis*, it will only be
with a view of returning with higher enjoyment to the
pursuit of Literature and Philosophy—but enough of
myself any otherwise than as that account may be connected with the mention of your business. The scene of
my illness in England was the place I am now in, namely
Alma Mater [*illegible*] where about five weeks ago, Sir
Gilbert Elliot [1] called upon me, and where General
Maitland; most obligingly came to see me on purpose, a
few days ago, and where Lord Loughborough called on
me the day before yesterday: so that Oxford seems to
have been the place for a sort of Parliament of your
friends. [2]

[1] Sir Gilbert Elliot (1751–1814) ; Member of Parliament from 1776 ;
Constitutional Viceroy of Corsica (1795–7);   created Baron Minto
1797 ; Governor-General of Bengal 1807–13 ; created Earl of Minto 1813.
[2] Add. MSS. 37848 f. 51.

WILLIAM WINDHAM *to* THE EARL OF NORTHINGTON

Brooks's: December 18, 1783

You have probably heard from some other hand a better account than I can give you of the events that have taken place since my last letter. My information of things future may lose something of its credit, upon the receipt of a letter, which I put into the hands of a friend of mine, the other day, a Mr. Wills. I there predicted that the ministry were to be triumphant, in the House of Lords.[1] The failure of this prediction you are already acquainted with : I can only say in my own excuse that I took my ideas from the language of Fox, who at three o'clock the night before at Brooks's, where one supposes that no disguise is used, spoke with great confidence of having a majority of thirty. The effect which the real issue produced, I need not talk of to you, who must have seen a more curious scene on your side of the water. As curious will be the reverse, I hope, on the arrival of the news of yesterday.

You know probably the terms of the resolution : indeed upon recollection you will have them more correctly than I give them from the papers : so I will only say that, by all accounts, nothing has ever been known equal to the animation of the house, and the triumph of ministry. Fox according to the usual account, greater than ever ; Lord North, of whom that is not so constantly said, is universally agreed to have been uncommonly able and successful in both his speeches. Pitt, after a great deal of intemperate and virulent declamation, was at last

---

[1] "Before the second reading of Fox's India Bill in the Lords the King gave Temple a card, authorising him to say that whoever voted for the Bill ' would be considered by him as an enemy.' This soon became known, and, on December 17, the Commons voted by 153 to 80 that it was now necessary to declare that to report the King's opinion on any question pending in Parliament with a view to influence votes is a high crime and misdemeanour. Nevertheless the King's unconstitutional move was successful ; the Lords rejected the Bill."—" Political History of England," x. 250.

so beaten and struck down, that upon the second question; I hear, he could not even make up a speech. Whether the rashness, folly and presumption of your worthy predecessor[1] will venture to undertake the government under the present circumstances, and whether his Majesty's magnanimity will remain unshaken by these resolutions of the angry Commons, is now the subject of speculation among the learned. I will hazard no more conjectures : for which indeed I have a further reason than the fear of being proved wrong, namely, that I have hardly an opinion upon the subject. One confidence only I have, that good, either immediate or ultimate, must be the result : and perhaps the greatest would be that which should come through the medium of temporary confusion. The conduct by which the fate of the measure was turned, was happily so marked that people cannot mistake it ; and I hear accordingly that people in general speak of it with much indignation. On such accounts, however, one can perhaps lay no great stress : the most satisfactory intelligence, therefore, to you may be that Fox, who has just been here, is in an extasy of spirits. The substance of the Duke of Portland's interview with the King yesterday was to acquaint him with the reports and desire his Majesty's authority to contradict them. To which the King answered " *that he could give him no such authority, having never approved* the bill." The fact is that every possible attention was shewn in submitting to him the several parts of the business, as it went on : and desiring upon each his sentiments : nor was anything said that imported the least disapprobation, and much that implied satisfaction.

I write this from Brooks's, which presents a scene such as you have so frequently beheld here : I don't know that it would be a bad wish to say that I

[1] George Nugent-Temple Grenville, second Earl Temple (1753–1813), Lord-Lieutenant of Ireland in the Shelburne Administration The Duke of Rutland succeeded Lord Northington, but in 1787 Temple, now Marquis of Buckingham, again became Lord-Lieutenant.

should not be sorry, if you were soon to make part of it.[1]

WILLIAM WINDHAM *to* THE EARL OF NORTHINGTON

December, 1783

It is worth while to write you a few lines from Brooks's, if it be only for the sake of bringing the place into your thoughts, and giving you a momentary vision of a scene, which at most hours of the day, may have a chance of being more agreeable than the one that is before you. At present however there is further reason, that you may have the last, and probably the most authentick account of a report of no long standing, and not much vouched and supported; yet sufficient to excite considerable alarm. I must be brief, having deferred writing to the last moment, that I may relate all that is hitherto known.

Lord Temple, that terror of administrations, was with the King yesterday, for an hour and half after the Levee. That fact and that only is certain. Two evidences declare that Lord Lothian[2] yesterday, at dinner at the Prince of Wales's, related in their hearing that Lord Temple, on coming out of the Closet, told him that the King had authorized him to say that his (his Majesty's) friends would do a very acceptable thing to him, if they opposed the present Indian Bill. That is [what] he, Lord Lothian, declared repeatedly, and talked of during the whole of dinner.—Adam Alsop, and Andrew Stuart[3] told Fox that Lord Carmarthen[4] had reported the same declaration made by Lord Temple afterwards to him. These points therefore seem to be pretty well

[1] Add. MSS. 33100 f. 443.
[2] William John Kerr, fifth Marquis of Lothian (1737–1815).
[3] Andrew Stuart (d. 1801), lawyer; Member of Parliament from 1774 until his death.
[4] Francis Osborne, fifth Duke of Leeds (1751–1799), until his succession to the dukedom in 1789, known as Lord Carmarthen. He was an active politician, and Foreign Secretary under Pitt, 1783–91.

established, that both Lord Lothian and Lord Carmarthen related this declaration as coming from Lord Temple. On the other hand, Lord Lothian on being asked by Fox, denies that he had even seen Lord Temple since his leaving the King, and this account is confirmed by Lord Essex,[1] the Lord in waiting, who says that when Lord Temple left the King, no one else remained at St. James's. The presumption, therefore, is, that Lord Lothian had related a conversation that had passed before Lord Temple's going into the closet, as having happened afterwards ; and finding afterwards that he had got into a scrape, wished to recall his report : and that Lord Carmarthen might have talked loosely, and related as a matter which Lord Temple was authorized to declare, what he might have said only as his private opinion.— This seems to be the whole of what is known upon the occasion. No other circumstances appear to confirm the opinion of Lord Temple's conversation having produced any effect ; and on the contrary, all those of the King's friends whose support was expected, seem to continue firm in their purpose. Fox, who is just gone from here, and whose account I have taken, tells me to caution you against feeling at all alarmed. One circumstance might be thought suspicious, that the Archbishop who is understood to be a warm supporter, and who I know has the Bishop of London's proxy for that purpose, was sent for to the King either yesterday or this morning : but Fox does not seem to apprehend that anything is to be inferred from this. I shall let you know what I hear further of this, if I find that you have not got accounts from better hands.[2]

---

[1] William Anne Capel, fourth Earl of Essex (1732–1799).
[2] Add. MSS. 33100 f. 522

SECTION III
FIRST YEARS IN PARLIAMENT
1784–1793

SECTION III

FIRST YEARS IN PARLIAMENT
1784-1793

CHAPTER I

The downfall of the Coalition Ministry : Pitt Prime Minister :
Windham elected M.P. for Norwich : A regular attendant at
the Literary Club : His friendship with Dr. Johnson : Some
correspondence between them : Windham's accounts of his
last interviews with Johnson : Johnson's death : Windham
invites Fox to the funeral : The political pupil of Burke : Some
of Windham's friends : Mrs. Siddons : Windham's interest
in aeronautics : His ascent in a balloon with Sadler : Fitzpatrick's ascent.

THE opposition of the King to Fox's India Bill
having brought about the downfall of the Coali-
tion Ministry in December 1783, Pitt became
Prime Minister. As, however, the followers of
Fox and Lord North still formed a majority in the House
of Commons, Parliament was dissolved in the following
March. Windham was again nominated for Norwich, and;
after a fierce contest, was returned as junior member on
April 5 by a majority of sixty-four votes over the Hon.
Henry Hobart,[1] being one of the few supporters of the
unpopular Coalition Ministry who were returned to
Westminster.

---

[1] The figures were : Sir Harbord Harbord, 2305 ; Windham, 1297 ;
Hobart, 1233.

THE DUKE OF PORTLAND *to* WILLIAM WINDHAM

London : April 7, 1784

I am most sincerely obliged to you and give you my most hearty thanks for having caused the only very satisfactory event that has happened since this cursed Dissolution has taken place, and I desire you to accept my best congratulations on your Election which you have obtained with no less honor to yourself than with advantage to the Publick Cause. You have undergone much trouble, fatigue, uneasiness and vexation of every kind, but you have succeeded, and succeeded with every circumstance that should give you comfort and make you satisfied with yourself. As a publick man I must again repeat my thanks to you, and in the private and more grateful capacity of a Friend I share with you the joy which you ought to feel, and which ought to be the effect of the Conduct you have observed.

I cannot like Westminster, nor can I say that my mind is at ease respecting York and Yorkshire (but this is to yourself). I trust Norfolk will afford me a better prospect. No pains shall be wanting on my part to realize this hope, but I desire that you will suggest any thing in which my endeavours can be thought to be of service.[1]

Now more than ever before Windham stayed in London, and in these years of his life he found the metropolis a very pleasant place. Previous to going abroad in 1778 he had been elected a member of the Literary Club, and now he was a regular attendant at its meetings. He made the acquaintance of the whole circle, and Dr. Johnson had a great liking for him. When it was that Windham first made Johnson's acquaintance is not known ; but it is clear from Boswell's " Life," that as early as 1776 they

[1] Add. MSS. 37845 f. 3.

were on intimate terms. At the end of 1783 Dr. Johnson founded the Essex Head Club, whereof Windham was an original member. That the two men had a very tender regard for each other there can be no doubt, and it is certain that they were as much together as circumstances permitted. " After dinner," Windham noted in his Diary, May 15, 1784; " took Johnson an airing over Blackfriars Bridge, thence to the Club ; present, Boswell, Murphy, Brocklesby, Berry, Mr. Bowles, Hoole, and his son, and a son [1] of Dr Burney, he that was expelled Cambridge."

DR. JOHNSON *to* WILLIAM WINDHAM

August 1784

The tenderness with which you have been pleased to treat me, through my long illness, neither health nor sickness can, I hope, make me forget ; and you are not to suppose, that after we parted you were no longer in my mind. But what can a sick man say, but that he is sick ? His thoughts are necessarily concentered in himself ; he neither receives, nor can give delight ; his enquiries are after alleviations of pain, and his efforts are to catch some momentary comfort. Though I am now in the neighbourhood of the Park, you must expect no account of its wonders, of its hills, its waters, its caverns, or its mines ; but I will tell you, dear Sir, what I hope you will not hear with less satisfaction, that, for about a week past, my asthma has been less afflictive.[2]

That Johnson was sincerely grateful to the younger man he has shown in a letter to Dr. Brocklesby, written from Ashbourne, September 2, 1784. " Mr. Windham has been here to see me," he wrote ; " he came, I think,

---

[1] Charles, second son of Dr Burney.
[2] Boswell, " Life of Johnson " (ed. Hill), iv. 632.

forty miles out of his way, and staid about a day and a half; perhaps I make the time shorter than it was. Such conversation I shall not have again till I come back to the regions of literature; and there Windham is, *inter stellas luna minores.*" It was on this visit-that Windham, as the Doctor put it, endeavoured to " wheedle " him into paying a visit to Oxford as the younger man's guest.[1]

DR. JOHNSON *to* WILLIAM WINDHAM
Lichfield : October 2, 1784

I believe you had been long enough acquainted with the *phænomena* of sickness, not to be surprised that a sick man wishes to be where he is not, and where it appears to everybody but himself that he might easily be, without having the resolution to move. I thought Ashbourne a solitary place but did not come hither till last Monday. I have here more company, but my health has for this last week not advanced ; and in the languor of disease how little can be done ? Whether or when I shall make my next remove, I cannot tell ; but I entreat you, dear Sir, to let me hear, from time to time, where you may be found, for your residence is a very powerful attractive to, Sir, your most humble servant.[2]

WILLIAM WINDHAM *to* DR. JOHNSON
Oxford : October 6, 1784

I returned to this place two days ago, not without a secret hope, that you might be here before me ; and that I might find myself at once in possession of your company, and of an evidence of your improving health. Those pleasing expectations, your letter has for a while suspended, but I hope not dispelled. From accounts

<hr>

[1] Boswell, "Life of Johnson " (ed. Hill), iv. 356.   [2] *Ibid.*

Sir *Joshua Reynolds, pinst.*   *Wm. Doughty, sculpt.*

DR. JOHNSON

which I received from Mrs. R. Burke [1] and from **Dr. Brocklesby**,[2] I cannot help flattering myself, notwithstanding the languor you describe, and the retardation of your recovery during the last week, that you are upon the whole gaining on your complaints, and that when next I have the pleasure of seeing you, I shall be able to congratulate you and myself, on evident marks of your advancement.

The interruption given to my residence here by the love of [*illegible*] which carried me for some time to London, would incline me to protract my stay for a fortnight longer, till increase of numbers shall render living in the University less agreable.   My continuance here has, however, no certain limits but my own inclinations, and they will not suffer me to depart, as long as I have any prospect of being favoured with your company.[3]

Johnson's health did not improve, and on November 16 he returned to London.   His friends were unremitting in their attentions, for it was evident that his strength was failing day by day, and all knew that his life was ebbing fast ; Windham was one of the most frequent visitors at Bolt Court, and on December 7 he had a long and interesting conversation with him, as he records in his " Diary."

After waiting some short time in the adjoining room, I was admitted to Dr. Johnson in his bedchamber, where, after placing me next him on the chair, he sitting in his usual place on the east side of the room (and I on his right-hand) he put into my hands two small volumes (an edition of the New Testament) as he afterwards told me, saying, *Extremum hoc munus morientis habeto*.   He

---

[1] Wife of the son of Edmund Burke.
[2] Richard Brocklesby (1722-1797), physician ; the friend of Burke, and also of Dr Johnson, whom he attended in his last illness
[3] Add MSS. 37914 f. 18.

then proceeded to observe that I was entering upon a life which would lead me deeply into all the business of the world ; that he did not condemn civil employment, but that it was a state of great danger ; and that he had therefore one piece of advice earnestly to impress upon me—that I would set apart every seventh day, for the care of my soul ; that one day, the seventh, should be employed in repenting what was amiss in the six preceding, and for fortifying my virtue for the six to come ; that such a portion of time was surely little enough for the meditation of eternity.   He then told me that he had a request to make to me, namely, that I would allow his servant Frank to look up to me as his friend, adviser, and protector in all difficulties which his own weakness and imprudence, or the force or fraud of others, might bring him into.   He said that he had left him what he considered an ample provision, viz. 70*l.* per annum ; but that even that sum might not place him above the want of a protector, and to me, therefore, he recommended him, as to one who had will, and power, and activity to protect him.   Having obtained my assent to this, he proposed that Frank should be called in, and desiring me to take him by the hand in token of the promise, repeated before him the recommendation he had just made of him, and the promise I had given to attend to it.

I then took occasion to say how much I felt, what I had long foreseen that I should feel, regret at having spent so little of my life in his company.   I stated this as an instance where resolutions are deferred till the occasions are past.   For some time past I had determined that such an occasion of self-reproach should no longer subsist, and had built upon the hope of passing in his society the chief part of my time, at the moment when it was to be apprehended we were about to lose him for ever !   I had no difficulty of speaking to him thus of my apprehensions ; I could not help, on the other hand, entertaining hopes ; but with these I did not like to

trouble him, lest he should conceive that I thought it necessary to flatter him.   He answered hastily that he was sure
I would not, and proceeded to make a compliment to the
manliness of my mind, which, whether deserved or not,
ought to be remembered that it may be deserved.

I then stated that among other neglects was the omission of introducing, of all others, the most important,
the consequence of which particularly filled my mind
at that moment, and on which I had often been desirous
to know his opinions.   The subjects I meant were
I said, ' natural and revealed religion '   The wish thus
generally stated was in part gratified on the instant.
For revealed religion, he said, there was such historical
evidence as, upon any subject not religious, would have
left no doubt.   Had the facts recorded in the New Testament been mere civil occurrences, no one would have
called in question the testimony by which they are
established.   But the importance annexed to them
amounting to nothing less than the salvation of mankind,
raised a cloud in our minds, and created doubt unknown
upon any other subject.   Of proofs to be derived from
history, one of the most cogent, he seemed to think, was
the opinion so well authenticated and so long entertained
of a Deliverer that was to appear about that time.
Among the typical representations, the sacrifice of the
Paschal lamb, in which no bone was to be broken, had
early struck his mind.   For the immediate life and
miracles of Christ ;   such attestation as that of the
apostles, who all, except St. John, confirmed their testimony by their blood ;   such belief as their witness procured from a people best furnished with the means of
judging, and least disposed to judge favourably ;   such
an extension afterwards of that belief over all the nations
of the earth, though originating from a nation of all
others the most despised, would leave no doubt that the
things witnessed were true, and were of a nature more
than human.   With respect to evidences, Dr. Johnson

observed, we had not such evidence that Cæsar died in the Capitol, as that Christ died in the manner related.[1]

On December 11 Windham was again admitted to the sick chamber, and of this meeting also he has left a record.

After promising that I considered what I was going to say as a matter of duty, I said that I hoped he would not suspect me of the weakness of importuning him to take nourishment for the purpose of prolonging his life for a few hours or days. I then stated what the reason was, that it was to secure that which I was persuaded he was most anxious about, viz., that he might preserve his faculties entire to the last moment. Before I had quite stated my meaning, he interrupted me by saying that he refused no sustenance but inebriating sustenance, and proceeded to give instances where, in compliance with the wishes of his physicians, he had taken even a small quantity of wine. I readily assented to any objections he might have to nourishment of that kind, and observing that milk was the only nourishment I intended, flattered myself that I had succeeded in my endeavours, when he recurred to his general refusal, and begged that there might be an end to it. I then said that I hoped he would forgive my earnestness—or something to that effect : when he replied eagerly, 'that from me nothing would be necessary by way of apology'; adding with great fervour, in words which I shall (I hope) never forget—'God bless you, my dear Windham, through Jesu Christ', and concluding with a wish that we might meet in some humble portion of that happiness which God might finally vouchsafe to repentant sinners. These were the last words I ever heard him speak. I hurried

---

[1] Windham's "Diary," pp. 28-30.

out of the room with tears in my eyes, and more affected than I had been on any former occasion.[1]

This was the last meeting between them, for when Windham went to Bolt Court the next afternoon, the dying man was sleeping, and he did not enter the room. In the evening Johnson passed away, a man so eminent in literary annals that even to have been his friend is sufficient for immortalization. The sad news was brought almost at once to Windham, who thus commented upon it :

While I was writing the adjoining articles, received the fatal account, so long dreaded, that Dr Johnson was no more. May those prayers which he incessantly poured from a heart fraught with the deepest devotion, find that acceptance with Him to Whom they were addressed, which piety so humble and so fervent may seem to promise.[2]

WILLIAM WINDHAM *to* CHARLES JAMES FOX

Brooks's : December 18, 1784

You have heard, no doubt, that to the great men who have departed in our time one more instance is to be added ; and that learning and virtue have sustained a loss, equal to any they have ever known, in the death of Dr. Johnson. Though you have never cultivated his acquaintance nor lived much in his society, you have so much respect perhaps for his genius and character, as to feel a satisfaction,—which is all that can be said,—in doing an act of honour to his memory. His particular friends, including The Club of which you are a member, mean to attend his corpse on Monday morning from his house in Bolt Court, Fleet Street, to its place of interment in Westminster Abbey. You are not too much of a philo-

[1] Windham's " Diary," p. 31.   *Ibid.* p 33.

sopher to share in the vulgar prejudice, that leads men to pay honours to the dead. If you can make it convenient to you to be in Fleet Street by 11 o'clock, or in Westminster Abbey by 12, I trust you will put on a black coat, and show yourself among the mourners at his funeral.[1]

Windham was one of the pall-bearers at Johnson's funeral, the others being Sir Joseph Banks, Sir Charles Bunbury, Edmund Burke, Langton, and George Colman. Subsequently he took an active part in erecting a memorial to his friend. " Last Sunday," Boswell wrote to Temple, November '28, 1789, " I dined with Malone, with Sir Joshua Reynolds, Sir Joseph Banks, Mr. Metcalfe, Mr. Windham, Mr. Courtenay, and young Mr. Burke, being a select number of Dr. Johnson's friends, to settle as to effectual measures for having a monument erected to him in Westminster Abbey."[2]

Windham was almost as intimate with Burke as with Johnson. He became his political pupil. He was also the friend of Malone and Reynolds, who painted his portrait.[3] Of the relations existing between these men something will be shown in these volumes ; whilst others whose names frequently occur at this time in his Diary are Fox, Fitzpatrick, Hare, Selwyn, Sheridan, Gilbert Elliot, Lord Spencer, the Duke of Portland, Lord Townshend, and, among theatrical folk, Mrs. and Miss Kemble, and Mrs. Siddons.

[1] Add. MSS. 37843 f 220.
[2] Letters of Boswell to the Rev. W J. Temple (ed. Seccombe), 263.
[3] " The two portraits which Sir Joshua Reynolds has lately painted of Mr. William Windham of Norfolk and Richard Brinsley Sheridan are so like the originals, that they seem almost alive and ready to speak to you. Painting in point of resemblance, can go no further "—Prior, " Life of Malone " p 358.

WILLIAM WINDHAM *to* MRS. SIDDONS [1]

Oxford : October 10, 1784

I sincerely congratulate you on the victory obtained over malice and brutality the first night of your appearance. From Mr. Lawrence, a friend of Sheridan's, who was present upon the occasion, and who is just come down here, I have received the whole account. Nothing had pleased me more than the style of your address, which completely removed any regret for the necessity of delivering it. It spoke the only language proper for the occasion—the language of innocence, disclaiming favour and calling only for justice against calumny and outrage. I regret that I was not in the house at the time. You will now resolve, I hope, that the matter shall end, and that nothing shall provoke you to further explanation.[2]

MRS. SIDDONS *to* WILLIAM WINDHAM

January 1, 1785

I wish you many happy returns of this day, and hope you will not be engaged this evening to tea, as I am to have a little music ; but my party does not exceed two gentlemen, who perhaps you know, with my own fireside. I am sure you would like it, and you can't be to learn that I am truly sensible of the honour of your society. I am flying to rehearsal, and shall flatter myself that you will give me the happiness of seeing you.[3]

---

[1] Mrs Siddons, who had been touring in the provinces, reappeared at Drury Lane Theatre on October 5, 1784, in the character of Mrs. Beverley in "The Gamester," and to her great astonishment was hooted when she stepped upon the stage. This unusual reception of a favourite actress was the result of rumours which had been circulated while she was away, that as a reward for appearing at the benefits given to Digges and Brereton she had extorted a share of the receipts. The fact, generally known, that she was extraordinarily careful of her money, made the public believe the story. Kemble led her off the stage, but she insisted on returning and denying the allegations, which were, indeed, soon proved to be unfounded.

[2] Windham, " Diary," p. 24.   [3] *Ibid.* p. 39.

Windham was at this time on very friendly terms with Mrs. Siddons. Sir Gilbert Elliot, writing to his wife on March 14, 1787, of a ball at Miss Adair's, mentions that the actress was the principal person there. " She did not dance," he remarked, " but was attended unremittingly by Windham on one hand, and Tom Erskine [1] on the other, and sometimes young Burke in front and young Adams in rear." [2] Windham's intimacy with Mrs. Siddons did not endure, however, for in his Diary, for May 27, 1805, after noting that he went to see her in " Zara," he added : " Had not seen her for years : impression of her excellence not less than formerly."

JOHN HELY-HUTCHINSON [3] *to* WILLIAM WINDHAM

Palmerston : August 12, 1784

Your kind letter has given me very sensible pleasure : it confirmed an opinion which I had formed after some consideration, and in which I had the mortification of standing single, and it flatters me with the hopes of the continuance of your friendship, on which I must set a high value whilst I have any regard for cultivated talents under the direction of virtue and candor, and under the influence of the finest feelings. These qualities would have certainly made their way through the thorny and entangled labyrinth of the Castle, but are more pleasantly exercised by the member for Norwich, who will serve his discerning constituents with the same spirit and integrity that animated his elegant and manly address for their suffrages. With them you are to answer only for your own conduct, in which you and they may always justly confide, but God knows for whom and for what a

---

[1] Thomas, afterwards Baron, Erskine (1750-1823), Lord Chancellor 1806

[2] " Life and Letters of Lord Minto," 1. 136.

[3] John Hely-Hutchinson (1724-1794), Provost of Trinity College, Dublin, 1774. An active politician, and an advocate of Irish independence and Catholic Emancipation.

Sir Wm. Beechey, R.A.

SARAH SIDDONS

Secretary to a Lord Lieutenant may be responsible. I hold this to be the most troublesome office in the British Empire, which, comprising every department in the Church, Law, State, Army and revenue, and both houses of parliament, is made more troublesome by the wild turbulence of the times. There is no intermediate body of men between the Castle and the people. The men of property and in great offices have not the power of restraining, because they have little or no influence. These disorders, as you justly observe, may by their excess work their own cure. There have been some favorable appearances of that kind in the metropolis and in other parts of the Kingdom. The great difficulty lies here · this country is become free and must be governed, if peaceably governed, by considering its interest as the primary object in all public deliberations. Of the interest of Ireland that of Great Britain should be certainly considered as an essential part ; but if the interest of the latter is to be preferred in the Irish parliament, I fear much for the public peace. The situation of Ireland is new ; the maxims of her government should be different from those adopted when the circumstances of the country were different. The commercial system should be form'd on principles of exact equality : Ireland to encourage the staple manufacture of England, the woolen in the same degree that England encourages our staple manufacture, the linnen, which we ought to encourage to the utmost extent, and it is capable of being doubled in value, to prevent, as far as possible, all jealousy between the two countries in adjusting this equality, justice requires that a liberal compensation should be made to England for the superiority of her markets. The difficulty above stated has occasioned the present disturbances. Administration had stood the parliamentary reform without receiving much damage ; and might have weather'd out protecting duties by yielding a little to the blast, and not steering directly against it. Temporary expedients,

such as premiums on the exportation of certain coarse
goods, were recommended, and would probably have
given time for future adjustments between the two
kingdoms.   Meeting these motions with flat negatives,
without proposing present expedients, or holding out
future expectations, much irritated the people. , The
censure of the Lord Mayor, which followed, administered
fuel to the fire, and offended the Magistracy and the
Citizens of Dublin.   The press teemed with the most
violent abuse.   The House of Commons wag'd war with
the printers, and the press bill spread the flame through
the Kingdom ; these circumstances immediately following
each other, have raised the fever of parliamentary reform
to the highest pitch.   Whilst those measures were carrying
on by Administration, the cry was, if you stop now they
will say you are afraid—but I think and always thought,
that true fortitude was seen in temperate councils which
wisdom warrants and when Justice guides—and that a
man, not conscious of fear, is never to act lest he should
be suspected of such a motive.   But do not suppose that
I impute all these things to the Lord Lieutenant or his
Secretary—by no means—they came here in haste, they
found men were in haste to get into great offices—*aude
aliquid si vis esse aliquis*, is sometimes the maxim of
better men than Juvenal had in view.   A most absurd
notion has prevailed in a certain great Kingdom that no
man can be a friend to English Government who is not
detested by the Irish people.   An unpopular Government is not quite so advantageous to a Lord Lieutenant
and his Secretary as it is sometimes made to those who
act with them.   The worst administration for the followers
of it was Lord Chesterfield's ; he kept clear from the policy
of the Lords Justices, whose first object was to commit
every chief Governor that they might have had the merit
of extricating him from difficulties which themselves had
raised.   It requires no great ingenuity to raise difficulties at present ; but he who can remove them will be

a friend indeed to both countries. Till those disturbances arose I have often lamented your retiring from us, but since the storm has arisen, I have rejoiced that you were on shore, both on your account and my own : for if you had been at the helm I should have been ever on the deck ; and tho' I have lost much in losing the assistance and society of a most valuable and amiable friend, yet we have both been gainers in ease and tranquillity.

I hope your health is firmly established and that you will not always stay in the House to very late hours, which I know to be highly injurious, but I also hope you will not follow the example of another friend of mine in your house who keeps all his talents for his friends in private but brings nothing of all his great store into the public streets. Pray remember me as a man who is proud of being obliged to you because he has the highest respect for your character and an earnest desire to hold a place in your friendship.[1]

Windham was much interested in ballooning, which in the early part of 1785 became a craze that attracted a considerable section of society. In March, he noted in his Diary, he " went out in order to attend the balloon in which Zambeccari and Sir Edward Vernon were to ascend " ; and soon after he decided that he would make a flight. That he was aware of the risk he ran is shown by the fact that he made his will, and wrote the following letter (which is especially interesting because it contains Windham's confession of religious faith), that, however, was only to be delivered in the event of his death.

WILLIAM WINDHAM *to* GEORGE JAMES CHOLMONDELEY
May 4, 1785

There is some difficulty in sitting down in earnest to write a letter, to which the occasion would hardly have

1 Add MSS. 37873 f. 98.

been given, if a good hope and confidence had not been entertained that it was never likely to be read. Something, however, must be said in case of the worst, that I may not leave the world without one affectionate farewell to him, who in the final evanescence of all worldly objects must be the last to remain upon my sight. · I must not suffer my imagination to dwell on a subject which it would quickly render too big for utterance ; but dispatch in a few words, such matters as are immediately present to me.

Some notice must be taken of a circumstance, which, however innocent, sits uneasy upon my mind, as it is a deception practised towards you. I mean the concealment from you of my present purpose, and the means by which I was obliged to effect that concealment. My motives to this you cannot mistake or be displeased at ; and, I think, will not condemn my determination. The hope that the news of my landing might, from the precautions of secrecy I have used, be the notice you would receive of my flight, prevailed over the wish of parting from you as my last earthly object, and of gratifying a similar wish, which I conceived would exist with you. Should you receive this letter I shall have wished that I had acted otherwise : should the event be as I hope, I shall be glad that I acted as I have. Something likewise must be said of my motives to this adventure. From the moment of my hearing of Balloons, I felt, in common I believe with every man of the smallest imagination, the wish of adventuring in one, and as early as the beginning of the winter before last, concerted with Dr. Fordyce that we should build one and go up together. The dissolution of Parliament joined to my own and his dilatoriness delayed the execution of the purpose ; till during my residence at Oxford in last September I got acquainted with Sadler ; with whom I should then have gone up ; but that before I knew him sufficiently to trust him with my intention, he had inserted an advertisement, which, as you may hear from a letter which I happened to write at the time to Legge, fixed him, he thought, to the necessity of going up at Oxford. I give you this detail, that you may vindicate me against the imputation either of doing this from ostentation, or, of having chose to wait, till experience should have done away any great apprehensions of danger. The credit to one's resolution that would have attended such an adventure some time ago, I should not have been insensible to : though I may safely say, that that was but a part of my motive, and the fear of its being supposed the whole or the principal part, was on the other hand one of the chief obstacles to the design. At this moment I should be desirous to go, though not a soul should know it : long since, the fear of blame. and appearance of coveting a foolish distinction. were the causes that created the chief difficulty. So much for this.

Let me now speak of another matter of infinitely greater importance to me, as it affects my opinion of your virtues, in itself, as it relates to the happiness of one, with whose character neither yours nor mine would stand in any advantageous comparison. If I have been desirous to hurry over the whole of this letter, that the general purport and occasion might not melt me into tenderness, I must dwell as little upon this part of it, lest it should betray me into sensations very inconsistent with what I would wish to feel at this moment—the subject I mean is the history of your Conduct *to Cecy*.[1] You have in that instance, done an injury to a fellow-creature, which no means now left you can probably ever repair, and for which hardly any degree of contrition and humiliation, which you can feel, will ever atone. You have undone a great and noble mind, whose only weakness has been too fond an attachment to you,— by a course of conduct utterly irreconcileable to justice and duty : and as little creditable in the motives as justifiable in the act. That you should prefer a life of vanity and

---

[1] Cecilia Forrest, who married Windham in 1798 *See ante*, p. 15 (note).

voluptuousness to a connection with such a woman as
Miss Forrest, is no very honourable mark of your choice
of happiness : That you should think yourself at liberty
to pursue that choice, to the utter ruin and extinction of
her peace of mind, is, in the circumstances, in which you
stood, no very favourable evidence of your regard to duty.
I forbear to push this matter any further than to say, that
her original, fatal attachment for you, has, I have reason
to be assured, and notwithstanding the most heroic efforts
to lock the secret from the knowledge of her nearest con-
nexions, continued with so unhappy a force, as to have
destroyed the very spring and power of happiness : and,
after a struggle supported with a degree of constancy
which redeems the weakness of the occasion, to have
proved in the end too hard for her bodily strength, and to
be now drawing her apace towards the grave. Do not
imagine, however, that what I here say, or a provision
which you will find in my will, is intended to invite you
to do from remorse and compunction, what you ought
long since to have done from principle and from choice.
I have too high an opinion of her to suppose that in such
circumstances she would condescend to accept you. I
should hope that from her pride : I fear there is a principle
still stronger, which would equally prevent her, an unlimited preference of your happiness to her own. Could
she ever be prevailed upon, I am far from sure, that I
should wish such an event to take place. I fear you have
not virtue enough to make such a connexion a source of
happiness ; and I am sure her love is of a quality too
exalted and noble, to admit of happiness under any other
condition. Here let me end this painful subject, and
having discharged, what I have thought it incumbent on
me to say, and what perhaps I shall say, even though
this letter should not be received, let me banish it for the
present entirely from my thoughts, and keep in view those
parts of your character, where my affections may be
unmixed.

That I preserve to the last the same sentiments towards you, my dear Cholmondeley, as at any period since the first bloom of affection was past, the disposition newly made in my property (which by the way is left at Cocks's) will sufficiently testify. If it appears in one respect less favourable than a former one, the reason will be understood from what is said above. I am sorry to have been obliged to cut down the bequest, till it ceases almost to be considerable · but I have not done more, than a regard to the merit, the wants, or the virtues of the parties, rendered, I thought, incumbent on me. All my papers are left to you, with perfect confidence, that any of a secret nature, which are not numerous, nor perhaps important, will be destroyed, without further inspection than is necessary to ascertain their nature. They will be found chiefly in a deal box, which has stood for some time past, in the front room above stairs.—More need not be said about these, nor about other such particulars. My literary papers are clearly of no consequence, and will only bear witness to the *strenua inertia*, in which I have suffered a life that might have been distinguished, and talent of which I believe something might have been made, to be wasted and trifled away.

The best, the greatest, the most solemn office I can render in a letter of this sort, is to extort you to a steady contemplation of divine truths, and a sincere endeavour to confirm in yourself that faith, which after various fluctuations I believe to be the true one, and which, independent of evidence, is supported by too great authorities ever to be rejected with confidence. Whatever may be the diversity of opinion as to the particular nature, I believe Christ to be a person divinely commissioned, and that faith in him affords the fairest hope of propitiating the great author of the world. Cultivate in your mind this persuasion. and dwell upon it till it grows into a principle of action. May it avail both to the purposes of final salvation. Nothing more remains to be said but that you will preserve of me such a tender remembrance, as it would be my joy to think should outlive me, and as may animate you during your continuance in this world, to such temper of mind and government of action, as may advance you to some better state hereafter. Farewell, my ever dear friend, and look up to God as the fountain of all good !

May He take you into his protection ! [1]

On May 5 Windham ascended from Moulsey with James Sadler, one of the earliest British aeronauts, who on this occasion made his last flight.[2] This exciting episode was duly recorded by Windham in his Diary :

Much satisfied with myself ; and, in consequence of that satisfaction, dissatisfied rather with my adventure. Could I have foreseen that danger or apprehension would have made so little impression on me, I would have insured that of which, as it was, we only gave ourselves a chance, and have deferred going till we had a wind favourable for crossing the Channel. I begin to suspect, in all cases, the effort by which fear is surmounted is more easily made than I have been apt to suppose. Certainly the experience I have had on this occasion will warrant a degree of confidence more than I have ever hitherto indulged. I would not wish a degree of confidence more than I enjoyed at every moment of the time.

EDMUND BURKE *to* WILLIAM WINDHAM

May 7, 1785

What time will you receive the congratulations of your Terrestrial Friends on your return to Mortality ? *O*

---

[1] Add. MSS. 37914 ff. 27–30.
[2] Windham in 1796 stood sponsor for a son of James Sadler by his second wife, who was christened William Windham Sadler, and achieved fame as an aeronaut. In Add. MSS 37925 will be found some notes on Windham's ascent made by himself

pater anne aliquas—iterumque ad tarda reverti corpora?
The rest does not hold exactly in the words.   I really long
to converse with you on this Voyage, as I think you are
the first rational being that has taken flight.

> *Adieu, Star triumphant, and some Pity show*
> *On us poor battlers militant below.*[1]

COLONEL RICHARD FITZPATRICK *to* WILLIAM WINDHAM

Grosvenor Place, London
June 27, 1785

I have gratified my curiosity in a flight from Oxford,
where your protegé Sadler (who, by the by, I consider as
a Phenomenon) behaved very handsomely, and finding
his process not answer his expectations and the balloon
only capable of carrying up one person, very obligingly
gave me up his place, and after receiving some hasty
instructions, I ascended by myself, in view of all the
University, as well I believe as of the whole county.   Some
of your friends there, Mrs. Croft and Mrs. Burgess, were
particularly civil to me, and did their utmost to keep the
spectators in order, but in vain, for the curiosity and
eagerness of the crowd was not to be restrained.   The
thermometer was broken, and your barometer had a
narrow escape.   I ascended with 7 bags of ballast,
the weight of which I did not then know, but which was
about a hundred pounds.   I had told Sadler that I
would not take his balloon very far, and my intention
was to have flown about two hours, but as I wished to
ascend as high as possible without danger to the balloon,
after having first try'd the valve to see if I was master of
the use of it, I continued rising for three quarters of an
hour, when I suddenly perceived from my flag, that I was
descending.   I discharged gradually five of my bags of
ballast, throwing out papers between each, without finding

---

[1] Add. MSS. 37843 f. 9.

that I appeared to diminish the velocity of my descent, till the 5th, when the paper I threw out floated instead of rising, to my great satisfaction, since I perceived something had happened of which I was ignorant. I then determined to reserve my two last bags till I was certain of being very near the earth, and fixed one of them to the anchor in order to drop it and break the fall of the machine. When I saw the shadow of the balloon increasing very fast, and could plainly distinguish objects, so small as horses in waggons and in the fields, I threw out my sixth bag, but unluckily when I was preparing the seventh upon the anchor, it slipp'd off, and fell without it. Within a very few seconds I came to the ground on the side of a steep hill, in a corn field. The shock was trifling, but the unevenness of the ground overset the Car, and rolled me gently out. Disentangling myself from the cords, I held fast the side of the car, and with some difficulty held the balloon till some country people came to my assistance. I then perceived a large rent in the lower part of it, which accounted for my descent, and which, I suppose, by a more judicious use of the valve I should have prevented. The curiosity and astonishment of the country who flocked in by shoals were prodigious. I got Sadler's balloon, however, safe in a stable, and waited at a little publick house two hours for his arrival. We were then conducted with great triumph about 5 miles to Wantage in Berkshire, where we dined, but as I did not admire this triumphal mode of travelling, I declined making *my entry* in to Oxford, and got on by myself as far as Henley, and came the next morning on to London. The field where I descended was 20 miles from Oxford, and I was just an hour on the voyage. I shall endeavour to promote our grand project both for our own amusement, and I hope for the advantage of Sadler, whom I really consider as a prodigy, and who is oppressed, to the disgrace of the University, I believe from pique and jealousy of his superior science. Adieu, Dear Windham. I confine myself to the subject of aerostation and refrain from earthly considerations, which I hope you are coming to look after, as it seems parliament is likely to sit the whole summer.[1]

After Fitzpatrick's flight it was some time before another amateur made an attempt. The craze ended abruptly when the news came that on June 15 M. Pilatre de Rosière and M. de Roman, in their endeavour to cross the Channel from Boulogne, had, owing to the balloon catching fire, been dashed to the ground from a height of about three-quarters of a mile and killed.

[1] Add. MSS. 37914 ff. 32-33.

CHAPTER II

1784–1792

Windham's early speeches : His attack on Warren Hastings in connection with the Rohilla war : Speaks in debate on the impeachment of Hastings : Wraxall's appreciation of his powers of oratory : Appointed a manager for the Commons of Hastings' trial : The King's illness and the question of the Regency : The commencement of the French Revolution : Windham opposes Parliamentary Reform : His views not entirely in accord with those of his constituents : Doubtful of the safety of his seat : Secures re-election 1790 : Extract from Windham's Diary : Publication of Burke's " Reflections on the French Revolution " : Rupture between Fox and Burke : Windham angry with Burke : They soon become reconciled : A letter to Mrs. Crewe : His attitude towards Parliamentary Reform : The political breach between Fox and Windham : A section of the Opposition supports the Government's repressive measures.

WINDHAM spoke for the first time in the House of Commons on February 9, 1785, in the debate on the Westminster Scrutiny, but in his Diary there is only the bare mention of the fact. On that occasion he rose after Pitt, and was followed by Fox, who congratulated the House " on the accession of the abilities which they had witnessed." To his second speech, on May 12, there is a more extended reference in the Diary : " Spoke for the second time in the House for the adjournment of the debate on the Irish Proposition. Felt more possessed than on the former occasion, but thought my performance inferior, and conceived that others thought so too. I have found since that they were inclined to think well of it. They are so

84

good as to be cheaply pleased. It was a mere effusion;
though delivered in a forcible and perhaps graceful
manner, containing nothing more than any one would
have thought of in conversation."

Windham entered the House of Commons with a considerable reputation for ability, and he soon showed that
rumour had not magnified his gifts. Not a great orator;
he always spoke well and sensibly and to the point ;
and was listened to with attention. He was soon
regarded as a rising man, a man marked out for office;
and the first proof of this general recognition is that to
him was entrusted by his party the conduct of the attack
on Warren Hastings in the debate on the Rohilla War.[1]

EXTRACT FROM WINDHAM'S DIARY

June 1, 1786. Day of motion on the Rohilla War.
. . . I there [at Brooks's] got from Long the report of
the Secret Committee, in which I found great advantage,
and settled to come the next morning to Sir Philip
Francis[2] to breakfast. I have seldom found myself more
clear than during my visit to him, and afterwards, till I

---

[1] Faiz-ullah Khan, one of the Rohilla chiefs, had been permitted by
treaty, after the conquest of Rohilkhund in 1774, to retain possession of
Rampore as a vassal of the Nawab of Oude   In return for being
permitted to maintain a small army for his own protection, he was
bound to place at the Nawab's disposal, whenever called upon, a body of
troops, the number of which should not exceed three thousand   In
1780, the Nawab, acting on Hastings' instructions, demanded from
Faiz-ullah Khan five thousand horse   As this was more than he could
supply, and as the demand was unwarranted by the terms of the treaty,
Faiz-ullah refused ; whereupon Hastings informed the Nawab that he
might take possession of Rampore, and add it to his kingdom. This
scheme was not, however, carried out ; and in 1782 Faiz-ullah Khan
paid Hastings a sum of money to procure his exemption from supplying
any troops at all.

[2] Sir Philip Francis (1740–1818), the reputed author of the Letters
of Junius, had, as a member (1774–1780) of the Council of the Governor-
General in India, on several occasions opposed Hastings, with whom,
in August 1780, after many quarrels, he fought a duel at Alipore, and
was dangerously wounded.

went to the House : but somehow, by the time I got there, my mind had got into some disorder, and my spirits into some agitation ; and by the time Burke had finished, I found myself in no good state to speak. The same state continued, though with a little amendment, till the time of my rising : yet I contrived somehow to steady and recover myself in the course of speaking, and so far executed what I had prepared, that I conceive it to be the fashion to talk of what I did as rather a capital performance ! 'Tis a strong proof on what cheap terms reputation for speaking is acquired, or how capricious the world is of its allotment of it to different people. There is not a speech of mine which, in comparison of one of Francis's would, either for language or matter, bear examination for one moment ; yet about my performances in that way a great fuss is made, while of his nobody speaks a word.

In the following year Windham spoke again in a debate on the impeachment of Hastings, when he dealt with the same charge. This task he performed, says Wraxall, " with that logical perspicuity, characteristic of his frame of mind, as well as of his style of eloquence, which always borrowed aid from metaphysical sources."[1] The impeachment was voted on April 3, 1787, and Windham was named as one of the managers of the trial for the House of Commons. He accepted the task, but was not very happy over his appointment. " This day—for which we have all been waiting so anxiously, so earnestly," he said to Fanny Burney, " the day for which we have fought, for which we have struggled—a day, indeed, of national glory, in bringing to this great tribunal a delinquent from so high an office—this day, so much wished, has seemed to me, to the last moment, so distant,

---

[1] " Posthumous Memoirs " (2nd ed.), ii. 276.

E. Burney, delt. *S. Bull, sculpt.*

FANNY BURNEY

that now—now that it has actually arrived; it takes me as if I have never thought of it before—it comes upon me all unexpected, and finds me unready!"[1] Windham was not one of the most active of the managers of this famous trial which, beginning on February 13, 1788, lasted until the spring of 1795, when Hastings was acquitted by a large majority on all counts of the impeachment.

In November the King showed such obvious indications of mental disorder that Parliament had to make arrangements for a Regency. The Prince of Wales was, of course, the person marked out for the office of Regent, and Fox at first made the blunder of stating that his Royal Highness had the legal right to be appointed, a position from which he retreated hurriedly on discovering that the powers of appointing a Regent are vested in Parliament. All parties, however, were agreed that the Prince was the proper person, but the question was hotly debated in the House of Commons whether he should be given a full or a restricted authority. Windham spoke on December 19 in favour of a Regency without restrictions, but the House decided otherwise. Before the Prince took up the office, however, the King recovered.

WILLIAM WINDHAM *to* ————
Hill Street : November 26, 1788

I wish it had occurred to me sooner, that from motives at least of general anxiety, if not from any concerns of business capable of being effected by such causes, you might have been glad to receive the best accounts, that were to be had, of the King's situation. It has been the fashion hitherto, and till lately was not an improper one, to speak of His Majesty's disorder in such obscure terms,

[1] Fanny Burney, "Diary" (ed. Ward), ii. 116

as left the nature of it quite uncertain ; or, if it was mentioned more particularly to describe it as a fever. It were much to be wished, that fever had more to do with it : but the fact has long been understood to be, that, whatever fever His Majesty has had, has been only symptomatick, and not at all the cause of his disorder, which is pure and original insanity. The symptoms of this have been increasing by slow degrees, and for a considerable period. There is reason to think that before even his journey to Cheltenham, some of these had appeared and been noted : and there is no doubt, that, immediately after, the appearances were so strong at his levee, that the foreign ministers all remarked them, and thought them of such consequence, as instantly to write an account of them to their courts. The immediate occasion of the Physicians being called in, and means being taken to prevent his Majesty being seen any more in Publick, is said to have happened, during an airing He was taking in a phaeton with the Princess Royal. If there were any hopes of the King's recovery from this state and so speedily as to render the substitution of any other government unnecessary, his situation could not be concealed with too much care, but the moment that ceased to be the case, too much care cannot be taken to make it known publickly and authentically. The greatest aggravation, which such a calamity could receive,—and a calamity certainly it is so far as relates to the feelings of every one who hears it,—would be that it should be subject to any doubt and suspicion. If the King of a country is completely out of his mind, whatever sorrow may be felt for that event, the extent of the evil is, however, known : It is, for the time it lasts, just as if the King were dead. The same person must, upon all principles of reason, and all views of the Constitution, carry on the Government, as if the King were actually dead—should he again be restored completely to his senses, the case is then equally clear : he must be restored completely to his government. Whatever other opinions are broached or thrown out in conversation by persons on either side, this seems to me to be the plain sense of the Matter, as we may possibly have to declare or act upon at least, before many days. The only case of danger and distress is when the sanity or insanity of a monarch should be not clearly ascertained or not generally known. To guard against that, in the instance now before us, I think accounts should have been given less ambiguous, less sophisticated and less false, than have been industriously propagated for some time past: and whatever motives of delicacy and prudence might have prevailed at first, as undoubtedly there were many, the case seeming now to be so decided, the actual insanity to be so complete, and the hopes of its ever ceasing so small, that any attempt further to disguise it will lye open to very uncreditable suspicions.[1]

During the previous year, from the end of August to the middle of October, Windham had been abroad travelling with Sylvester Douglas (afterwards Lord Glenbervie). Again this year, 1789, with the same companion he went to France for about a month from August 12. It is scarcely necessary to state that France was at this time in the early throes of the Revolution, that the Tiers-Etat had constituted itself the National Assembly on June 17; and that the Bastille had been destroyed on July 14.

EDMUND BURKE *to* WILLIAM WINDHAM
Beaconsfield : September 27, 1789
It is very true, that I promised myself the satisfaction of seeing you very soon after your return from the Land of Liberty. I am sure I was very glad of your *safe* return

---

[1] Add. MSS. 37873 f. 159.

from it ; for though I had no doubt of your prudence, where no duty called you to the utterance of dangerous truths, yet I could not feel perfectly at my ease for the situation of any friend, in a country where the people, along with their political servitude, have thrown off the Yoke of Laws and morals. I could certainly wish to talk over the details and circumstances with you. But the main matter consists in the results, upon the general impression made upon you by what you have seen and heard ; and this you have been so kind to communicate. That they should settle their constitution, without much struggle, on paper, I can easily believe ; because at present the Interests of the Crown have no party; certainly no armed party, to support them ; But I have great doubt whether any form of Government which they can establish will procure obedience : especially obedience in the article of Taxations. In the destruction of the old Revenue constitution they find no difficulties—but with what to supply them is the opus. You are undoubtedly better able to judge ; but it does not appear to me, that the National assembly have one jot more power than the King ; whilst they lead or follow the popular voice, in the subversion of all orders, distinctions, privileges, impositions, tythes, and rents, they appear omnipotent ; but I very much question, whether they are in a condition to exercise any function of decided authority—or even whether they are possessed of any real deliberative capacity, or the exercise of free Judgement in any point whatsoever ; as there is a Mob of their constituents ready to Hang them if they should deviate into moderation, or in the least depart from the spirit of those they represent. What has happened puts all speculation to the blush ; but still I should doubt, whether in the End France is susceptible of the Democracy that is the spirit, and in a good measure too, the form, of the constitution they have in hand : It is, except the Idea of the Crown being Hereditary, much more truly democratical than that of North America.   My son has got a letter from France which paints the miserable and precarious situation of all people of property in dreadful colours.   Indeed, the particular details leave no doubt of it.   Pray let me hear from you again for I fear it will not be in my power to go to you or to our friend Dudley North—and I wish much to know whether the manes of the Enemies of honour and common sense have made any way at Norwich ; for I had much rather you were the Spectator, than the victim of popular madness.   Adieu, my dear friend, and believe me, ever with the most sincere attachment,

Truly yours,

EDM. BURKE.[1]

Windham was constant in his attendance at the House of Commons.   On March 4, 1790, when speaking in opposition to Flood's motion for the Reform of Parliament, he aptly put the question, " What, would Mr. Flood recommend you to repair your house in this hurricane season ? " On this occasion he was supported only by Burke among his political associates; Fox and the rest of the party being inclined to countenance the measure.   Pitt, too, was favourable to reform, but thought with Windham that this was not the time to discuss it calmly, and at his request the motion was withdrawn.   This was the first occasion on which there were signs that Windham was drifting away from the notions he had earlier entertained.   It will be seen later that he who was in his youth an advocate for reform, in later days could with difficulty be brought even to consider any measure involving constitutional reform.

In June of this year there was a dissolution, and Windham, not without reason, for his views on some matters

[1] Add. MSS. 37843 f. 15.

were not in accord with those of his constituents, was of the opinion that his seat was shaky. "After a good deal of business done in Norwich, in the way of calling, came away at half past twelve," he had noted in his Diary on March 16. "From some accounts which I heard, cannot help entertaining some doubts of the security of my seat. Will it not be advisable to put the question to people by a species of select canvass? It is very fair to say, that they never know enough of me to be able to make up their minds, and that I may reasonably expect, they should declare their minds, while time is yet left to me to look out for other situations." Windham was, however, re-elected, in spite of some opposition.

EXTRACT FROM WINDHAM'S DIARY

July 24, 1790. I felt that strong sense of the unhappiness of my own celibacy; that lively conception of the pleasures I had lost; that gloomy apprehension of the conviction, which I should feel of this hereafter, clouding all my prospects, relaxing all my motives, and, in an especial manner, destroying all enjoyment, that I might ever have in residence here,—that unless I could resolve manfully to fight against such images, and force my mind from the contemplation of evils admitting no remedy, the most fatal mischief must ensue, both to my happiness, and to my powers. Of this resolution the necessity was not at first foreseen, nor the resolution of consequence fully taken. These images, accordingly, continued to pursue me, during the time of my absence at the Assizes. The effect of their continuance, during that time, was sufficient to point out the necessity of putting a speedy stop to them; which has, accordingly, since then, been pretty effectually done. It is, indeed, sufficiently plain that wisdom must condemn the thinking on uneasinesses, which thinking cannot mend: the hint or symbol for enforcing that truth, may be the reflection on the broken tea-cup in Rasselas.   The precept will not come with less weight, for coming from Dr. Johnson ; nor will it be unsatisfactory, to me, to owe to him, what may alleviate some of the sorrows of life.[1]

EDMUND BURKE to WILLIAM WINDHAM

October 27, 1790

I have seen a letter of yours to Mr. Joshua Reynolds, which was one of the pleasantest I ever read, except in one short Sentence, or rather part of a Sentence.   The pleasant part, you may think, was your desire of the publication of my Letter of which you had seen the beginning.[2]   But though this was flattering to me on every account, I hope you will think I speak of the general Tenour of your Letter, and not the little which touched my selfish feelings.   If you had seen the middle, and end, as well as the beginning of my Book, you would have given me such lights, as might make you perhaps the less repent of your wish of my holding up my hand to be tried by my Country : God send me a good deliverance.   To you, I do not send it to be tried, but to be protected : It goes to an Asylum and not to a Court of Justice : for I should be sorry, that you were as well qualified to be my Judge by your impartiality, as you are by your penetration and your skill.   You dropped a word, as if you thought I had not been quite fair in some of my representations.   This gave me a good deal of uneasiness.   In this Vein I looked over what I had written with some attention.   It is possible enough, that in the infinite variety of matter contained in my original Subject I may have made some Mistakes, and I wrote sometimes in circumstances not favourable to accuracy.   I wrote from the memory of what I had read ;

---

[1] Add. MSS. 37921 f. 21.
[2] " Reflections on the French Revolution "

and was not able always to get the documents from whence I had been supplied when I wished to verify my facts with precision. But I hope my errors will be found to be rather mistakes than⁻ misrepresentations. I am quite sure, that in most of my statements, I have rather shot short of the mark than beyond it. However, where I have erred, I wish to be corrected ; and shall certainly, if the Letter (now a Book) which I send you should come to a new Edition, I shall thankfully avail myself of the advice I may receive from you. Accept then this mark of my sincere respect and affection, the last. I sincerely hope of the kind, with which I shall ever trouble my friends or the publick.[1]

WILLIAM WINDHAM *to* MRS. CREWE [2]

Felbrigg : October 30, 1790

I have behaved very ill in point of correspondence, and very undeserving of all the merits you have shown towards me. The cause has been, not as before, any uncomfortableness of mind that disinclined one to exertion, but good genuine dilatoriness, such as makes one often defer things that are upon the whole pleasant, as well as those that are unpleasant. It is so long since I received your letter, that I hardly remember distinctly the points in it that I ought to answer. The time fixed for your going to Welbeck was the 18th, I think. I was not without thoughts of joining you ; but finding upon enquiry, that it was a hundred and eighty miles from here, my heart failed me, and I resolved upon grubbing on quietly where I was. You must know that in one respect the longer I stay here, the longer I feel disposed to do so : for though, after a length of solitude, company becomes

---

[1] Add. MSS. 37843 f. 19.

[2] Frances Anne Crewe, died 1818, the daughter of Fulke Greville, and the wife of John, afterwards Baron, Crewe. She was a noted beauty, a keen politician, and an intimate friend of Fox, Burke, Sheridan, and Windham.

more pleasant, there is both in long continuance in one place something that incapacitates one for moving ; and to me here, an occupation in various pursuits, which the more time I have to engage in them the more hold they take of my mind, and the more unwilling I am to quit them. In London these things have never time to attach ; but here they have nothing to weaken and dissipate their effect, and, as they were my first love, recover all their original empire. It would have been better for me, perhaps, that I had never meddled with anything else ; or, meddling with other things, that I had begun to do so sooner. From some cause or other I am now a little of two characters, and good in neither : a politician among scholars, and a scholar among politicians. As Dr. Johnson said from Pope, of Lord Chesterfield, " a wit among lords, and a lord among wits."

Under the present half of this divided empire, I am very sorry that Parliament is to meet before Christmas ; and look with great concern to the termination that is to be put in three weeks' time to various schemes which I fancy now, if time was given me, I could pursue to some effect. Of the business that we are to meet upon I am as ignorant as need be, and don't at all know what the right judgment is about Pitt's proceedings, or what the points on which principally he is to be attacked. I have, in fact, for some time past, nearly forgot that I had anything to do with it : though a late great politician, who has been unexpectedly thrown upon this coast like a whale, has within these few days a little awakened my political ardour. The little fishing town that is within two miles of me has contained no less a man than Colonel Barré.[1] The history of his coming here is not a writ of outlawry nor any warrant issued against him for treasonable practices, but his having been on a visit to Lord Townshend, and been

[1] Colonel Isaac Barré (1726–1802), fought by Wolfe's side at Quebec. He retired from the Army in 1773, and devoted himself exclusively to politics. John Britton in 1848 wrote a volume to prove that Barré wrote the letters of " Junius."

tempted to proceed thus far, on occasion of some of the children having been sent hither to bathe. To you who don't know the seclusion of this corner of the world, but who live in all the resort of the Palatinate, there may appear in this event nothing wonderful : but you cannot conceive to us what the appearance is of any one besides the natives, or, as we should describe it, of one out of the shires. As I could not prevail upon him to take up his abode with me, I must go down, I think, and see him again to-day.

One of the circumstances to render me less inclined to remove to London at this time, one at least of the motives wanting, is, I conclude, that we must not look for you there. I fear I shall hardly be able in the interval between the breaking up and the meeting of Parliament, again to get as far as Cheshire. I had an invitation the other day from Lord John, to renew my hunting in Northamptonshire, and I made during the winter a half promise to Lady Spencer to go at Christmas to Althorpe. But all this is dark and doubtful ; and nothing certain but death and taxes, and that Pitt will come out with new lustre from all the present measures, and heap new confusion on his oppositionists. Farewell ! I must live upon hope, with the aid of a letter now and then. Remember me, pray, to Crewe, and to all that are obliging enough to think of me ; my thanks to Mrs. Lane [1] and Mrs. Bouverie.[2]

EXTRACT FROM WINDHAM'S DIARY

November 7, 1790. On Thursday I conceive it was; that a material incident happened—the arrival of Mr. Burke's pamphlet.[3] Never was there, I suppose, a work so valuable in its kind, or that displayed powers of so

[1] Sarah, sister of John Crewe and wife of Obadiah Lane.
[2] The Crewe Papers : Windham Section, pp. 5-10 (" Miscellanies " of the Philobiblon Society, vol. ix.).
[3] " Reflection on the French Revolution," published November 1.

MRS. BOUVERIE AND MRS. CREWE

extraordinary a sort. It is a work that may seem capable of overturning the National Assembly, and turning the stream of opinion throughout Europe. One would think, that the author of such a work, would be called to the government of his country, by the combined voices of every man in it. What shall be said of the state of things when it is remembered that the writer is a man decried, persecuted, and proscribed; not being much valued, even by his own party, and by half the nation considered as little better than an ingenious madman?

The French Revolution, so far-reaching in its effects, had laid the foundation of the breach between Fox and Burke. Fox was enthusiastic about the French people, and on all occasions expressed his sympathies with the popular cause : Burke, on the other hand, was most bitter about everything connected with the Revolution and did not disguise his contempt for all who thought that something good might ultimately result from the terrible up-heaval. So far there had been no open breach between the statesmen, although it was clear that they could not long continue to work together. The quarrel came at last in a debate on May 6, 1791, on the Quebec Bill. In his speech Burke lamented the loss of friendship that arose from the view he took of the Revolution. To this the great-hearted Fox replied, that there was not, and could not be, any loss of friendship between them. " Yes, there is," Burke said. " I know the price of my conduct, I have done my duty at the price of my friend—our friend-ship is at an end." When Fox rose again, it is recorded that some minutes passed before he could speak for the tears that choked his utterance.

The conduct of both men was characteristic. It is not surprising, however, that the sympathy of nearly every

I   G

one went out to Fox. What Windham thought may be deduced from the brief entry in his Diary : " Fatal day of rupture with Burke." So deeply did he feel on the subject that he excused himself from dining on May 16 with Lord Petre if Burke was to be of the party. Windham was at the House of Commons the next day, when, he noted, " the only circumstance that did give me satisfaction was some overtures of reconciliation from Burke." [1] Soon they were again on excellent terms; which endured until Burke's death six years later.

WILLIAM WINDHAM *to* MRS. CREWE

Paris : September 15, 1791

I don't like to let another post go without a line, though I have not time enough to make a letter suited by its contents to be sent such a distance. 'Tis something, however, to know that your letter is received, Rue des Petits Augustins, at *Paris.* The most important information, however, in its consequences to me is, that a letter to find me here should be sent to Mons. Perregaux, Banquier. I hope I shall not be long without profiting by the communication. To earn my hopes by the readiest way that the time will allow, let me tell you that on my arrival I found at the Hôtel de l'Université, Payne,[2] General Dalrymple,[3] Lord Palmerston,[4] Lord Hardwicke [5] and W. Wyndham, Lord Egremont's 2nd brother. The two last had come over, leaving their wives at Spa, and are now both gone back. To replace them are arrived Sir William and (late Mrs. Harte, now)

---

[1] Windham's " Diary," May 16, 1791.

[2] (?) Captain (afterwards Admiral) John Willett Payne (1752–1803), an intimate friend of the Prince of Wales.

[3] Colonel Hew Whiteefoord Dalrymple (1750–1830), Lieutenant-Governor of Guernsey ; baronet, 1815.

[4] Henry Temple, second Viscount Palmerston (1739–1802), a member of " The Club "

[5] Philip Yorke, third Earl of Hardwicke (1757–1834), Lord-Lieutenant of Ireland, 1801–1800.

LADY HAMILTON

Lady Hamilton.   They came the day before yesterday and
I am going this morning to see them ; but, however I may
fear being too late, I will not miss the opportunity of
sending this.   There is another Lady also expected here
whose presence could not fail to make Paris very interesting to *me :* but as she was to come with Lady R. Douglas,
and Lady R. is said to be prevented by a miscarriage or
some increase of ill-health, we shall probably lose the
pleasure of her company.   This is all that I know of
company about which you will be much interested, not
having yet seen your son or knowing for certain whether
he is here.   I might have mentioned indeed Lord Thanet,[1]
who arrived the same day as myself, with a Hungarian
lady, whom as a brilliant achievement he carried off from
her husband at Vienna ; and who, as well as himself, is
now suffering for their sins, by the most complete weariness (as I should suppose) of one another.   Crauford
(James) is likewise here, and in the same hotel with
myself.   Hare[2] has likewise been here for some time.
Having begun, like a good Englishman, with an account
of the English company, I may now just mention the
little event that took place yesterday of the King's
acceptance of the constitution.   By the extreme friendly
activity of Noailles (ci-devant Vicomte)[3] I got a place
in the Assembly and was present at the whole ceremony.
There was great respect and great applause, but the
nature of the proceeding was necessarily humiliating, and
some circumstances in the conduct of it rendered it still
more so.   Before the King appeared, two very splendid
chairs were placed, one of which I was surprised to see
occupied by the president, who pronounced from thence,
he and the King being for some time the only persons

---

[1] Sackville Tufton, ninth Earl of Thanet (1767–1825). The Hungarian lady was, presumably, Anne Charlotte de Bojanoiwitz, whom he
married at St. George's, Hanover Square, February 28, 1811.

[2] James Hare (1749–1804), M P. for Knaresborough 1781–1804,
an intimate friend of Fox

[3] Louis Marie, Vicomte de Noailles (1756- 1804), fifth son of Philippe
de Noailles, Duc de Mouchy.

sitting, a long lecture, in which, besides the objection on account of its length, there was somewhat too much of " la nation," and somewhat too little of " le Roi." The principle of this equality between King and president was, no doubt, that the president represented the nation : but that principle followed up should have put the King upon the footstool, with the president's foot on his neck : for there is no doubt, to me at least, in theory as well as in their practice, that the nation, rightly understood, is all in all. It would have been much better, in my mind, if being bound in courtesy to remit much they had carried their courtesy a little further and remitted more. I hope that we shall be the people to keep up a little of the " vielle cour " in our manners, while we lose nothing of the solid advantages and privileges that the new system can promise.[1]

WILLIAM WINDHAM *to* W. J. GURNEY

Hill Street, May 2, 1792

My mind is so full of the measures which made the subject of our debate on Monday [2] that I can hardly forbear writing or speaking to any friend, who I think likely to have ideas at all similar to my own upon the subject. Though my declaration upon the occasion was not exactly what some of the papers have put in my mouth, that ' whenever or in whatever shape a motion for Parliamentary Reform was brought forward, I would oppose it ' (such a declaration exceeding even my objections to Parliamentary Reform, and being such as no man hardly would make), yet nothing can be more decided, than my hostility to the measures now pursuing nor than my determination to oppose them to the utmost extremity.

You will not be surprised at this determination, when

[1] The Crewe Papers : Windham Section, p. 11 ("Miscellanies" of the Philobiblon Society, vol. ix.).

[2] Charles (afterwards second Earl) Grey had given notice on April 30 that in the following session of Parliament he would introduce a measure of parliamentary reform.

I tell you, as I did to the House, though they have
omitted I see in the papers, that part of what I said, that
in my opinion this is little short of the commencement of
civil troubles.   I can consider it as nothing but the first
big drops of that storm, which having already deluged
France is driving fast to this country.   I have in general
been far from adverse to the principles and cause of the
French Revolution.   So much otherwise indeed, that
from the beginning almost, Mr. Burke and I have never
exchanged a word on the subject.   But when an attempt
is made to bring the same principles home to us, Principles
in a great measure extravagant and false and which at
best have no practical application here, I shall ever prove
myself as violent an opposer of them as Mr. Burke or any
one can be.

It is as the commencement of changes similar to those
that have taken place in France, that I view the measures
now declared ;   though far from being so considered or
intended, on the part of the authors of them, or of the
greater number possibly of those by whom they may be
supported.   I think, however, that this is the conclusion
to which they are directly and rapidly tending ;   and
which can only be prevented by a timely alarm spread
among all people, who may think the happiness which
this country has hitherto enjoyed too valuable to be
risked on experiments, hitherto unconfirmed by anything
like an adequate trial, nor recommended even by any
theory (if theory on such subjects were worth a farthing)
that has been known in the world till within these half-
dozen years.

Mr. Grey and some other gentlemen, men very respectable both for their talents and characters, and with whom
I am most closely connected, seeing this danger, and
feeling about it as I do myself, are of opinion, or rather
were, (for I am not sure whether already some of them
do not begin to be alarmed) that the only way to avert
this danger, was to anticipate its arrival, and by timely

concession, and changes temperately and judiciously made, to quiet the minds of people, and defeat the projects of those who may wish for changes of a different character. Undoubtedly this is a policy very easily understood, and that may in various cases be the best to be pursued. It would have been happy had this been followed in the case of America. It would have been wise to have done the same thing in the case of Ireland : it is to be wished that the same course were pursued with respect to the Catholicks of Ireland at this moment. But this policy, though often good, is like every other prudential measure, very often not so, and the question is, whether it is so or not in the present instance. I am setting aside for the present, all consideration of the measures themselves, which they propose, viz., the enlarging the representation and shortening the duration of parliament,—the former of which may possibly in a very moderate degree be desireable rather than not, and the latter of which, I conceive to be clearly hurtful. I am considering them merely with a view to the effect, which they propose by them, of defeating the schemes of those, who mean nothing short of a complete overthrow of the present constitution.

Now for this purpose, I am persuaded they will produce an effect directly the reverse of that which their authors intend ; and this opinion I ground upon the consideration, that their reform, should they ever introduce it, would only be one of many thousands, which others have proposed, who of consequence will be little satisfied with Mr. Grey's Reform or Constitution, as he or they may now be with the present one. You cannot with one measure satisfy all schemes. Your measure can be but one, your schemes are infinite, many of them the most discordant and opposite. Does he suppose for instance, that, by any plan which he will recommend, he will satisfy those who say that every Government is an usurpation upon the rights of man, in which every individual has not a vote ? Does he suppose, that he can ever form a House of Commons, from which influence, much of it undue, will be excluded, or on which, such influence, whether existing or not, may not always be charged ? When the principle of change, such as that now adopted, is once established, of change not founded on a comparison of a specifick grievance with a specifick remedy, but proceeding on a general speculation of benefits to arise from this or that mode of constituting a Parliament, what is there that is to put a stop to it, till we run the full career of all that the speculators of the present day may wish to drive us to ? We must not shut our eyes to the fact, that there is at this time a spirit very generally diffused, as it has been very wickedly excited, of changing the present constitution of things without any distinct view of what is to be substituted in its room. The promoters of this spirit call the means which they apply, an appeal to reason. But to whose reason do they appeal ? To the reason of those, who they know can be no judges of the question. To the reason of the very lower orders of the community, whom it is easy to make discontented, as their situation must ever render them too apt to be, but whom no man, not meaning to betray them would ever erect into judges of the first moral principles of Government, or of the advantages or disadvantages of great political measures.

It will be well worth the while of people not indifferent to their own interests, whatever experiments they may wish to make with those of other people, to consider, whether this practice of teaching all the world to submit to nothing but what their reason can satisfy them of the truth of, may not proceed in time to lengths which they will not much like ; and whether they do not conceive, that upon this doctrine of universal rights arguments might be brought, such at least as an audience of labouring men may think satisfactory, why there should be an equality of property as well as an equality of voting. Hints of this sort have already been thrown out, I think, in Mr. Payne's pamphlet. I am sure it would not be difficult to improve them in a way to make them circulate among the lower people, as rapidly as arguments about the principles of government are said now to do among the workmen at Sheffield. They have already abolished in France all titles and distinctions, a species of property surely as innocent as any that can be conceived, and which, on being given to one man, does not seem to take anything from another. They have abolished likewise in great measure the right of persons to dispose of their property by will. What are all the laws of property but the mere creatures of arbitrary appointment? And who shall be able to derive any one of them by a regular deduction from natural rights, so at least, as not to admit endless disputes about the authenticity of the pedigree? Suppose some one should take it into their head to write a work addressed to the labouring people, exposing to them the iniquity of that system which condemns half the world to labour for the other, and pleading for such a partition of goods, as may give to every one a competence and leave to none a superfluity. I am certainly not meaning to say that such arguments would be good ones : I am not meaning to say, that they might not be easily answered, but I should be sorry to undertake to answer them, in an auditory such as composes the majority of every parish in England. For some time the habitual respect which the laws have taught for property, would perhaps prevail : but when you have once well taught men to consider the power from which such laws proceed, as an usurpation, how much longer will the respect remain for regulations, unfavourable to their interests, which that power has ordained? How long will men acquiesce in laws, which condemn them to poverty, when they are to be maintained on no other ground than such agreement, as they can discern in them, with natural rights? Why publications of this sort should not be put forth, I don't see. You cannot punish them on any principles which permit the publication of many works now circulating ; and you cannot dispute the competency of the common people to judge of the question of property, when you allow them to be judges of what are certainly not less difficult, the first principles of Government.

But I will not tire you nor myself by going on with this subject, on which one might write volumes, without stating all the wildness and danger of the principles now abroad. My own serious opinion is that unless men of all descriptions write to say, that they will not, on mere general hopes of improvement, consent to change a state of things which has produced and is still producing a degree of happiness, security and liberty unknown hitherto in the world, we shall, before we are aware of it, be involved in all the horrors of civil confusion. If we are, it will be an example of human folly and madness, such as the world has never yet exhibited. That a nation great and happy as this is, raised to a degree of splendour that has made us the admiration of the world, enjoying the most perfect liberty united with all the blessings of order, possessing at this moment peculiar advantages from the distracted state of many countries around us, and seeing in no country any one advantage that we do not enjoy ourselves in a superior degree,,—that such a nation should at once, upon the mere assurance of certain persons that they can make us better, put all these blessings to hazard and risk the falling into universal confusion is a degree of extravagance which can be called by no name but that of madness. In such madness, as it appears to me, I, for one, will not be a partaker. I hope that among my friends at Norwich there are many that are in the same sentiments. Such sentiments are, I am sure, very much wanted : but there is nowhere that I should so much like to find them, as among persons with whom I am otherwise so much connected.[1]

[1] Add. MSS. 37873 f. 172.

The political breach between Fox and Windham grew wider, though they did not allow their differences in Parliament to interfere with their private friendship. In May 1792 the Government issued a Proclamation against Seditious Meetings. This Fox opposed tooth and nail, but the Duke of Portland, Lord Spencer, Lord Fitzwilliam, and Windham, with others of the party, thought it their duty to the country to support Pitt on this and similar occasions.

THE DUKE OF PORTLAND *to* WILLIAM WINDHAM
Bulstrode : October 13, 1792

I am not without my fears that this letter may increase the gloom into which the Duke of Brunswick's retreat has very naturally thrown you, because you will find no contradiction or any explanation of the event but what you have already seen in the Papers, which in my apprehension very sufficiently accounts for it, because since it took place I have not received a single line of intelligence from any person whatever. I met a person belonging to the Secretary of State's office, the beginning of this week, who assured me that everybody now knew as much of France as Ministers did, and probably more, for that Thelluson [1] received the earliest and best information from thence, and, he believed that what came to the Secretary of State's office was the last and the worst. All I have to send you, therefore, are my hopes, and they are confident and not wholly unfounded that there is too large a portion of good sense, or self-interest, or indolence, or indecision, or dislike of novelty, or attachment to old habits, or in short something that, if it is not good sense, will be a substitute for it which will prevent our being overrun by French Principles, and as for French *arms*, my dread of them will not disturb me

---

[1] Peter Thellusson (1737-1797), a merchant connected with the Paris banking house of that name.

much, for I do not believe that anything could so effectually animate and unite us as an armed attempt from France to force us to accept Anarchy. You see that I am of opinion that we have both vigor and wisdom sufficient to resist such an attempt; and that opinion is founded on the very general diffusion and distribution of property, the perfect security in which it is enjoyed, the great opulence and prosperity of the Country and the superabundance of employment and wages for the manufacturers of all descriptions, who are the most, and indeed the only, turbulent part of our community. The Army, small as it is, I believe to be perfectly safe, and to be depended upon and quite sufficient to support the Civil Power which, with that confidence it will derive from the military, is very able, with the assistance of the well disposed part of the Community, to preserve good order and defeat any hostile designs or undertakings against the present Constitution of our Government. I am sure there are *Men* in this Country (and there does not appear to have been *one* in France), for though it has been the system of the present Reign to annihilate them, in that it has not succeeded, and they still exist, and I trust and believe, there will be found enough to save the Country, even from being attempted I do not know whether you will concur with me on this point and perhaps it is as well you should not, for too much and too general confidence might ruin us. Do you therefore continue to despond and to exert yourself, and I will be sanguine and not idle.[1]

LORD MULGRAVE *to* WILLIAM WINDHAM
Harley Street: December 1, 1792

If I were to say half I wish on the various subjects in your letter, I should not save the post. I will, therefore, write more fully hereafter. I find the same timid

---

[1] Add. MSS. 37845 f. 5.

disinclination *to be first* amongst those to whom I apply, as you complain of in your part of the country, to which there is nothing to be said but that those who are the last to exert themselves in defence of their rights frequently are or always ought to be the first to lose them.   Government, however, are doing their part with vigour, by this night's proclamation (which I am in momentary expectation of receiving to enclose to you). You will find that in consequence of the tumult in Scotland, a part of the Militia is to be immediately embodied. A nice selection of the corps most to be depended upon is precluded by the locality of the grounds upon which the force is embodied. Eleven counties are to be called upon, amongst which Norfolk is to be one, and the first impression of the *Gazette* is to be sent to me to transmit to you, because my friends do you the justice to rely on your giving this measure the turn of encouragement to those who wish well to good order, instead of suffering it to have the effect of alarming them with apprehensions of unforeseen and latent dangers ; the consequence of this measure will of course be that the Parliament will assemble within a fortnight, when I trust that unanimity, firmness and exertion will dispel the Dangers which have been stirred up by desperate and unprincipled emissaries. The best mode, I should think, for giving effect to associations in the county would be to have standing committees in different parts who should consist of a small number and transact the business of the Association, without calling those together who have signed the Resolutions, unless any extraordinary circumstance should require the exertions, or influence of collected numbers.

I feel with you the propriety of the increase of Labourer's Wages, and the importance of that measure being kept distinct from the political circumstances of the time.   I am not prepared at this moment to give a decided opinion as to the mode of effecting that, but I will write more fully to you on this Head when I have more deeply considered it. The most ordinary or obviously legal means are certainly the most desirable : I believe there is a power in the Quarter Sessions to regulate the price of labour. The call of Parliament is so far fortunate that it will probably collect a considerable body of country gentlemen from different parts, amongst whom the best expedients may be determined upon. The alteration in the price of Labour must ultimately fall on the Landowners, and when they are convinced of the propriety and necessity of it, the concurrence of the Farmers, may, I should suppose, be easily contrived. These are, however, but the sudden thoughts raised by what I have read in your Letter and which I should wish to discuss further with you.

There is not the least foundation for the Report of Lord Chatham's[1] going to Ireland. Lord Temple and Lord Edward Fitzgerald[2] have been dismissed from the service for the part they have taken in the propagation of Republican doctrines. I hope you will not suffer discouraging ideas to intrude themselves upon you. I should be afraid the little justice you do yourself would induce you to suspect me of flattery, if I were to say how much I think the strength and success of our cause depends upon your appearance and exertions in it, and how very much chearfulness will be given to any struggle I may endeavour to make, by my doing it hand in hand with you.[3]

[1] John Pitt, second Earl of Chatham (1756–1835), First Lord of the Admiralty, 1788–1794.

[2] Lord Edward Fitzgerald (1763–1798) was cashiered from the Army for joining in Sir Robert Smith's toast to the abolition of all hereditary titles, given at an English dinner-party at Paris in October 1792.

[3] Add. MSS. 37873 f. 183.

CHAPTER III

1793

O N the eve of the declaration of war against France, Thomas Grenville wrote to Windham regarding the invitation that he, in common with other prominent politicians, had received to meet at Windham's house to confer as to the advisability of forming a coalition between Pitt and the Duke of Portland.

THOMAS GRENVILLE *to* WILLIAM WINDHAM

February 10, 1793

I received your letter to-day at five o'clock, and being obliged to go out to dinner have not till

WILLIAM PITT

now been able to send you any answer; being desirous of seeing the Duke of Portland upon the subject, I learn from him that you had this morning apprised him of its being the wish of many persons, who concurred with him in the necessity of supporting the war in which we are engaged, to meet and communicate together this evening at your house; I learn also from him that he expressed no sort of objection to any concert of his parliamentary friends for that purpose. I have, however, read in your letter with a good deal of concern that, a proposition was to be made for a determination to set aside for the present all views of opposition.   It is true that a proposition of this nature was discussed at the beginning of this session, but you will I am sure recollect that the Duke of Portland, Lord Fitzwilliam,[1] many other persons, and myself amongst them, expressed the most distinct dissent from that proposition, and that it seemed to be the wish of all those persons to pledge themselves to no support of government or suspension of opposition, except in those particular instances which were effected by and comprehended in the very peculiar dangers of the times.   Under these circumstances, of which Mr. Fox was likewise informed and upon which communication was constantly had with him, tho' he differed in opinion the general course of conduct seemed understood to be, that those who saw internal dangers from republican principles, and dangers arising from the growing power of France, would resist them by supporting those measures of the government which were meant to counteract the dangers at home, and such support; too, of war with France as might make it most effectual if war proved to be necessary.

For my own part I own I much wish to see again at Burlington House[2] those meetings which it has always

---

[1] William Wentworth Fitzwilliam, fourth Earl Fitzwilliam (1748–1833).

[2] The property of the Duke of Devonshire from 1753 until 1815.

given me so much pleasure to attend there, and which I am persuaded have been of the greatest publick benefit ; least of all can I subscribe to any notion of devising any project for not engaging the Duke of Portland to take his old place at the head of those who act upon his sentiments, because he appears to me to have kept that place with honour to himself, and I am persuaded too with the most perfect satisfaction to all his friends.[1]

W. BANKS *to* WILLIAM WINDHAM

Soho Square: March 17, 1793

You need not have informed me that you respect the rights of adversaries, because I well know that you respect all rights except perhaps the rights of those whose watches have gone better than Mudge's ever did go and , who in that case certainly have a right to the Public reward you seem determined to confer on your Devonshire Friend.[2]

As an adversary I claim however one right, which is that if the Committee to-morrow should find themselves satisfied with the truth of Mr. Mudge's allegations and make up their Consciences to report them to the House of Commons as proved according to the Standing orders, a reasonable time may be allowed before that Report be carried up, in order that these who think that public money cannot with justice be given to the second-best while the most deserving is left unrewarded, may have an opportunity of explaining the comparative pretensions of these to whom the public are indebted for the improvement of time-keepers.

This right of an adversary I hold that you cannot in

---

[1] Add. MSS 37849 f 204

[2] Thomas Mudge (1717–1794) invented a chronometer, for which he claimed a reward from the Board of Longitude, which was not granted Subsequently a Committee was appointed on which sat Pitt, Windham, and others, to consider the matter Convinced of the value of the timekeeper, they recommended a grant of £2500, a decision that the House of Commons confirmed.

justice deny, for, as your mode of Proceeding allows the smallest possible number of Periods for explanations to take place that the Constitution of Parliament recognises, each period ought to have a greater interval than is necessary in the Conduct of an act of Parliament to allow to the Corresponding one.[1]

W. Banks *to* William Windham

Soho Square: March 18, 1793

Being of Opinion that neither you nor the rest of Mudge's Friends are aware of the Pretentions other artists have, to be rewarded in Preference to him, I have been induced to draw up the inclosed paper which I mean to circulate to the members on the day the report is to be received. I think it candid to communicate it to you forthwith, but I do not mean to bring it out to-morrow, because I understand it is not customary to make a serious opposition in the Commons for proving allegations.

I beg to have it understood that I do not mean to Combat Mr. Mudge's pretentions on any other Ground than the Defence of the Decision of the Board of Longitude and the pretentions of Mr. Arnold and such others, if such there are, whose time-keepers are better than Mr. Mudge's. If the House chose to extend their Bounty to Reward him, I am sure that I shall lay no obstacle in the way of their generosity Provided they give due attention to the claims of those who have excelled him.[2]

William Windham *to* John Coxe Hippisley (*at Rome*)

London: March 28, 1793

I have already much to answer for in having delayed so long to write; at a time when you must be so impatient for letters, and when you have given yourself such a claim to them from me, by the numerous ones which I have received. It is the sense of my obligations in

---

[1] Add. MSS. 37°'4 t. J .   [2] Add. MSS. 37854 f. 47.

that respect, and the ideas conceived of what I ought to do in return, that has, till now, repressed my endeavours, and threatens, without care, to throw me into as bad a state, as during the time of your absence in India.[1]

An experience of that danger makes me resolve to break my chains by times. I have accordingly seized my pen this morning, determined to write a page before I pull off my night-cap ; and not to go out of the house, till I have got upon paper such a quantity, as I may venture to send off by next post, should I be unable even to make any additions to it. Where shall I begin ? And what order shall I follow ? What shall I consider as most important ? And where shall I consider you as most uninformed, and most desirous therefore of information from me ? The points probably most necessary, will be those, that you can least learn from public accounts ; and such will be the history of our domestic and party politics, particularly as affecting that class of men about whom you are most interested.

You know, what the state of my mind was respecting the situation of Europe, and the progress to be apprehended of those changes which were gaining daily new strength, and which were never likely to stop of themselves, till they effected the dissolution of all the subsisting governments. The reasons for these fears went on increasing, in respect both of the progress of the French Arms, and of the corresponding opinions in this country, till some time, as I recollect, after your departure they seemed then to be brought to a sort of crisis, at which some immediate explosion was to be apprehended. I am not sure whether this was just before, or just after your departure, but it was towards the end of November.

You must consider this as a sort of fixed point, with references to which the history of these times is to be graduated. The despondency of those who have been

---

[1] Hippisley had been in the service of the East India Co. in India, 1786–9.

distinguished since, as the sect of Alarmists[1] was then at its lowest ebb. Among those who happened to be at that time in London, I was among the most eager for calling together whatever force of counsel could be collected, in order to consider what should be done. The general opinion was, that an intimation should be given to the Ministry, serving in our view as a menace, and in another as an encouragement, that those, by whom they had been supported at the time of the Proclamation,[2] would not fail them in any measures, which they might think it necessary to take in the present circumstances ; and that, in the opinion of the persons comprehended under that description, measures, vigorous and decisive, both internal and external, ought to be taken. This was accordingly done ; and though the intimation so conveyed was not so explicit nor so strong, as I could have wished ; it is not impossible, that on that little circumstance much of the subsequent conduct of government, much in consequence of that of the dispositions and plans of foreign powers ; and much, therefore, in the end of the fate of Europe, may have turned. I have always been a great tracer of the effect of little things ; and the opinion, that this step seemingly so inconsiderable : may have led to consequences, thus important, is a reflexion of great comfort and satisfaction to me, who had some share in it, and who rejoice so much in those consequences.

The sentiments of Fox, in the meanwhile, remained in a great measure unknown. He had been absent from Town during the greater part of the Summer, and little more was known of his sentiments, than what I had collected in a short conversation in my way from Norfolk to London, previous to the retreat of the combined Army, and to those events, which made so large a part of the present crisis. My own expectations were not very

---

[1] Burke and others opposed to the French Revolution were called " Alarmists."

[2] The Proclamation against Seditious Meetings, &c,

sanguine ; and the result of three or four conversations, to which he seemed to be dragged rather unwillingly, gave me an early impression, that our difference was not of a temporary or superficial sort, but such as was likely to lead us, without some unexpected turn of things, wider and wider from each other.   It was not a difference capable of being reduced to specific points, and of being confined, therefore, within precise limits, but a general difference of feeling that pervaded all our sentiments on the present state of the world.   This opinion, admitted as you may suppose with great reluctance, and at first with considerable hesitation, has alas ! been growing stronger, as the scene has opened ; till now that we have passed the question of War, without being able to find in that an occasion of union, there is nothing, as far as the eye can reach, that affords a prospect of our coming together.   The situation in which we stand, and the persons comprized in one or other description, you know probably partly from the accounts of the debates, and partly from private letters.

It may be more necessary to say something of the situation and sentiments of the Duke of Portland.   For his sentiments have been on all occasions, except on the Bill now depending to prevent treasonable correspondence &c. the same as Sir Gilbert Elliot's and mine, who have never differed yet in any instance.   His opinion and feelings on the affairs of France, his ideas on the state of this Country : his wishes for war, and his intentions of supporting the Ministry, till he was talked out of them by other counsellors, were all the same as ours ; But his situation is such as no nicety of conduct can make consistent with itself, and as has been the parent of all his difficulties, and all his perplexities, and of such loss of personal consequence as it will be difficult ever to repair. He has conceived that his present difference with Fox could be treated as a difference on a particular point, and be reconciled with a continuance of party connection.

The consequence of which is that he is acting in party
with a man with whom he never agrees, and is joining
with him to overturn the power of those by whom his own
system is supported.   One of the effects of this situation,
illustrating the original falseness of the conception, is
that he can take no step to aid and co-operate with those
with whom he concurs in opinion.

To obviate so strange a consequence was the object
of that conference, which produced the declaration from
Sir Gilbert Elliot, about which you have heard probably
a good deal, and which has drawn upon him a great deal
of enmity from that side.   It was proposed to the Duke
to put himself at the head of those, whose sentiments
he agreed with ;   and to allow them still to consider
themselves as acting under their original chief.   To this
it was thought at first, that we had an explicit consent :
but all was afterwards embroiled, and confused, till, in
point of fact, we all find ourselves now acting without a
leader, and with no other concert, than that which we
have been able to make out among ourselves.

The only meetings, therefore of the party that have
taken place on our side, have been at my house.   Much
against my will I have been obliged to act as a sort of head
of a party, much in the same way as some Colonel or
Serjeant may now be doing with the remains of Dumouriez's Army.[1]   This, however, can last only for a short
time.   It may serve to keep us together for a while ;
but if the Duke cannot be prevailed upon to return to his
station, of which I see at present no prospect, and hardly,
indeed, the opportunity, we must dwindle away and be
dispersed in various channels till the very name and idea
of the party will be lost.   The credit and consequence that
has been lost by this conduct, first of Fox, and then of
the Duke, is dreadful to think of.   Had Fox determined

---

[1] Dumouriez had been defeated at Neerwinden, March 18, by the
Au᷐trians under Saxe ·C᷐ bur᷐, and driven out of Belgium.   Dumouriez
deserted to the Allies, April 4.

to have taken part with us at the close of last year, had he disclaimed the Friends of the People, and sided with those, who had certainly the best claim to be considered as his friends, there is hardly a doubt that he might, at this time, have been a Minister. Had he even taken part with us at the beginning of this Session, there is little doubt, though more than before, that his authority in the Country, might have been equally or nearly as great. As it is he has put himself in a situation, in which, as far as can be foreseen, nothing less than a Revolution can ever make him Minister.

The Duke of Portland upon a smaller scale has judged equally wrong, and with consequences equally injurious. By this attempt of continuing to act with·Fox, while they differed on questions such as those now depending, he has disappointed the expectations of his friends, and of the publick, and lost much of that reputation for firmness and decision, which is so necessary to the head of a party, and may be so much wanted hereafter for the purpose of recovering Fox. The opinion that the Duke had a will and a judgement of his own, and could firmly act up to that judgement, would be the best cure for that distrust, which otherwise may for ever exclude Fox from Office. The situation of the Duke was, I confess, difficult. To have taken the course, which I recommended, would undoubtedly have changed what was one party into two, with each its head and members and separate functions ; acting without enmity to each other, but moving in different directions, and forming each its own system. But the course which is now taken leaves us no party at all. The only body that lives and acts is an heterogeneous mass, formed hardly in any degree of the materials of the Duke of Portland's friends, (though it has derived from them its life and energy) and pursuing habits and instincts altogether its own. It is a little gilded and venomous insect, with great force of wing, which has sprung from the carcase of the old party. which

it leaves to moulder and grow putrid in the eyes of the
Publick. If I were a Man of ambition and activity and
talents for such a situation, now is the time when I might
become a great leader, all the world being ready to hail
the course I have taken, and which I laboured, with most
earnest endeavours, to make the course also of the Duke
of Portland. I have no such disposition, did I possess
even the powers, so that the party seems to be melting
away, with no one growing up to replace it, but such
as must derive all its strength and nutriment from the
misfortunes and mischief of the Country.

This is the best picture which I can give you of the
state of internal politics as confined to public men. The
evils of this I feel less acutely, from the consideration of
the promising appearance which things seem to assume
upon the Continent, where the progress of the mischief is
at least stopt, with as good hopes of further reduction of
it, as can be entertained in a business of such extent and
complexity.

The representations which you made of the state of
opinions in the Southern parts of France, combined with
other accounts confirming the same ideas, makes a very
considerable part of the hopes, which I allow myself to
indulge. You will have heard all the accounts, which
we have as yet got of the complete success of the Austrian
Arms in Brabant, such as give already full assurance for
the security of Holland, and leave little, or no doubt, of
the entire evacuation of Flanders. We know as yet
for certain (March 27th) only of the Victory of the 18th.
these are Accounts seemingly pretty authentick of a
continuence of the same successes, amounting to nearly
an entire dispersion of the whole of the French Army.

What we want now is a Naval force in the Mediterranean, such as might give heart and protection to the
sentiments which you describe as existing in that part of
France. Similar aid is wanting towards Brittany ; where,
as you will see by the French papers, a very general

dissatisfaction prevails.   In both these cases, indeed, there must be a land force to co-operate with that by sea ; and such I conclude in the course of the Summer must be found.   At all events an English Fleet should be or rather should have been, in the Mediterranean, to give that succour and protection, which I conceive all the Countries upon those Shores are looking for at our hands, and which it would be a proud distinction in us to grant. I long to think that Rome, our common mother, should owe her safety, if danger must approach her, to the protecting justice of Great Britain.

Amidst so much said of our political differences, it may be necessary to state in what degree they affect private and individual intercourse.   You may imagine, that those who lived together chiefly as politicians, do not continue much to do so, when their politics disagree.   The secession likewise from the Whig Club, of which you may have seen an account in the papers, has been a subject of greater complaint than any difference in voting or speaking.   But none of these have led, in my case, to any change of manner in private, nor in my own mind to any change of private regard.   I retain all my former opinions and kindness for Fox, though I see, with regret, that his sentiments and wishes on the changes now going on in the World, are more remote from mine, than I had formerly supposed.   The list of the persons who side with him on these points you know pretty well by the list of the division.   Those, who do not appear there, may be presumed, in general, to be on the other side.[1]

[1] Add. MSS. 37848 f. 59.

AN UNKNOWN CORRESPONDENT [1] *to* WILLIAM WINDHAM
The 1 *of June* (1793)
Philadelphia at M. Morris,
Member of the Senate, Market Street

The affectionate attention you honoured me with during the time I spent in England induced me to think that you would hear with satisfaction of my happy arrival in the Unitate States. I had good companions on board, among which I will mention the respectable familly of M. Duché, M. Talon, a member of the first constitutionel assembly, under an accusation of the convention, M. Bonnet, a French clergyman banished, and M. Devillaine, a French officer who made the last campaign with the Princes. The number of our fellow passengers was eighty and against the common rule of sea travellers we lived on board ship and parted on the most friendly terms.

We found the sea so much covered with your vessels that I thought its Empire belonged entirely to Great Britain. Your men-of-war seemed to me very well disposed to protect your Trade, and stationed with a peculiar Knowledge of the French coast. Some of them came near our vessel but your sea officers, able to distinguish the form of every ship, never stoped or prevented us from continuing our course. We desired our Captain to shew his colours to every ship we met with ; by this precaution we had an opportunity of speaking with several of your Merchantmen and acquainting them that hostilities had taken place between France and England, and of telling the Captains of those vessels the lattitude and longitude where they would receive the protection of your men-of-war.

---

[1] This letter is taken from a copy, the original not being among the "Windham Papers." In the copy the signature is omitted, but the presumption is that the letter was written by a French Royalist, and one of no little importance, since, as will be seen, he was on terms with the most important men in the United States.

I landed at Philadelphia the third of May and went immediately to M. Washington. He inquired with peculiar attention concerning the Officers who served in America during the War and more especially concerning M. de Lafayette. I looked upon this first enterview as a good presage of M. Washington's public sentiments and in private conversation I was confirmed in my opinion that the President of Congress disliked the System of the New Republicains as much as might be expected from a man sensible of the true principles of a good government and anxious for the happiness of mankind.

To give you a just idea of the opinion of the people of the Unitate States, I must have a retrospect to the beginning of the French revolution. When the *états généraux* was called, the Americains expected the improvement of our government. The revolution of July 1789 received the general aprobation of the people. Every one thought it was the struggle of despotism in the Aristocraty of the clergy and nobility against the principles of liberty. However, some men of ability escaped this common enthousiasm and thought that the basis upon which the legislature of France proposed to elevate the constitution was not that which was proper to suport the foundation of a large empire. Had not the unhappy Lewis the 16th adopted the bad proposition to go to Varennes, leaving before the National assembly the fatal writing which led to doubt of his faith, the sentiment I mentioned had received the greatest credit and every one had aprouved of the refusal of the King to take care of *a helm ready to break in his hands.* The French constitution as it was formerly accepted, leaving some means of amelioration, obtained at last the consent of the Americain's people.

The conduct of the first legislative assembly changed sudently this favourable disposition. People found in the discussion of October, 1791, all the character of a faction which wanted to give humiliation to the throne and to ruin the Kingdom. The declaration of war against the house of Austria appeared useless, impolitic, and rather disposed to destroy the liberty of the people than to strengthen it. In short, the revolution of the tenth of August divided America into two parts well distinguished and almost fixed by the different states. Those which are called the eastern, and extend from the boundaries of Canada to the Southern part of Maryland, looked upon the events of that time as prepared by the ambitious pretentions of some individuals, conducted against the interest of the people and compleated by all species of crimes. The Western States, which are comprehended between the Southern part of Maryland to Georgia, have approved openly the conspiracy against the King and the Monarchy. And it is very remarkable that the states which admit slavery were all more in favour of equality and licentiousness.

The manifesto of the Duke of Brunswick,[1] his attack on France with Prussians, and particularly with Hessians, to give laws to the French nation again united the wishes of the people in favour of the French arms, and on that account the massacres of the second and third of September have not provoked the indignation that one might expect from a people gentle, sensible, humaine and compassionate as are the Americains. But when, after the retreat of the combined armies, the system of a general republic became the politics of the national convention, when it decreed that it would no more admit of the ties of religion, of Kings, of tribunals, proprietory probity, fidelity in the most sacred engagements, that it had the intention to oppose the poors to the riches, crimes to virtues and to carry its infernal doctrine into every country, a sentiment of indignation took place and was manifested particularly in the Eastern States. They

---

[1] Frederick William, Duke of Brunswick, who took an active part in the war against France. He fell at Quatre Bras, at the head of his troops.

regretted the rejoicing made in favour of such victories as ought to put the present age into mourning and leave indelible impression on the future. The murder of the King augmented those sentiments and gave new ennemis to the chiefs of the French republic. A general mourning would have been worn in the *union* but the public spirit, badly directed by the newspapers, prevented America from paying to the King of France the tribute of gratitude which his virtues, his private and public endeavours to support the cause of America most undoubtedly entitled him.

To me the discussion which took place at the meeting of your British parliament, the division between the Eastern and Western States of America, has been more remarkable and form two partis in the *union*. In a constitution well established government gives the impulse to every one, but in the infancy of a constitution men of various character have the greatest influence in the governement. I must then make you acquainted with the leaders of this country.

The representatives of the people receive the impression from those which give them qualification and carry it to Congress, to the Senate and to the administration. Both houses, that is, the Senate and Congress, have a certain majority at present in favour of a well-regulated governement. It is more numerous in the Senate, it is a strong body which oppose every improper means in the present crisis to alter the neutrality. The executive power is shared between the two partis which divide the Unitate States. At the head of the first in favour of an exact neutrality is Hamilton, minister of finances,[1] general Knox, war minister,[2] Randolph, attorney general ;[3]

---

[1] Alexander Hamilton (1757-1804), American soldier and statesman, took an active part in the War of Independence, and, after the death of Washington in 1799, became Commander-in-chief of the United States army. From 1789 for five years he held the important office of Secretary of the Treasury.

[2] General Henry Knox (1750-1806), took a prominent part in the War of Independence.

[3] Edmund Jennings Randolph (1753-1813).

Jefferson, minister of foreign affairs,[1] is the leader of the second party which wishes a more intimate connection with the french republic. Hamilton is a man of a great understanding, fine talents, a communicative genius, an untainted probity, an absolute disinterestedness. With the desire of reputation he is so indifferent with respect to the possession of his office that he would leave it rather than abandon an opinion or an object useful to his country. Hamilton has created a System of finances which everybody admires on account of its advantages and of its Simplicity. General Knox is a man of good judgment and intirely influenced by Hamilton. Randolph is a well informed man and possesses some ability. His conversation proves a man attached to the opinion that it is impossible to govern an extensive Kingdom without an executive force which must not be prevented, except when it acts against the constitution of the country. In a conversation I had with M. Randolph he told me that he had very little to expect of security and happiness in a constitution where the chief of the executive power was elective ; that everybody in America, except M. Washington, in several circumstances of the greatest importance had been obliged to conform his opinion to that of Congress, though directed against the public advantage. I induced M. Randolph to confess that our suspensive *veto* is a chimera when it is not supported by the dissolution of the legislative body, that without it, the use of the *veto* will determine the civil war, and the destruction of one of the two powers. M. Randolph's opinion in point of constitution advise me to rekon him among the ministers who are favourable to the good principles, what is important because it offers a majority of three with the president against one ; but M. Randolph

---

[1] Thomas Jefferson (1743-1826), drew up the Declaration of Independence. In 1785 he went as United States Minister to Paris, where he remained for four years. Returning home, he became Secretary of State under Washington, and in 1801 was elected (third) President.

is a Virginian and in consequence of it attached by interest to the party which wishes to support the odious system of the French republic.

Jefferson is the chief of the jacobin party ; had he the talent and capacity of Hamilton he would acknowledge with him that there is no prosperity for a great Empire without a repressive force directed against every one who wished to rise above the law and that the support of criminal principles cannot promis any advantage to a new country which can only florish by just regard shewn to public and private virtue : but the unhappiness of representative government is that inferior talent with great ambition and little probity cannot suport the credit which obtain those of the first order and try by every mean to supplant them. As people don't admire the genious of Jefferson, his eloquence, his fine speaches, his happy repartee in public discussion, it is necessary to fixe its attention with the favourable idea of Jefferson's excessive love for liberty, of his immoderate attachement to the people's interest, of his ardent zeal in favour of democracy. It is by the consideration he pays to jacobin's principles that he is called the democratic or whig minister. Those who suport his doctrine have a peculiar cathechism. Their principal articles of faith are that the death of the King was a necessary sacrifice to the intire liberty of the people, that the massacre of the second and third of September must be considered as the inconveniency which belong to a great revolution, the daily convulsion of the empire, as an evil which cannot be prevented. As this party dare not aprouve publickly of all the crimes committed in France; it says that being obliged to take the alternative of the duke of Brunswick on the French nation, it preferes the second, it calls French nation the union of legalité, *Marat* and three or four thousand murderers. The success of Jemappe[1]

---

[1] At Jemappe, on November 6, 1792, was fought the first battle in which the French, under Dumouriez, defeated the Austrians.

had made a great number of proselytes, but Prince Cobourg [1] and general Clerfait [2] have diminshed the zeal of the belivers. Jefferson in a close conversation don't answer the expectation which his partisans give of him. I suppose him to be in an intimate correspondance with the party which govern the convention, whilst the diplomatic affairs pass by the chanel of governior Morris,[3] who is intirely opposite to his sentiments.

It is probably with the leaders of the *jacobins* that the success of citizien Genet,[4] the representative of the French Republic, has been prepared in this country. He has been preceded in it by an Americain who was thought influent ; he had learned in Paris the doctrine of the new republicains and had promised to buy all the grains, corn and flower that France wanted for this year ; he promised to send in France eigthy thousand arms ; he had also engaged his credit to determine America to pay at once the debt contracted with France. The first part of his mission has succeded, the second is now suspended and the third has completely miscarried. I have no doubt that proper dispositions will be taken to carry to England all the guns proposed to France.

[1] Frederick Joseph, Duke of Saxe-Coburg (1737–1815), Austrian Field-marshal, commanded the Imperial forces from 1789 until 1795, when, having sustained several defeats, he resigned his command.

[2] François Sebastien Charles Joseph de Croix, Comte de Clerfayt (1733–1798), Austrian Field-Marshal. In 1792 he commanded the Austrian contingent in the Duke of Brunswick's army. In the following year he opened the campaign in the Netherlands with the victory of Aldenhoven and the relief of Maestricht, and he was largely responsible for the defeat of Dumouriez at Neerwinden.

[3] Governor Morris (1752–1817), appointed by Washington, in January 1791, to negotiate with the British Government regarding certain unfulfilled articles of the treaty of peace. Shortly afterwards, until 1794, he served as United States Minister to France.

[4] Edmond Charles Edouard Genet (1765–1834) went to America in 1793 to endeavour to secure for the French Republic the assistance of the United States. In this he was not successful. Washington decided to issue a proclamation of neutrality. Genet, however, continuing his activities, Washington on the following year demanded, and secured, the envoy's recall. Genet then resigned his mission, but remained in the United States and became a naturalized citizen

I think it useful to inform you with respect to the debt of America to France that it amounted after the war to eigtheen hundered thousand pounds sterlings, that now a million of it has been paid and that for the rest of the sum America is indebted to France. The executive power of this country is determined not to draw near again the moment fixed in former time to pay the sum that is due. It has resisted all the requests which have been made by the executive power of France to change that disposition, but the month of September, October and November next are the epochs fixed for paying two hundred thousand pounds sterlings in hard money. This sum will be of great assistance to the republicains, perhaps employed to renew the massacres which took place in several circumstances and to continue the war.

The representative of the French republic is very anxious about it : his first step in this country has been imprudent, criminal and will not answer his expectation. You knew before I left England that citizien Genet had the command of a sum of eighty thousand pounds sterlings to make new friends and four hundred commissions to arm vessels and send them as cruizers against your trade. It was certainly calculated by the executive power of France that M. Genet should land at Charlestown in order to raise the spirit of the people of the Western States in favour of the pretentions of the french republic. Citizien Genet at his arrival was very well received in the State of Carolina ; he armed a privateer which was an Americain bottom and filled it with an Americain crew. The administration of the State refused its consent to the departure of the privateer but Citizien Genet made a peculiar application to the governor of the State and obtained an order to let the privateer go out of the harbour ; she went out and since made five prizes. One is of a very great value. The conduct of the governor of Carolina is very much against the neutrality which America promised your minister to observe and directly against the wishes of its inhabitants. The fitting out a privateer is quite contradictory to the proclamation of the President of Congress which (it is true) came out after the privateer of Citizien Genet went to sea. The proclamation is wrote in the following terms :

" Whereas it appears that a state of war exists between Austria, Prussia, Sardinia, Great Britain and the United Netherlands, of one part ; and France, on the other, and the duty and interest of the Unitate States require that they should with sincerity and good faith adopt and pursue a conduct friendly and impartial towards the belligerent powers;

" I have therefore thought fit by these presents; to declare the disposition of the Unitate States to observe the conduct aforesaid towards those powers respectively; and to exhort and warn the citizen of the Unitate States carefully to avoid all acts and proceedings whatsoever which may in any manner tend to contravene such disposition;

" And I do hereby also make known; that whosoever of the citizen of the Unitate States shall render himself liable to punishement and forfeiture under the law of nations, by committing, aiding or abetting hostilities against any of the said power, or by carrying to any of them those articles which are deemed contraband by the modern usage of nation, will not receive the protection of the Unitate States against such punishment or forfeiture ; and further that I have given instructions to those officers, to whom it belongs to cause prosecutions to be instituted against all persons, who shall, within the cognizance of the courts of the Unitate States, violate the law of nations, in respect to the powers at war, or any of them, &c."

Their proclamation is sufficiently expressive; but the new republicains don't care for the forms which are fixed in the governements established and pretend to make the happiness of mankind their object. Citizien Genet;

I   I going on his travels in the eastern States; opened his system ; it convinces people that he had the intention to obtain a majority in Congress and by its assistance to countrive America to join France in the war ; in case this plan could not succeed to make the executive power of America unpopular and to suport the party of the French republic in raising Citizien against Citizien, State against State.   His atrocious politics have obtained some success among that classe of people which enjoy tumult and troubles in every country.   But the prudent and wise inhabitants, irritated by this machiavelous conduct, have endeavoured to prevent its consequence : those even who were in favour of the French republic found it against the dignity of America that a French minister, after his landing without mentioning any thing to the president of Congress or to the ministers, fitted out privateers and send them out.   The place the Citizien Genet chose for landing augmented the discontent, and now it is certain that the English ships which have been taken will be restored, and that the character and the mission of Citizien Genet will be covered with all the contempt both deserve.   I had opposed his success but my constant opinion always was that it " is more advantageous to let a fool do for himself than to help him."

A proof of the general sentiment of the people of America is the conduct of the inhabitants of Philadelphia about the proclamation.   An address of thanks has been presented to M. Washington to felicatate him upon the steps he had taken to prevent America from engaging in a war against the combined powers.   This disposition will take place through all America.

Some individuals without character have met few days ago in a tavern and have presented an adress to Citizien Genet at the instant he came to town.   This adress contains very reprehensible expressions and also the answer of the Citizien, but you most look upon it as dictated by people without influence and just as if the people of the *Canon tavern* in London had presented a petition to Citizien Channelin.

So far as I can judge of the disposition of this country; it will maintain a neutrale system. The cases which perhaps might raise the discontent of America are those I mentioned to you during my stay in England.— 1°. considering France as a fortified town besieged, you should by all means avoid protracting the war, render it more cruel, and upon this principles seize all ships loaded to France with corn or flower and send them to British harbours to sell their cargo at the prise market in favour of the owners. 2°. take any French ship armed with an Americain captain and an Americain crew. My opinion upon these two prepositions is that, suposing you should be determined to act in this manner, America will make some reclamations. In this case do not threaten or come to a war.

Perhaps to prevent France from receiving any assistance of this country, your minister will it find expedient to buy the crop of next year and to send it under an American colour to England. I believe your country would find a great advantage in it and sell the corn of America with an immense benefit to all the people of Europe.

I think that with respect to the debt of America to France and particularly to that part which is to be paid in the fall of this year; it would be expedient to advise the regent of France to send an agent in order to claim the money which is owed. I should supose America would not find any difficulty to suspend the moment of paying that sum. The people's choice for the negociation must be a man of character and of determination. The people as Citizien Genet have comonly the mob of all countries at their commands.

I believe it will be prudent also to take some measure to prevent the murderers of the King, those of the second, third of September and other days from being admitted in this country. If you are victorious, of which I have no doubt, I supose America will not refuse to grant a favour requested by all powers of Europe. If you suffer that infernal fire which has reduced France to ashes to burn in any part of the world, it will be revived and inflame it.

After having examined America in its interior politics; in its afinity with France, I must make out the real situation in which it may be considered relative to the European powers.

The population of America, white and black; is near four millions : it encreases so rapidly that without the emigration of Europe in fourtheen years it double in the eastern States and in twenty in the western. There is now a system of finances regulated upon the rules of England. The debt of the Unitate States is fifteen millions sterllings. Part of the taxes is appropriated to pay the interest of the debt and cannot be disposed to an other object. The taxes are of two sorts—upon importation which gives upon almost every article ten for cent, and upon distilling liquors. These taxes are suported by rich people and of so little consequence that every body consents to pay them. The expence of the country is nothing. Fifteen thousand pounds in each State pays the salary of people employed in the administration. The army directed against the Indiens is paid upon the general taxes and without any augmentation to them. The debt of the Unitate States will be certainly extinguished in the course of twenty years and probably much sooner. America has an arsenal of two hundred field pieces; of hundred pieces of Artillery siege all brass, moreover howesters, mortars, &c., hundred and twenty stands of arms. The principal arsenal is at Westpoint in a very good order. I intend to go and visit it.

The situation of America enables it to oppose every State of Europe which would attack its liberty : but it cannot attack any. I suported this opinion against the

most obstinate of this country and proved to them that
a nation in the situation of America cannot be looked
upon as an offensive power. For that it is necessary to
have an excess of population to recruit the army, a
treasury or an established credit to supply it, a naval
army to transport it, and America wants these advantages. However, it is not indifferent to England that
America should keep the most exact neutrality. If it
would declare in favour of France, it would give the hope
of success to a great number of French people attached
to the republicain party who desire to come to a good
issue and perhaps find new friends. All the crop of
America would be sent to France and some of the ships
loaded with it would come in its harbours. The Americain
privateers would do great injury to the trade of England.
The war with France would certainly continue longer.
During its continuance, America would loose the habit of
trading with England, raise a number of manufactures
which France would encouraged. It is then, by the
motives above mentioned, the interest of England not
to quarrel with America, as it is the interest of America
to keep not only the most exact neutrality but a perfect
harmony.

Commissaries have been sent from this country to treat
with the Indiens in order to make peace. People of
America think that England encourages the Indian war.
My opinion about the treaty now offered by the Unitate
States is that it will not take place, and that, if they agree
with the Indiens upon the present terms, war will com-
mence again in less than two years. I firmly believe also
that, if war continues now, the Indiens will be succesful
and that on account of the bad dispositions and foolish
plan of operation admitted by the Americains. I should
think very easy for this country not only to defeat the
Indiens but to oblige them to retire as far as Missipy.
America never will have a long peace without it.

To give you a general view of the situation of America,

I must now consider it with respect to the ressources it offers to speculations. The main things are 1°. trade, 2°. acquisition of cultivated land, 3°. the loan upon private individuals, 4°. the loan upon the Unitate States, 5°. the reestablishment of French colonies, 6°. the acquisition of uncultivated land.   1°. The trade of this country is attainded with difficulties and to carry it on with succès it is necessary not only to have studied the theory of it in the infancy but to have continualy practiced it. It is also indispensable to give a part of your confidence to merchants established in Europe and to Americans houses in the Unitate States.   The trading people of Europe are continualy exposed by political events and those of this country by the enterprizing genious of its inhabitants and as it has but an insuficient number of manufactures, it is indispensable to bring from Europe every things which they fournish.   The means America offers to exchange are corn, flower, timber : the first article, the most productive, cannot be transported in time of peace and offers but momentareous advantages. The importation of things manufactured obliges them to make advances in money. They are sold with difficulty and require a great lengh of time because every body in this country being merchants order every kind of goods it wants. The best trade is that of commission: it produce some advantage and offers little danger. 2°. The acquisition of cultivated land is of very little benefit. The most interet you may receive is five for cent. The plantors who have commonly a great number of tenants find much difficulty in being paid their revenu. It is very often the case in a representative governement where the people have acquired to extensive a share of the politicals rights. In such a governement those who are at the head of the administration wants a great popularity and to obtain it they favour every claim of the multitude. To the difficulty which keeps the tenants from paying their rentes it is necessary to add the inconveniency which arises from tittle not well ascertained, which is very often the case. In short, the rentes are so small and the expences of justice so great that the proprietor had rather give up his rights than have recourse to the law. 3°. The loan is permitted upon security or privilege ; the deposit authorised by the law is inscribed upon a public register. so that it is not possible to be deceived. It is one of the best methods to make use of money. You may receive as much as seven for cent. 4°. The loan upon the United States gives an interest now of seven for cent, but the principal sum you deposit suffers all the mutation which please those who play upon public founds and the discredit which the instability of the fortune of this country and the uncertainty of its governement incite in Europe. 5°. The reestablishement of French colonies is uncertain, and perhaps the moment it will take place far from the present ; but the instant it shall take place be very favourable to the possessors of land in this country. 6°. The acquisition of uncultivated land is of a very great advantage. The settlement of few families doubles directly the capital sum and two years after the first cultivation one receive four times what he has expended. To succeed with a certainty it is necessary to choose very good land, springs, naviguables rivers and to dispose of such people as are determine to give you all their time and industry. I had the peculiar advantage to met with people of that description. Resuming my opinion about what concern this country; I think it will not come to a way that the people is very much divided in political sentiments, that the majority of representatives and of the executive power is well disposed to your country, that the governement of the Unitate States uncertain and fearful against the multitude cannot now sufficiently assure the property and liberty of individuals, that the revolution of France had a fatal influence upon the constitution of America; and so much that if the French republic could be established, it might overturn that of this country or divide the federacy in two parts, that this country offers rather occasion to reestablish some broken fortune than to make people in general happy.

After I will have seen the opinion of the Americain fixed with respect to the affairs of France, what I hope will not be long, I shall make a journey in the country, with several of my friends able to judge the value of the land. I shall go as far as Niagara, Montreal, Quebec and see all your new settlements. My absence will be more useful to confirm the opinion I want to see prevail in this country than my stay in Philadelphia. People at last might believe if I should continue in town that the expression of my sentiments are dictated by some other object than public happiness.

I have often seen here your Minister, M. Hammond,[1] and your consul. The first is an exceeding good man, true, open, very much attached to the interests of his country. I believe the second in the same disposition and of a good intelligence with M. Hamond. Lord Grenville has not sent the letter mentioned to you. I am astonished that he has not performed his promise.

I should beg your pardon for writing so long letter, did I not think that it contains some particulars useful to the cause you suport and that my former knowledge of this country has rendered me able to observe. What I mentioned relative to the employment of founds may be serviceable to those of our countrymen who may be desirous of an establishment here. Many of those who came lately have expended without judgement the remains of ther fortune.

I preserve, dear Windham, the hope of seeing you in London before January next.

---

[1] George Hammond (1763–1853), First British Minister at Washington (1791–1795). Subsequently Under-Secretary for Foreign Affairs in the Pitt Administration (1795–1806), and in the Portland Administration (1807–9). He was a friend of Canning and joint editor of *The Anti-Jacobin*.

I wrote in English to prevent you to read a bad French hand. My best compliments to one's friends.[1]

WILLIAM PITT *to* WILLIAM WINDHAM

Downing Street : June 14, 1793

Mr. Pitt presents his Compliments to Mr. Windham, and wishes much if Mr. Windham will give him leave to have some Conversation with him before Monday on the Subject of the Motion of which Mr. Fox has given Notice for that day.[2] It would also be a great Satisfaction to Mr. Pitt to have an Opportunity, if it is not disagreeable to Mr. Windham, of stating confidentially to him some Circumstances arising out of the present State of Politics, and which Mr. Pitt rather wishes to communicate Personally to himself than thro' any other Channel. It is hardly necessary to add that if Mr. Windham has the Goodness to comply with Mr. Pitt's Wishes in this respect, any thing which may pass will not transpire any where, without Mr. Windham's particular Permission. Mr. Pitt will be at Leisure any hour either to-morrow or Sunday, at which Mr. Windham would find it convenient to call in Downing Street.[3]

WILLIAM WINDHAM *to* LORD CHATHAM

Hill Street : August 1793

I take the liberty of submitting to your Lordship the name of a near Relation of mine, Mr. Lukin,[4] who having served as yet in no capacity but that of a Midshipman, cannot be known to your Lordship, but by means of such a communication.

He was about the age of twelve when He was sent to sea, and passed for a Lieutenant about four or five years since. His wish for service could not have been sooner expressed, as He is but just returned from Abroad.

---

[1] Add MSS. 37855 f. 29.

[2] Fox's motion against the war, which was defeated.

[3] Add. MSS. 37844 f 7.   [4] William, afterwards Captain, Lukin.

If in case of any promotion of Midshipmen; Your Lordship will have the goodness to inquire into his character from different Captains with whom He has served, I should esteem it a mark of obliging attention : and have no doubt, that his pretensions and merits, whatever they may be, will meet from Your Lordship all the consideration, that shall be their due.[1]

On July 10, 1793, Windham left England for the Netherlands, with the object of seeing for himself the state of the Army under the Duke of York. He went to Valenciennes, then being besieged by the Allies, and with characteristic but somewhat reckless courage, spent some time in the trenches under fire.

EXTRACT FROM WINDHAM'S DIARY

July 19, 1793. This was the day of our seeing the French camp from the little mound with a pole upon it. To St. Arnaud, the Abbey, the Vicoque, and Bonne Espérance, and back by Augin. This was the day following the preceding, and that on which they fired some cannon shot at us, by one of which Phipps' horse was wounded. I shall never fail to regret my foolish dilatoriness, and want of consideration, in not having decided then to take my leave. Had I gone then I had stayed a blessed time ! By suffering myself to stay on beyond that, I have outstayed my interest, and left myself with a doubt upon my mind, for which, before, there could not have been a pretence, whether something more should not have been done. I had seen the trenches the day of the truce ; and when there was no danger, I had then gone down twice besides, once by daylight and once by night ; at the former of which time there was a good deal of fire of cannon and shells, and at the latter of musketry. It was at the latter of those times that a sergeant of the

---

[1] Add. MSS. 37914 f. 5.

14th had his head shot off. I had rode about everywhere, and, as it happened, had run some risk. I had done enough to satisfy myself and to show to others, what, if it is very necessary to be conscious of oneself, it is pleasant also to have known. By not going to the storm by the covered way, though I forbore only, what every one would have said it was absurd to do, except at least a few people, whose opinions perhaps are not worth much, yet I felt something below what some might have expected. One way of putting it may be, Was it a thing, which would have been more praised or blamed, had it been done ? Would it, considering all circumstances, have raised the character of the actor or have depressed it ? It is the hope, that it might have had with some good judges even the latter effect, that can alone reconcile me to the not having done it. The decision taken of avoiding any intermediate course, if I was not wholly to engage, was, I think, right. I observed at least a distinct line, that of keeping throughout with the Duke of York. It is most fortunate for my own satisfaction that the Duke went into the trenches and not amiss, that there was, during the time, a pretty smart fire. The head of an Austrian was knocked off, who was walking a few paces before the Duke, and a Guardsman was knocked down while we were standing near the battery.

Windham was still with the Duke of York when the garrison of Valenciennes surrendered on July 28.

EXTRACT FROM WINDHAM'S DIARY

August 1, 1793. Up at six in order to be present at the grand ceremony of the troops marching out, and laying down their arms. Few scenes in life can be conceived of equal magnificence. Such a union of troops drawn from countries the most remote, and considered as of the first character at this time in Europe ; such a display of officers, of the highest rank, and most distinguished reputation, such splendour of appearance, such variety of character, such a combination of strong interests, can hardly be imagined to have been found on any one occasion. In the midst of the general feeling excited by such a scene, it was a fine thing to have had as parts of it, corps of the British troops who had either had their share of honours in the preceding duties, or were calculated to do credit to the country, by their appearance and equipment.

The day which at first was cloudy, turned out afterwards, to be as brilliant, as could be wished. Nothing was wanting to me, to the *feel* of enjoyment of the occasion, but that I should have been party to the service which immediately produced it, or should at least not have been in a situation in which I could have been party to it.

SIR GILBERT ELLIOT *to* WILLIAM WINDHAM

Minto : August 4, 1793

I cannot tell you how much I am obliged to you for your letter, nor how much pleasure it has given me. I am extremely glad that you was present at the catastrophe and that your specimen of military life has thus been complete in all its parts. I enjoy as highly as it is possible to enjoy, *per alium*, all the pleasure and all the sorts of pleasure which this expedition has given you. I need not tell you that I should have liked to be there, nor that my relish of the thing would have been amazingly heighten'd by a participation in it with you. But there is nothing like envy in my regret for this loss ; for on the contrary the enjoyment you have had in it is not only agreeable to me in itself, but is a sort of compensation to me for my own absence. Your way of seeing and enjoying such things, I am willing to flatter myself is so much *akin* to my own, that I feel as if it was gone in the *family* though it did not fall to my own share. I am

G. *Chinnery, pinxt.* W. J *Edwards, sculpt.*

SIR GILBERT ELLIOT, FIRST EARL OF MINTO

exceedingly gratified indeed by your understanding so justly the sort and degree of interest I take in *all* that concerns you ; not only in your welfare, in your fame, in your interests, but even in your own feelings about yourself.   I am also highly delighted with the unlimited confidence you are willing to place in me, of which you could offer no proof more perfect than your readiness to have told me faithfully your feelings in the trenches, even if they had been different from what they proved.   If they had been of the other sort, and you had told me so, I should have given you credit for courage, not less in degree, and of a much higher kind, than that which no man could doubt in you but yourself, even without the experiment. For as the mind is superior to matter, so is magnanimity; or the valour of the mind, to that of the nerves.   But I am still better pleased to know that you have both.   I know that you resolve almost all questions of conduct; small as well as great, into questions of *duty ;* and if you sometimes hesitate when others would see no room for doubt, it is in a great degree because you are more anxious to be right ; and the *chance* of being wrong is more uneasy to you than to almost any man I have ever known.   I honour this principle too highly to quarrel even with any little *error* in the *going of the machine* that may be incident to it.   My indulgence is, indeed, the cheaper, as I cannot refuse myself the justice to *claim kindred* with you here also.   But I have thought of a compensation piece, or rather a balance to steady these little fluctuations and to render the motion more uniform; which I dedicate to you as a Patron of such improvements,[1] hoping to give no offence to Sir George Shuckborough[2] or the Astronomer Royal.   The invention has this presumption in its favour, that it is perfectly simple.

[1] A humorous allusion to Windham's service upon the committee appointed to investigate he claim of Thomas Mudge.   *See ante,* p. 112 *note.*

[2] Sir George Augustus William Shuckburgh-Evelyn, Bt. (1751–1804), the author of a number of mathematical treatises.

It is only a certain degree of *hardiness* in acting on what appears to be right on *balance*. Suppose a scale of Right in which 20 is the highest number. Take, then, an alternative to decide on, of which one side shall stand in the scale at 10—the other at 9. I say, act on 10, as firmly as if 9 did not exist. You will say this hesitation is occasioned by the difficulty of observing correctly at what number each side stands, not by want of firmness afterwards. I am not sure of this. Hesitation is often occasioned by what you say, and then it is right ; but there is also in many cases a subsequent hesitation, and fluctuation, as if the two sides of the question were pulling, not uniformly and constantly one against the other, so that the strongest should be sure of prevailing, but separately and alternately, so that tho' the strongest pulls *furthest* at each pull, yet in the interval of its action; the weaker pulls back again, and great part of the work must be perpetually repeated, and then the question is determined not by who pulls strongest but who pulls last.

When I mention'd your anxiety to be right, I did not mean to talk of any *error;* on the contrary, it is to this excellent part of your character that a great proportion of that homage which the whole world is paying you, ought to be ascribed ; and amongst the rest it is to this virtuous principle that for one I profess to give the *very* high esteem which you know I have for you, although I beg you to remember that I claim friendship and affection with you on many other grounds of private endearment and early habits. I mention'd your anxiety on these points, only to say that I enter entirely into it on this occasion, and am very happy to give you my *clear* suffrage both for what you have done, and what you have omitted. You was certainly right to visit the Trenches. You would have *certainly* been most exceedingly culpable for mounting a breach, or otherwise exposing your life to considerable and, in your case, wholly gratuitous, and *impertinent* hazard. If others did so, in my opinion they were wrong ; but no two cases are alike on this question; and taking all circumstances into the account, publick and private, it would have been more blameable in you than any Englishman, or perhaps any other man alive.

It is now time to talk to you of something else, not less important perhaps than the scene you have left, tho' less splendid and animating. But it is the proper sphere of your action ; and one in which you are not a spectator, but called by God who gave you the means, by the world which wants the use of them, by yourself and friends towards both of whom you have an account to render, to perform a principal part. I seem to be threatening you with the subject *at large ;* but altho' I wish to do so; and I know I could find no time more favourable than when you are just returned from witnessing great exertions in the same common cause, and must, therefore; be the more impressed with the duty and desire to *be doing* yourself, and to take your share in these great concerns of the world, yet I must for want of time confine myself to one part of the subject which does not admit of delay. I left London the day before you ; on my arrival here I reflected on what had passed between us concerning Lord Spencer,[1] and the possibility of his acceptance. This was not known to ministers, who thought on the contrary the thing *over*. They might therefore take such steps towards another arrangement as might *fix* some much worse choice. Thinking, as I do, that Lord Spencer's filling that most important and critical station is of real and urgent consequence to that country, to this country, and, considering the sort of danger to be apprehended from thence, to the rest of the world, I judged it absolutely necessary to let Dundas[2] know the *possibility* of his going to Ireland. I did so by letter, but with every sort of caution which could prevent

[1] George John Spencer, second Earl Spencer (1758-1834).

[2] Henry Dundas (1739-1811) ; Home Secretary, 1791-4 ; Secretary of War, 1794-1801 ; created Viscount Melville, 1802.

Lord Spencer from being *committed*. I desired Mr. Dundas to wait for your return before any step should be taken towards renewing the proposition to Lord Spencer. He promised to do so in his answer, but presses me to lose no time after your arrival, in getting you to bring the subject forward. If you receive this letter in time, you had much better see Pitt or Dundas on the subject immediately. If not you will, I am sure, feel the importance of the matter sufficiently to use such means as occur to you with Lord Spencer *instantly*. The Irish arrangement stands entirely, still on this account; and Government is naturally, I believe, impatient to settle it.

I received your letter this morning and have time for no more. I presume you will be in England before this letter reaches London. Lady Malmesbury is here on her way to Kinnaird, Sir David Carnegie's. Lady Elliot sends you her kindest compliments and is happy to hear that your tour has give you so much satisfaction, but she *will not* repent of my having resisted the same temptation. I hope when you answer this to hear that your health has not suffer'd, and that you have recovered the extraordinary fatigue you have been exposed to.

Do not delay the Irish business; but if you have leisure, pray write your present thoughts and intentions on what relates to your own situation. The enemies of all good, as you so will call them, seem to have hopes from Ireland. Your stout cooperation in England will be wanted, and I confess I look forward with comfort to the prospect of acting in consort with you, tho' on a different stage; possibly of corresponding with you directly on, this great work.

[P.S.] Lord Spencer need not and I think, should not know of my letter to Dundas.[1]

---

[1] Add. MSS. 37852 f. 212.

SIR GILBERT ELLIOT *to* WILLIAM WINDHAM

Minto : August 13; 1793

Not having heard from you; I presume you are taking steps with Lord Spencer, and that you will not write till you can tell me the result. I am so far off, that a great delay will be occasion'd by making me the medium of your communication with Dundas on this subject ; and as I advised you to go directly to him, I have now advised him to see or to write to you on the subject. I thought it right to let you know, however, that I have done so. The more I hear of Ireland the more important I think Lord Spencer's mission, and the more anxious I am for his acceptance of it.

You know, or if not, I tell you in confidence that Lord Malmesbury [1] is extremely desirous of *Ireland*. I shall speak to *you* quite frankly, on the subject. Lord Spencer's character and name is *of the sort* that is wanted there, and being united with understanding and talents; I consider him as precisely what the occasion calls for; and cannot help feeling that the country has a strong *claim* to his services. If it should happen, however, that they cannot be obtained, and he is put out of the question, not knowing any other person of *the same description* on whom the choice can fall, I presume it will be made on a different principle, and they will either fix on some *friend* of a *negative* quality ; or employ some able man of business. The latter would be the better principle, provided *character* is not *too much* forgot in the choice. Looking through the Peerage, I believe impartially that they will find none so well qualified by ability, official habits and the great talent of knowing and conciliating men as Lord Malmesbury. The entire cordiality and confidence between him and me would undoubtedly be another very favourable and useful point ; and if there

---

[1] James Harris, first Baron Malmesbury (1746- 1820), diplomatist and politician ; created Earl of Malmesbury, 1800.

I   K may be supposed any difference between his general views and mine of Publick Principles and dutys, I will venture to say that in the sort of business that belongs to that office, he will be more likely to approach to me than to draw me after him. In a word, after Lord Spencer I should prefer him, and I am persuaded he is amongst the best, if not the best qualified. I feel, however, the impossibility of my suggesting either him or any other. I mention all this to you, both for the sake of saying *every thing* to you which I think, and also that if you should happen to agree with me and an opportunity should occur in which that opinion might drop from you, it might not be lost. I pledge my *Faith* and *Honour* to you in the mean while that Lord Malmesbury shall never know of his name having been mentioned to you, unless it should hereafter prove agreeable to you ; so you can feel yourself under no embarrassment of delicacy on this subject.

I long to have Valenciennes in detail from you ; but that will not be to-morrow.[1]

WILLIAM WINDHAM *to* THE DUKE OF PORTLAND

Felbrigg : September 3, 1793

I was more unfortunate than your Grace can conceive in missing the pleasure of seeing you at my return from the Continent. Lord William had told me so confidently that you would certainly be at Welbeck that I was careless about inquiring the first day of my arrival : and the day afterwards, I think, had the mortification of finding that, if I *had* inquired, I should have been in time.

Among my reasons of regret on this occasion is the missing an opportunity of talking to your Grace on subjects which, however little to me, I am sure, and probably even to your Grace, are not for that reason less necessary to be consider'd. I fear the return of such ques-

---

[1] Add. MSS. 37852 f. 216.

tions as that which I mentioned to your Grace at the close
of the last session, which, though laid asleep for the
present, will probably be brought up again ; and I wish to
put myself in as good a state as I can, for forming a firm
and satisfactory judgement upon them. The situation
beyond all comparison most agreeable to me would be
that of a mere member of Parliament, maintaining from
time to time my own opinion in debate, and giving to
Ministry, in a cause which I approved, the benefits of a
support which would become of some value from its total
exemption from the suspicion of any undue motive. The
thought of any closer connection is one from which I
shrink with perfect dread : yet I am far from being
convinced that it may not be necessary : and for that
reason am anxious to be provided as much as possible
with the opinions and views of those to whose judgements
I am accustomed to look up, and with a view to whose
conduct I should wish to regulate my own.

It is plain that the plan of those who are friendly in
different degrees to the French system, is to endeavour
to rescue it from final overthrow, by rendering the war
unpopular here, and thus to destroy the confederacy
which at present threatens it, and which, when once
dissolved, is never likely to be again united. If this
plan succeeds, there is an end in my opinion to all hopes
of maintaining the constitution of this country, or of
preserving anything like regular and orderly government
in any country in Europe. Should it even fail, I do not
conceive it will fail so completely, or the success of the
opposite system be so entire, as not to leave Europe
exposed for a series of years to the danger which now
threatens it, and not to require all the exertions which
wise and well-intentioned men can use to keep down the
operation of opposite principles. The differences, therefore, that now separate people in their political conduct
are not only of the most important kind, but likely, as
I conceive, to be of very long continuance. To me it

seems that the world in my time is not likely to be in a state in which, with such opinions as I conceive Fox to have; and with such persons as he will probably be for ever connected with; I could wish to see him Minister of this Country. The only choice; therefore; that will be left to me and others who are of that opinion; will be either to remain a third body; or rather a third, independent collection of individuals; supporting Ministry but not joining them ; or to incorporate ourselves; at some period and in some circumstances; with those to whom; as party men; we have hitherto been opposed. This question, on which there is probably much diversity of opinion; among those even who admit it to be the only one remaining; and on which much may be said on both sides; might safely perhaps be deferred, and left to the decision of future circumstances; if it was not for that part which involves the consideration of Ireland. The situation of Ireland is so important and so critical that it forms an epoch by itself ; and may be a reason for anticipating a decision which otherwise it might be very desirable to keep for some time in suspense.

The views which open on this occasion; if Ministry are fairly desirous on their part of establishing a government on a firm and constitutional basis; and restoring to the Aristocracy of the Country the influence which they have so much contributed to strip it of, and if it is thought on the other that such a union ought to take place; would be; of course, that some person of proper consideration should go to Ireland; while a corresponding weight; sufficient to ensure an honourable support; should be placed in the Cabinet here. Persons proper for all those stations are certainly not wanting; nor would an arrangement for their admission seem to be difficult, supposing Ministry to have a real view to the Interests of the Country; and not to be seeking merely to break and disunite those who might in future be opposed to them. The wishes of Ministry have hitherto seemed to point only

to Lord Spencer ; but if the grounds on which this wish
has been formed have been good, it would apply not more
to him than to others of similar description; could they
be induced to take that situation. At all events; Lord
Spencer would hardly be induced to place himself there;
nor would well indeed be advised to do so, without a
better assurance of support at home, than there appears
at present the means of forming. If Ministers are not
sincere or not honest in their views,—an opinion which
I should have no particular difficulty of admitting—
nothing remains but to continue the course which one
is at present pursuing : but if the fact be otherwise, and
that they are really desirous, though for purposes of their
own, of forming an administration on its true bottom, it is
a matter certainly to be well consider'd whether such a
disposition ought to be frustrated, and an opportunity
lost which may never again return with equal advantage
to the country.

I am sure I am as impartial upon this subject as a
person can well be,—as impartial, at least, if I may make
a good bull, on one side : for there is really nothing that I
dread so much as the necessity of taking any part in a
measure which I seem to be recommending. Though
I have brought myself to the state of being *ready* to do
whatever should be necessary, I am very far from having
prepared myself equally in point of inclination : My
likings are all the other way, and are yielded only to
arguments which I don't know well how to resist.

If Welbeck were not so distant, or my desire so strong
of enjoying for some time a state of perfect retirement, I
should like to wait upon your Grace, and talk over these
matters more fully than can be done by letter. Your
Grace, however, may be as well satisfied not to hear of
them : and it may be necessary rather to apologize
for having said so much, than to regret the want of an
opportunity of saying more. At all events I will desist
here. It would have been pleasant to me to have seen

your Grace when I came fresh from seeing Lord William ; and to have told you how much his character appears to advantage, as it is more and more discovered. Though such testimonials you must have had from many other persons, I am happy to add mine to the number.[1]

H.R.H. The Duke of York *to* William Windham

[Address illegible] September 4, 1793

I take the earliest opportunity in my power to acknowledge the receipt of your very obliging Letter, and to express to you how glad I am that you are pleased with your stay among us.

We are busily employed at present in preparing everything to begin the Siege of Dunkirk, and I hope in a very few days to be able to open the Trenches. Ever since the affair of the 24th the Enemy have left us exceedingly quiet ; firing, only a few random shot and shells every day, which, however, have done no mischief whatsoever. I am exceedingly anxious to get this town into our possession, as I think it of great national consequence and besides that it will render the rest of the campaign very easy.

We are given to understand here that there is a very considerable revolt among the Peasants between Aire and St. Omer, and that they have already beat the garrison of Aix, which marched out against them, they have risen in consequence of the decree of the Convention to force every person from the age of Sixteen to Sixty to serve.

We have no account as yet concerning the fate of the poor Queen of France,[2] though from the last newspapers I have seen I am affraid that there is very little chance of Her being alive at this moment.[3]

---

[1] Add. MSS. 37845 f. 13.
[2] Marie Antoinette was tried on October 14, and executed two days later.
[3] Add. MSS. 37842 f 63.

EARL SPENCER *to* WILLIAM WINDHAM

Oxford : September 14; 1793

I met with your Letter of the 12th here on my way back from Althorp from Hampshire, and having a leisure quarter of an hour before bed time, avail myself of it to thank you. I confess I expected pretty much that the Person whose Opinion you speak of in it, could entertain those Sentiments, and perhaps though I entirely agree with you in not having the least hope of a reunion with the Quarter alluded to, they are such as I cannot either be surprised at, or altogether disapprove, considering all circumstances ; for that Person having always professed so strong a diffidence of those in power, has surely no great reason for wishing a connection with them from anything that has happened very lately, and on the contrary may probably be less inclined to it, from what must at least to him have appeared in the Light of Endeavour to detach from him as many as possible of those of his friends, whose sentiments were the most like his own, and who was the person most likely to have co-operated with him in support of those sentiments. I agree with you in being decidedly of opinion that I could not go the least out of my way upon a hope of Reunion with the other Gentleman whose opinions, if they are really such as his late Conduct would lead me to infer, are such as I shall be extremely sorry to give my countenance to. The other part of your intelligence may possibly be here, and if it is will (as it appears to me) circumscribe the Part we have to take in this very narrow Limits indeed, as it will put it out of our power to think of any other than an *unconnected* support of Government : while at the same time the state of affairs will probably call for a support the most decided. Since you wrote; your Opinion upon the Dunkirk Expedition will not have been rendered more favourable, though I am in hopes by the News of to-day s Papers, that it is not so bad as we had great reason to apprehend ; but if the Plan was a bad one, the Execution of it does not appear to have made amends for the Error, and I am afraid that all those who wish to defend the Continuation of the War; will be a little put to it to give you an account of the Conduct of it. I have not heard since from the Army, and I conclude that my correspondent either does not like to enter unpleasant Accounts, or that he has lately been too much upon duty to have an opportunity of writing. The Accounts from Toulon seem to be confirmed in the Paper of to-day, with so many particulars that I hope we shall find them true, but I don't quite understand what is to be done about it, as I have no idea of Lord Hood's having Land force sufficient to defend the Place, and the manner in which it seems to have been taken would I should think, scarce permit of his making the sort of use of the Capture that an Englishman would wish, that is, to take possession of, or destroy their Ships and Naval stores there. I hope, however, his Lordship will send a more distinct and intelligible account of his transactions than your friend Sir James Murray does, who I really think improves in obscurity and mysteriousness every dispatch he writes. I am very glad you have not yet sent me back C. Fitzroy's Letter, as it will be another opportunity for you to write something with it, and now I have drawn you into a correspondence, I shall be very unwilling, I assure you to lose any occasion, of encouraging you to the continuance of it.

I was in town for a day last Saturday, and I saw Sir Gilbert Elliot in the Street. I was in a great hurry at the time, or I should have stopt to speak with him. What can have brought him up from Scotland so soon ? I hear that Parliament is to meet on the 29th of October. I hope I shall be able to see you before that time, and shall be glad to know whether you are to be at Felbrigg about the 6th of that month, because I am not quite sure

GEORGE JOHN, EARL SPENCER

whether I could not then contrive to call on you for a day.[1]

EARL SPENCER *to* WILLIAM WINDHAM

St. Albans : September 18, 1793

I sit down to write to you without having very well considered in my own Mind what I am to write, but, having a little leisure, cannot avoid communicating the apprehensions I have been forced into from observing the very awkward predicament in which we seem to have got; the difficulties of which appear to increase and grow more complicated every day. I was this morning for a few hours in London; where dissatisfaction and dejection seemed to me very apparent in the face and language of every one I happened to meet with. The late total failure of the Dunkirk scheme has been a great cause of this, and the very censureable neglect or mismanagement or perhaps both together, so conspicuous in the Admiralty, has not a little added to it. It is Currently reported that the Duke of Richmond[2] has justified his own share of the business in a manner unanswerable by producing the minutest and exactest detail of all the Orders received and executed in his department. The necessary consequence of his justification appears to be Lord Chatham's[3] condemnation, and between them they have been the means of crowning a rash and ill-concerted plan with a lame and inefficient execution. My chief reason for making all these reflections is that I foresee we shall, by and by, when these matters are, as they certainly will be, brought before the publick with all the exaggeration and aggravation that malice and ability can give them, find ourselves in a most distressing position, either obliged to defend what we cannot in conscience think defensible,

---

[1] Add. MSS· 37845 f· 112.

[2] Charles Lennox, third Duke of Richmond (1735–1806), Master-General of the Ordnance, with a seat in the Cabinet, 1782–1795.

[3] John Pitt, second Earl of Chatham (1756–1835), First Lord of the Admiralty, 1788–1794.

or if we join in the Clamour, which I very much fear will soon become a popular one, give strength to those whose strength will be the Ruin and Subversion of everything which we the most wish to preserve.

It will be too much, I doubt, to expect from Mr. Pitt; that he will have public spirit enough to sacrifice his Brother if he is really to blame, and if he does not sacrifice him I shall be almost afraid in the present circumstances of his falling himself; but if he does fall, where are we to look to supply his place? only to those who would (if they are in truth acting upon principle) plunge us into a System which would lead, for ought I know, to all the Horrors and Miseries of France: for as to looking if any third Party, of strength and weight enough to make head against the joint abilities of Pitt and Fox with all their respective supports and appendages, it would, I think in the present state of the country, be perfectly chimerical. To set against all the bad part of our Prospect, I see nothing but Toulon, and there is something about that which I am a little at a loss whether to be satisfied with or no. I have always had a great aversion to engaging in defence of any particular System of French Politicks, and Lord Hood's declarations are directly and absolutely in favour of the Constitution of 1789, which Constitution, if we are to trust to Burke, whose predictions have been verified by Experience, contained in it the Seeds of all the bitter fruit that followed. How do we know, that if all France, or at least a great majority of the country, were to declare themselves for that Constitution, and it should in consequence be established and sworn to as it was in 1789, how do we know that it might not tend like the former one to the confusion and escapes which the ill-contrived balance of that Constitution gave rise to before? I own I am as much puzzled in my own mind whether to be glad or sorry for the Capture of Toulon, circumstanced as it is, as ever I was in my life; and I am much tempted to think that perhaps the best event of that undertaking for England would be that they should do something which might justify Lord Hood in destroying their Fleet and Arsenal there, notwithstanding the Treaty. You see, my dear Windham, that I am taking a great liberty with you, by actually thinking upon Paper to you, for I am now wiiting just as they occur to me the crude Ideas that suggest themselves upon what I have read in the Newspapers. I should be happy if these Ideas of mine might draw from you some better conceived and better digested opinions, and lead you to point out some plan of operation for us in the ensuing parliamentary Campaign which we might pursue with Credit from the publick, with satisfaction to ourselves, and with advantage to the Cause we wish to support.[1]

SIR GILBERT ELLIOT *to* WILLIAM WINDHAM

Spring Gardens : September 18, 1793

Since I wrote to you a change has happen'd in my destination which will prevent Elliot[2] and me from visiting you as we hoped to do. I have not left myself an instant to write the many things I have to say and must reserve it for a post or two hence. In the mean while, and in two words, I am going to *Toulon*.[3] My duty will be to conduct our civil and political affairs in that *Region,* and to improve to the best advantage the unlook'd for good fortune which has befallen us there. This is an important commission but a most anxious one. It is impossible, however, to imagine one more consonant with all my wishes, feelings and principles. Pray keep this information secret till my actual appointment or departure. Elliot goes with me, and I believe we shall go in a week. I *wish* most devoutly I could receive my instructions

---

[1] Add. MSS. 37845 f. 114. [2] William Elliot of Wells.
[3] Elliot had just been appointed Civil Commissioner at Toulon. On December 20, however, Toulon ceased to be in the possession of the English Elliot then went to Florence on a special mission for the British Government.

from *you*. However; if that must not be; I am yet highly gratified and delighted with the opportunity of taking my post, and lending my hand, such as it is, in this great Labour of the World. A distrust of my powers, in this very arduous service, alone diminishes the pleasure, or checks a little the alacrity, with which I enter on this duty. But something must always be hazarded. All notions of neutrality, or even of inaction, have, I confess, long since *gone against* me, and although your zeal is quite equal to mine, as your exertions have been far greater; yet I tremble and grieve most sincerely to think how radically the course of our minds seem to differ in those points which lead to our *practical* determinations. I am not so much blinded, however, by ardour, and still less so much misled by confidence in my own opinions; as to oppose them to yours without real and unaffected distrust, as well as regret. I have caught myself now and then writing to you in a *form* of confidence in myself; which might bear even the appearance of censure on your opinions, which would have been most completely unwarrantable, if intended. I wish; therefore, that you should believe I have no other adherence to my own sentiments against yours than that which is imposed on me by the very nature of an opinion, which is not subject to the will and cannot be commanded. That in such a case as the present, I *must* act on my own is certain. I cannot yet quite forego the hope that as the *Gruel thickens*, or, to speak without metaphor, as the danger of the world increases, you will come to think *action* the first duty, and responsibility pretty nearly a point of honour. I protest I think it so. I cannot divest myself of an opinion that, all things considered, a distinct; separate, and unresponsible corps, even supporting Government, is in effect a formidable opposition. It is certainly a great drain for that confidence of the Publick; the whole of which should be turn'd to the acting and executive Power of the country at this crisis. Pray do not consider this as a letter on this subject. I have been sucked in; unprepared. I hope to write again soon.[1]

SIR GILBERT ELLIOT *to* WILLIAM WINDHAM

Spring Gardens: October 2, 1793

I am still here and do not expect to set out for Toulon before Thursday, the 10th inst. I promised, not to you but to myself, that I should write you a long letter, but have had my thoughts as well as the whole of my time forced another way; and now I flatter myself that I may yet have the pleasure of talking over with you instead of writing many things that appear to me extremely interesting. In this hope, however, you may very well tell me that I perhaps reckon without my host, as it depends wholly on your doing what you may think it very unreasonable to expect, and what at this moment you have possibly no thoughts of. It is nothing less than your coming to Town. I will tell you very fairly, as I must do very shortly, that I really wish you extremely to come; and that the occasion is, I am persuaded, sufficiently grave to deserve this sacrifice of your present comfortable leisure for a few days. It has got very much about that you are not only dissatisfied with some things that have passed during this campaign, but that you have expressed so indiscriminately that opinion, as to evince something like an intention of following it up in publick. The greatest possible uneasiness is entertained on that account by those who may, indeed, have a sufficient personal interest in the question, but who also think such a measure certain of producing the most fatal consequences to the common cause. It is the duty of a private as well as a publick friend to offer an opinion, if it is decided, on matters of real moment. Therefore, my dear Windham; excuse me; consider me as speaking still as one linked in publick as well as private friendship with you, and not

---

[1] Add. MSS. 37852 f. 218.

as already entered on my diplomatick functions, if I say that I most deliberately and entirely agree with them in thinking that what they apprehend would be fatal to the publick cause and interests. In one opinion you will I am sure agree with me, as soon as it is stated, viz. that not only a publick and formal opposition in Parliament on these grounds, but that *any* intimation of a strong opinion from *you* on that subject, is a *measure*, and cannot be classed as the casual conversation of indifferent men. If it is a *measure*, it should be taken on deliberation, and as a fair decision of your judgment. For this reason it is that I wish you to come to Town—to enquire where your information may be authentick, and to deliberate with those with whom you are accustomed to hold counsel what your conduct should be, on any result of your enquiries. Dundas knows that I meant to write this letter but he does not know what I say to you. I mention this only that I may not seem even to myself to avail myself of your kindness and of our friendship for the purposes of others, without telling you distinctly all circumstances. In truth, I feel that this question is not only so very important for the Publick, but so full of *delicacys* with regard to yourself that I have no hesitation in pressing you to come. If you do come, I *must* hope on a thousand other grounds that it may be before I lose this last opportunity of embracing you, and carrying with me your advice and kind wishes.[1]

WILLIAM WINDHAM *to* MRS. CREWE

Felbrigg : October 5, 1793

You show a sad pusillanimity in wishing to coax the persons you mention ; and seem yourself too much inclined to give in to their opinions. In foreign affairs I see nothing to make one despond ; and against the folly and wickedness of people here one has nothing to do but

[1] Add. MSS. 37852 f. 220.

to make stout fight.   What can make your Mr. Wallis (?)
talk any language which you can construe as democratical ? if he really does do so, I shall think less favourable of his understanding.   Never surely was a time when
the French system has less to recommend it, and, on the
contrary, showed more how monstrous it was in all its
parts ; and as to those who, condemning that system,
do yet talk against the war, they do really manifest a
degree of folly, bordering upon the weakness of infancy.
Be of good heart and cheer.   Resist open attacks, and
don't be led away by their cant.

I wish I could give you more assistance than I shall be
able to do in your subscription ; but I will do all I can.
My hostility to Jacobinism and all its works, weak or
wicked, is more steady and strong than ever.   If Pitt
is the man by whom this must be opposed, Pitt is the
man whom I shall stand by.   If I do not act with them
in office, it is only because I think I can be of more use
as I am.   Sir Gilbert's acceptance of the appointment
offered him has my perfect concurrence.   Farewell ! I
will write when I have anything that I think you
will like to hear.   By the way, your friend and admirer,
Mr. Malone,[1] is going somewhere into your neighbourhood,
and would be very glad, I am persuaded, of any encouragement to make you a visit.   Will you authorize
me to give him such, or, what would be still more
gracious, write him a line yourself ?   I wish I were able
to accompany him.[2]

WILLIAM PITT *to* WILLIAM WINDHAM

Hollwood : October 13; 1793

I received yesterday the favor of your obliging Letter,
enclosing several Papers from Mr. Hippisley, the Substance of which I had before learnt in some Measure, but

---

[1] Edmund Malone (1741–1812), a member of the Club and one of
the Johnson circle ; editor of the works of Shakespeare and Dryden

[2] The Crewe Papers ; Windham Section, p 15 (" Miscellanies " of the
Philobiblon Society, vol ix.).

less fully from the Lord Chancellor. Allow me to return you my thanks for the Communication, and at the same time to beg your Permission to retain the Papers for a few days, in order to examine them more at Leisure than I have yet been able to do. I partake thoroughly in your Sentiments both with respect to Toulon, and to the Person with whom the Political Concerns arising out of the Possession of that Place are entrusted.

This Event seems to me to furnish a better opening than could have presented itself in any other Way for facilitating the Restoration of regular Government in France; and for terminating the War satisfactorily, perhaps speedily. In Sir Gilbert Elliot's hands, I am sure every Advantage will be improved to the utmost. I need not say how happy I should have been if your Concurrence of Opinion on the great Questions now depending, had led you also to take an active share in conducting the affairs of Government. At least, however, I have the Satisfaction of knowing from Experience how much the Public may benefit by your Exertions even in your present Situation. The Check before Dunkirk is certainly much to be regretted. But unless any Impression should be produced by it at home to impede the Vigor of future Operations, the Mischief will, I trust, be little felt in the General Scale of the War. We expect in a few Days important Accounts from Maubeuge.[1] Success in that Quarter would in a great Measure relieve us from any further Anxiety on the Side of the Netherlands, and lead to further vigorous Measures, either before the End of this Campaign or very early in the next. I have enquired about the Paper transmitted from Norwich,[2]

[1] Jourdan attacked the Prince of Coburg on October 15 and compelled him to raise the siege of Maubeuge.

[2] " You have received from Norwich probably an account of a seditious paper, which made its appearance immediately on the miscarriage at Dunkirk, but which drooped and died away on the news of the success of Toulon : so little true is it that the progress of arms has no influence on that of opinions."—Windham to Pitt, October 11, 179
(Add. MSS. 37844 f. 11).   3

which I understand was immediately referred to the Attorney General.[1]

WILLIAM WINDHAM *to* LORD GRENVILLE

Felbrigg : October 22; 1793

It would have been better that the papers inclosed with this had been sent to your Lordship in the first instance; as I fear that the explanation; which Mr. Hippisley seems to look for from me, will hardly compensate for the delay of transmitting them through my hands.

Mr. Hippisley, in his letters to me, appears very anxious, lest any wrong construction should be put upon his conduct : or lest the pains which he has taken,—certainly from the best motives, and seemingly with the best effect,—should be deemed unseasonable and officious. He has sent me numerous documents showing both his reasons for acting, and the probable share, he has had, in exciting and promoting, those dispositions towards this country, which at present prevail in the Court of Rome. But I cannot think it necessary to trouble your Lordship with any of these vouchers for the purpose of Mr. Hippisley's justification. His interference; as far as it went, could not have been otherwise than advantageous :—His application, I mean, for the supply of our fleet with grain : and it will not be thought less so, because persons jealous of their own consequence, and of interests probably more substantial, seem to think it matter of complaint, that the service was performed too soon; and was not retarded in order that it might pass through their hands. Mr. Bartram's letter contains a reprimand, which might have produced a more impatient reply than that which Mr. Hippisley has given to it.

In a letter lately to Mr. Pitt on the same subject I could

---

[1] Add. MSS. 37844 f. 13.

not forbear expressing my hopes, that it might be found consistent with the interests of this country to join in the sentiments thus manifested by the Court of Rome ; nor to point out Mr. Hippisley as a man proper in various respects, to serve as a vehicle for any communication that might be intended, and who might be employed advantageously for that purpose.[1]

EDMUND MALONE *to* WILLIAM WINDHAM

London : October 30, 1793

I am delighted to find you; what I had no doubt you would be, so warm and zealous on the subject of the war ; the most necessary and honourable that ever was undertaken. I would not only part with my coat, but strip myself to my skin, to carry it on. The paltry attempt to rouse all those who are solely bent on gain to impede its progress, will I hope be the daily topick from the moment parliament meets. I see it is prorogued to the 10th of December.

There have been some apprehensions these two days past for the fate of Ostend. Some of the troops there were to have gone to the West Indies ; but Sir Charles Grey[2] is by this time at Ostend not to take away their troops, but to head them and to defend the place. The West India expedition will not be ready these ten days. Nothing had arrived last night from Ostend ; but a messenger is every hour expected. I will not, therefore, send this away, as perhaps I may hear some particulars in the course of the day—"Each hour is now, the father, not of some stratagem," but of some atrocity greater than the former. Does the history of any age or nation

---

[1] Add. MSS. 37846 f: 1:

[2] Sir Charles Grey (1729–1807), created Baron 1801, and Earl 1806. In 1793 he and Jervis were about to sail to endeavour to conquer the revolted French Indies Before the expedition started, however, the Duke of York had retired from before Dunkirk, and Nieuport was in danger. Grey was at once despatched with a small relief force.

Sir Joshua Reynolds, pinxt.

EDMUND MALONE

furnish us with anything half so calamitous as the last moments of the unfortunate Queen of France. Even the vilest and the most criminal of the human race have in their last moments some person near them to hear their last wishes and to receive their last pledges ; she had not near her one mortal that she could trust ; not a servant of her own choice ; not a single bosom on which she could drop a tear, or from which she could receive the smallest consolation ; not one whom she could charge with a lock of her hair or any the slightest memorial for that faithful sister-in-law, who had so long shared her sufferings, except the infamous pleader, whom in mockery they had assigned to her as her defender, and who by his own confession examined her only to betray her. Surely Heaven will presently " put a whip into every honest hand to lash these villains naked through the world." You know, I suppose, that the faithful Edgeworth [1] was not allowed to come near her ; and to mortify and disgrace her, they placed by her a constitutional priest, with whom she could have no communication. Like Charles in the same situation, all that was left to her to say was, " You may pray for me if you please, but you shall not pray with me." They have set a price on Edgeworth's head.

A minute fact has lately come to my knowledge, that may possibly be of consequence, if attended to. A very furious Jacobin, who was an ambassador from a wild Club at Derby to the National Convention, but within these six months has returned to England, has by some means or other, perhaps by the recommendation or some oblique interference of Lord L——e, got a commission in a new Scotch Regiment, and is either actually sailed to London, or under orders for it. His name, I am told, is Tweadle. Now as he has held this commission for sub-sistance, and has no doubt all his former propensities; would it not be worth while to give Sir Gilbert Elliot some

---

[1] The Abbé Edgeworth.

intimation with respect to him, that he may at least watch his motions ?

Thus far I had written yesterday, and afterwards wandered out with the hope of picking up some intelligence for you ; but there was not any to be had for love or money. All the good I did was to pick up Sir William Scott [1] at the Commons and to engage him to dine with me to-day. He may perhaps bring some news with him and therefore I will keep my letter unsealed. It depends entirely on the Wind, which has been for some days westerly, and detained the packets.

You will receive to-morrow the Manifesto of last night. I hoped it would have been more strong and have contained mere invective. I wanted " words that burn."— But perhaps this would have been less royal.—Nieuport is supposed to be safe by the adjoining country being two feet under water. Lady Lucan's news yesterday, which she said she derived from a foreign letter, was, that Prince Saxe-Cobourg was deceived by false intelligence that the French had turned his Army, which occasioned him to retreat when he was really victorious, as appears by the great number of Cannon which he took.

.   .   .   .   .

Instead of Sir W. Scott, I have just received an excuse from him, so I may now conclude. Boswell and Courteney were to have met him ; and I hoped with the authority of the King's Advocate to have kept the *Citizen* in good order. However, we must do as well as we can. It is astonishing that a man in no other respect hard-hearted, should still adhere to these cut-throats : he does, however, most lamentably, as far as decency will permit.[2]

---

[1] Sir William Scott (1745-1836), lawyer; won high distinction as ecclesiastical and Admiralty Judge; created Baron Stowell 1821.
[2] Add. MSS. 37854 f 127.

EDMUND BURKE *to* WILLIAM WINDHAM

October 1793

I do not exactly know, though I think I can partly guess, in what manner the present situation of things appears to you. To me it is the subject of the most serious anxiety. I went to Brighthelmstone, thinking to pass from thence to Portsmouth, and on through Winchester, home. But the news of the fresh defeat in the Netherlands brought me hither. Yesterday a sort of Message came from Macbride,[1] announcing, that this defeat had been followed, on the part of the Allies, with a great and decisive Victory. I have seen the Lieutenant dispatched by Macbride with this News, which has many particulars inducing one to believe that it is founded. But as the account particularizes neither time nor place, I am obliged, however reluctantly, to suspend my entire reliance on its truth. This day will clear up the matter.

I trust, that the good Event of this affair will enable us, (though such an event rarely disposes us) to a calm and unprejudiced review of the whole plan of the War—which in my opinion has been totally wrong—and that the bad military plan has arisen from the false political principles on which it is formed. If we have succeeded, I must consider it as a great escape. No Victory, however great, can reconcile my Mind to this Business of Maubeuge; no more than it could to the affair of Dunkirk, where, indeed, Victory was in a manner impossible. I feel no great pleasure in the Expedition against Martinico—if that should be, as I greatly fear it is, finally resolved upon. All these, and many more considerations, give me, at times, more uneasiness than I am able to express. But the fault is not only in our ministry, the whole Body of the Alliance is concerned in it. Things can never be brought to a decision, in the way they proceed

---

[1] Rear-Admiral John MacBride (died 1800), at this time commanding a frigate squadron off Brest.

in, by any Victory or Victories. However, I wish you to consider these hints of mine as for your own breast ; into which I wish more fully to unbosom mine—praying to God, that no hasty word from you or me, may give an advantage to the Jacobin Enemy here. If we criticize let us criticize to amend, to help, to supply—even possibly to encourage. But let us strengthen the principles we support, and give no advantage to those who find fault with conduct because they are utterly irreconcilable to principles. Our principles are antijacobin. We cannot be neuter. We are on the stage : and cannot occasionally jump into the Pitt or Boxes to make observations on our brother actors. Such are there, at home or abroad; who abhor Jacobinism as we do, and who act against it; bona fide, though with a thousand Errours. I have written something to the Ministers, and I have twice seen them, and spoken my sentiments very freely and very fully. I think we do not disagree in any principle nor in any Measure ; but in the time, the order in which Measures are to be taken and pursued, to be sure we differ —and this I take to be a very important part of the consideration. Here I am without any assistance, out of my own walls, to correct or to advise me, or to co-operate with me. In the world, as well as in the House of Commons, no motion is received, that is not seconded. I do most earnestly wish to see you. Clouds lower all over the Horison; which alarm, but do not dispirit me, if you keep up your Vigour. *Heu quianam tanti cinxerunt aethera nimbi !—quidve pater Neptune paras ?*

Do not you think the new act of Regicide the smallest part of the wickedness ? Oh God ! the Charge ! and the last article particularly. All this is but the unfolding of the Germ of Jacobinism. For God's sake come to Town. Again and again I want consolation and assistance. You cannot withdraw yourself from the world, now in the Vigour of your Age and faculties, without a Crime.

I hear nothing to confirm the News. But there have

been three actions at La Vendée. The Royalists failed
in one, Noirmoutier—but succeeded in three others—all
very important.[1]

WILLIAM WINDHAM *to* EDMUND BURKE

Felbrigg : November 1; 1793

The desire of obeying your summons might be motive
sufficient to carry me to town, without allowing the reason
which you assign, if I could be sure that the meeting of
parliament would be delayed long enough to admit of my
coming back again. Till it shall be determined that
parliament is not to meet till after Christmas; I could wish
to defer a little, my going to London, that I may not begin
my winter residence sooner than is necessary. To go to
town from this distance, without a long period before one,
must be going for good.

I fear that *good* in that sense; is the only good which
would attend my going at present. I have no counsels to
offer but what I must learn from you ; nor any means of
enforcing them, but what they must have already from
your authority. Authority, probably, of any sort, can
now do but little. What remains of the campaign; and of
the fate of the armies, must be determined probably by
the events, for the result of which I am waiting with
the most anxious expectation. In a letter which I had
from Brussels of the 21st, great Anxiety was expressed
for the army of the Prince of Coburgh ; and, what
was worse, the same was said to be felt in the army
itself.

I have not the least doubt of what is right to be done
by us ; namely, to maintain the war, in and out of parliament, by every possible means ; But I tremble to think;
should disasters increase, how long this may be in our
power. Toulon and Weissenburg,[2] if they keep to their

---

[1] Add. MSS. 37843 f. 25.

[2] Weissenburg was captured by General Wurmser, October 15,
1793.

mark; will, it may be hoped, preserve the balance for this year.

The murder of the queen of France is an event that appears more shocking (I know not certainly for what reason) than even that of the king. The length of her sufferings, though urged commonly with a contrary view, makes one less endure that they should terminate at last in death. One hoped for some period in reserve, that might have softened the memory of her past woes, and brought some retribution of happiness in this life,—a little longer respite, and relief, one hoped, might have reached her. All is now extinct ! An act of such savage and unrelenting cruelty,—of such black and unprovoked guilt,—I suppose is hardly to be paralleled ; as a case can hardly be found of life ended in circumstances so dreadful, so destitute of all external support, so beset with every thing to embitter and sharpen the last agony. All that the imagination pictures of death had been hers for long past ;—seclusion, silence, solitude, ignorance of all that was passing, separation from all the visible world. Her pursuers seem, beforehand, to have plunged her into the tomb, that its horrors might have time to sink into her mind,—might pervade and occupy every region of the soul. It was wonderful how her courage was able to sustain so long a conflict ; or how, in fact, she contrived to preserve her senses. It is a strong proof of the vigour of her mind, and a presumption highly favourable to the virtuousness of her character. She seems to have retained her dignity and firmness to the last ; to have been wanting in nothing that the occasion required ; to have sustained, throughout, the part she was to act, worthily of herself, and of those whom she represented. The assertors of monarchy as opposed to modern doctrines, need wish for nothing better, than such a contrast as is formed by the conduct of the king and queen, compared with that of their destroyers.

In this solitary place, I have little communication with

the world, except occasionally by letters, and know but little, therefore, of the language generally talked. In fact, in matters of this sort, people seldom talk any language but what they are taught ; and, therefore, till they assemble in town, or parliament sets them a-going, they have no very decided opinions. To me the necessity for the war seems so impossible not to be seen by the commonest understanding, the motives for persevering in it to be so powerful, that I cannot but think it must be the fault of those who should direct the public mind, if the clamours against the war gain any great ground. The artifice of those who wish to conceal and give effect to their wishes in favour of the French system, under a pretended horror of war, is surely so easily seen through, that it can never produce much effect. Our first debates in parliament must be directed, I think, to strip the mask from this miserable hypocrisy ;—it surely cannot be a difficult task.

I shall, at all events, come to town before Christmas. If parliament does not meet, I shall be desirous of coming very speedily.[1]

WILLIAM WINDHAM *to* EDMUND BURKE

Felbrigg : November 7, 1793

You will have received, before this, my answer to your letter, and find that I am ready to come whenever my presence shall be necessary or useful. Though you give me, for the present, a dispensation, I am half inclined not to make use of it, but to yield to the wish of being for a while near the centre of counsel and intelligence. Your letter is written in a tone of dejection that makes me apprehend something worse than has yet reached me, or suspect that I have seen our situation more favourably than I ought. The worst news is undoubtedly from La Vendée ; yet unless you have further accounts, confirming

---

[1] Burke, " Correspondence," iv. 179.

those of the convention; I cannot abandon my hopes upon the strength merely of what they say. Besides the allowance to be made for exaggeration, and often for total fabrication, the war of La Vendée does not seem to be of a sort which temporary ill success will eradicate. One may hope that the whole of that country is so thoroughly impregnated with hatred and horror of the present system, for which new reasons; too, are arising every day, that they never can do more than stop its effects for the moment, and that the first opportunity will call them out again with their original vigour.

In all other quarters our affairs seem to be going on with reasonable success. No fears, I hope, are entertained, at least, no news or special ones, of our being forced from our hold on Toulon. The progress of the northern armies must, of necessity, be slow; they are thus riving the block at the knotty end. But I cannot but hope that at the southern extremity the work will go on quicker and that a rent may be made by our operations that will reach far into France.

What is your opinion of the declaration ? [1] I think in one passage, they are yielding too much to the adversary ; and by seeming to give up part of the question, making the defence of the remainder more difficult. Why is all right of interference in the affairs of another country, even without the plea of aggression on the part of that country, to be universally given up ? The more I have thought upon that opinion, the more satisfied I have been; that it is a mere arbitrary assumption wholly unsupported by anything in reason and nature, and in direct repugnance to everything which the maintainers of that doctrine would be compelled, and even ready, to allow. In other respects it seems to be judicious, and it is certainly well drawn, and I should hope will produce the best effects ;

[1] The Declaration issued by the British Government, October 29, 1793, in which the causes and objects of the war were set forth, as well as the circumstances which would enable the King to end it.

particularly if, as I see in the papers just received, the Austrians have taken possession of Alsace in the name of Louis XVII.

The poor departed queen ! How cheering would such intelligence have been to her ! How much does one wish that she might have lived to see herself and her son restored in part to their former situation ; or rescued ; at least, from the fangs of these hell-hounds ! How painful is the reflection, that whatever good may now befal, she no longer remains to enjoy it !

From the delay occasioned at Ostend, the West India expedition is, I suppose, laid aside. The opinion which you seem to have of it, has taught me not to regret its loss. The fever, too, that rages so dreadfully in some of the islands, might itself have been a reason, I should conceive, for not persisting in it.

Mrs. Burke, I hope, and all your family are well. Let me beg you to present my best respects.

[P.S.] The system of atheism will now, I think, not be denied. What say the religious dissenters to this ? The worthy bishop who believes that the God of nature and liberty needs no *intermediary*, will perhaps reconcile them. They are perfectly satisfied that there should be no religion, provided there is no establishment.[1]

WILLIAM WINDHAM *to* MRS. CREWE

Felbrigg : November 7, 1793

I have suffered my debt to you to rise to such an amount that I run the risk of being driven to despair; and abandoning all thoughts of paying it. Let me make an effort in time, and offer a small instalment, though in order to do that I must defraud another, and leave unwritten a letter which I ought to send abroad. You have a claim not from me only, to whom you have done so kindly, but from all lovers of good to be hailed and

[1] Burke, " Correspondence," iv. 189.

celebrated, and encouraged in the good work which you pursue so zealously. Don't be discouraged or discountenanced by any rebuffs. I don't know where must be either the hearts or the heads of those who can refuse to assist in it if they possess the means, much less who can attempt to find fault with it. I have another subscription in reserve, I formerly subscribed 25l., whenever it shall be most wanted. In the mean time I cannot say that I have contributed to you quite all the pains I might ; but I will from this time, and meant this very post to have written to Dr. Burney. I am glad that the pen of Madame Abry,[1] or whatever the name is, is going to be exerted in the cause.

There can be no necessity for stimulating your rage against the present system and its abettors. Its horrors are now of so deep a dye, have a cast of character so truly diabolical, that there is an end of all reserve and management : and all who support in any degree that system, are persons from whom I am separated by the widest gulph that can separate men on publick affairs.

To talk of condemning this system, and not supporting the war, is in those who are sincere in that language such extreme weakness; in my opinion, as can only be equalled by the wickedness of those who talk about it without being sincere. The fact is, that the greater part of those who lead on that side either care not what becomes of the world, so they can answer their purposes of ambition or enmity, or else they do really love this system, for that which to most men renders it an object of horror and detestation. All who are not of either of these descriptions are, in my idea, the most deplorable dupes that ever belonged to that fraternity. I cannot conceive any opinion so utterly devoid of common sense and likelihood, as that, if we were to withdraw from the present war, supposing it possible in common honour and honesty that we could do so, the whole of the French system

---

[1] Madame D'Arblay (Fanny Burney).

would not pour into this system, as certainly as the sea would into Holland, upon the removal of any of their main dykes. What at least is to be our security against this, if the French were to chuse to fraternize ; and who is to be our security that they will not chuse it ? If they are this irresistible people that some chuse to describe, and derive such new powers from their present condition, why may not part of this præternatural vigour be carried into their external operations, and make them equally formidable in offence as they are in defence ? In fact, with the aid of their principles they would be infinitely more so ; in so great a degree that the moment they should be let loose to act exclusively against us, I should be one of those to distrust altogether our powers of resistance. I must not go on, however, on this subject, which is end-less : we shall have enough of it when Parliament meets. In the meanwhile, let me thank you for your letters, exhort you to remain steady in the faith, extol you for your splendid exertions in behalf of the poor priests, and beg you to believe me, as always,

Your most faithful and obedient,

W. W.

I am waiting with great impatience for the papers. Things in Flanders seem to have got round again ; and Weissenburg opens the prospect, I hope, to great consequences. For Toulon, too, I hope no fears need be entertained. The Queen, the fate of the poor Queen, for whom now I begin to justify all Mr. Burke's enthusiasm, saddens even our prospects of success, so much I wish that she might have lived to enjoy them.[1]

EDMUND BURKE *to* WILLIAM WINDHAM

[*Circa : November* 7–14, 1793]

I received your second very kind, very satisfactory Letter, just as I was going to thank you for your first.

---

[1] The Crewe Papers : Windham Section, p. 18 (" Miscellanies " of the Philobiblon Society, vol. ix.).

I do confess, that I feel myself gradually sinking into something like despondency. It is not from the Events of War; which, as one might expect, have been chequered. A little security towards a defensive is promised to us in the Netherlands. The affair of Weissenburg seems to me one of the finest things in military History. I can scarcely, as an operation of War, imagine anything beyond it. But it is not from our defeats, that my hopes are damped, but from our successes. If we had been only beaten, better conduct and greater forces, with our share of the chances, might set us right again. But I see nothing, which all the successes we have had, and much greater than I dare to look for, can do towards bringing things to the conclusion we wish, as long as the plan we have pursued and still pursue, is persevered in. When I have the pleasure of seeing you, we will talk over this matter in the Detail.

I agree with you, that the proclamation is well drawn : Perhaps too well drawn, as it shows too much art. I admit that it seems, more than anything else that has yet appeared, to depart from the unfortunate plan of making war against France, and to direct it where it ought to be directed, to the relief of the oppressed, and to the destruction of Jacobinism. I wish, however, that nothing had been said about indemnity. It is a thing unheard of in this stage of a War : and as in fact we have no pledge whatever in our hands but Toulon, it looks as if we meant to keep that place, and the ships in that harbour for that indemnity though surrendered to our faith upon very different Terms. This precious demand of indemnity, which has a sort of appearance, (even so much as perhaps to hazard the whole effect of the Declaration) of Fairness, is yet so very loose and general that I scarce know what it is that we and the allied Courts may not claim under it. The worst of the matter is that the only object which we have hitherto pursued, is the previous security of this indemnification.

The thing however that perfectly sickens me in this
Declaration is its total disagreement with everything
we have done or (so far as I see) that we are going to
do. We promise protection and assistance to those
who shall endeavour the Restoration of Monarchy in
that Country: Yet, though Poitou is in a manner at
our door and they have for eight months carried on a War
on the principles we have pointed out—not a man, not
a ship, not an article of stores, has been yet sent to these
brave unfortunate people; all the force we can spare
was destined for our indemnity; and when now released;
I do not know with what prudence, from the Flemish
Service it is intended again to go to the West Indies.
No talk, nor no thought, of giving the least of the succour
we stand engaged for, and which common justice and
common policy ought to have induced us to send though
we were under no positive engagement at all. This,
joined with our refusing to recognise that Monarchy in
those who have a right to exercise its authority, is a
defeasance to our Declaration which nothing but a total
change of conduct can cancell. However, though I am
grieved beyond measure, and mortified at this proceeding, our only hopes are from these people. The
conduct of our late party is so absurd, contradictory, and
self destructive, that I cannot easily express it. But on
all these matters we shall talk seriously when we meet,
which I trust will be soon. Oh! what you say of
the Queen in your two Letters is like what I should expect
from your feelings on that, the most dreadful scene, that
ever was exhibited to the world! Stupified as I was at
the enormous wickedness of the actors, as well as at
the *nature* of it, which was worse, in my opinion, than
its magnitude, and astonished at the sustained fortitude
and patience of the sufferer, yet my indignation, at the
unfeeling manner in which it has been received by the
Princes of her own House, has perhaps been the strongest
of my Emotions on this occasion. The wicked faction at

Paris have obtained the only end they could have proposed to themselves by their savage proceedings, the rendering vile and contemptible the Royal Character. The execution of a King or Queen by the hands of the common hangman, as the lowest and vilest of criminals, will produce no more effect than one of the periodical hangings at the old Bailey. I am quite of your mind that there is something that mingles more of disgust, and of compassion, with our horrour in this Barbarity even more than in the murder of the King. In fact Women, and such Women, are more out of the Field in such contentions as brought on these Events—and the Circumstances themselves were much worse. Sure some Justice ought to be done to a character which does so much more than Justice to the nature we belong to.[1]

EARL SPENCER *to* WILLIAM WINDHAM

Wilderness : November 11, 1793

Though I cannot say that the general result of what I am going to communicate to you is of any very considerable importance, yet on the terms of perfect confidence with which you have done me the Honour to treat me, and on which I hope nothing will ever prevent our continuing ; I think it indispensably necessary to acquaint you that, having come here on a visit to Lord Bayham[2] for a night, I met Pitt. This meeting was not purely accidental but Lord Bayham who saw me in town at Lord Lucan's on Thursday asked me to come, and told me that Pitt was very desirous of having an interview with me, which he thought might be brought about more agreably by me in this mode than any other. I determined to accept of the invitation thinking that it might possibly be productive of some good, and could not of any harm, and at all events would probably afford us

[1] Add. MSS. 37843 f. 31.
[2] The courtesy title of the eldest son of Lord Camden. *See* vol i, p. 287, *note* 2, of this work.

some information on the present state of Affairs. I
confess that the Result of it has not in this last point done
a great deal, and in neither of the former considerations, it
seems to have been as nearly as possible indifferent : it
has, however, given me the opportunity of repeating to
him what you had already expressed for me, and of finding
that for the present, with respect to any internal arrangements, matters remain I think, much as your conversation with him at the end of the last Session left them, that
is to say, still open but not ripe for any decisive Step.   He
began by saying that he was desirous of having this
conversation with me in order to explain any thing
relating to the events of the last Summer that might have
left a wish for explanation on my Mind, and to give me
any confidential information I might desire to have;
and he might be able to give me, respecting any such
events and the general state of affairs. He then seemed to
expect me to point out the particular objects on which
I wished the conversation to turn. I own I felt very
awkwardly at the moment, owing rather to the finding
myself all at once in so very new a situation to me, and I
believe in consequence of this I did not explain myself at
first so clearly and intelligibly as I could have wished.
From this circumstance also it probably arises that I am
not able to give a very exact detail of what passed between us on this branch of the subject, the general substance, however, I think was, that the idea of taking
Dunkirk formed originally a part of the general Plan of
the Campaign, in which, it was hoped we might have
got into possession of that Port (stated by him to be
a considerable object as being a Port, and from the
nearness of its situation to us being more likely to give
a favourable impression of the war in their Country) of a
strong line of Frontier from thence all the way to Maubeuge inclusively, and even of having formed something
like a winter investment of Lille ; I collect from what
he said that it had been agreed that the Austrian Artillery

should have cooperated in the siege of Dunkirk; but as they insisted on conducting that of Quesnoy [1] at the same time; it become necessary for our Army there to be supplied from home, and a Requisition was accordingly sent, and answered in such a manner that he speaks with great confidence of being able by a new statement of dates to satisfy us that every exertion that could be made was made. As to the want of Gun-boats, the fact is that they had no idea that they would be wanted till a requisition was sent for them from the Army *actually before Dunkirk*, and then, of course, they could not come in time. All this, you see, in reality amounts to little more than saying that Dunkirk was attacked with an inadequate force, and, of course, that all that we lost both in time, in stores, in expences, in men, and in reputation by it was absolutely *en pure perte*. I dwelt a good deal (after I had recovered my nerves a little) and repeatedly in the course of our conversation on the expediency if it could possibly be done of making some satisfactory explanation at the opening of the Session upon these points, as they are likely to have taken some hold of the publick mind, and to have given strength to opposition in general. He did not say anything directly to this, but I think it did not pass without exciting his attention. He seems in general to look on the French as being at present in a Situation less likely to dispose them to yield than they were some months ago, owing partly to the Surrender of Lyons and partly to their successes in La Vendée, which he apprehends to be more decisive than they have ever been yet ; though he did not seem to state any very clear Intelligence having been received about them. The Ships that were sent away from Toulon to the other Sea Ports, which was a measure that has excited some Curiosity and no inconsiderable Surprize in many people, were sent by Lord Hood on his own Authority in order to remove about 5000 Seamen

---

[1] Quesnoy was taken by the Austrians, September 11, 1793. It was recovered by the French, August 16, 1794.

from the Place who were very ill affected and who might
have been capable of doing much Mischief, more particularly
before they were so much reinforced there, as they have
since been.   I think this is nearly the substance of what
passed with respect to past transactions. With respect to
the future, I found him fully determined on the most
vigorous exertions in the Prosecution of the War, in
which he seems to expect a very cordial cooperation on
the part of the Austrians; on that of the Prussians he is
not so sanguine, and even went so far as to say he should
not be much surprized if they were to withdraw altogether
from the Confederacy. The other Powers will act as they are
paid (the Dutch I think we omitted to speak of).   He
seems much inclined to the Opinion that there will be little
hope of putting an End to the War without penetrating
pretty far into the interior of France, and in order to [do]
that, it would seem that we must possess ourselves of all
the frontier strong Places (even including Lille) before
we can advance with any Security, the ostensible Object
of the War is, I suppose, to be consonant to the Language
of the Declaration, namely, such a Government in France
as the rest of Europe may reasonably depend upon for its
future Peace and Security, hinting then at the same time
that a Monarchy of some kind or other at least is the
most likely to attain those Ends.   On the Article of
Expence he talked very openly, and said that he should
want at least 12 millions for the Supply of the Year (I
suppose of course the extra supply for the War), but
from the situation of the Finances he hoped to be only
obliged to lay absolutely new Taxes to the amount of from
three to 400,000, and he hopes to lay them in a manner that
shall not be much felt.   He asked me whether I happened
to know anything of the Duke of Portland's present
Sentiments, I said I had heard that he was still disposed
to support the War. In the course of this part of the
Conversation; as he happened to mention your Name, I
thought it not a bad opportunity to find out whether he

had still any views similar to what he talked of with you last Summer on the subject of political arrangements, so I said that you had according to his desire as I believed, communicated to me at that time the Substance of what had passed between you, and that I also believed you had expressed to him our joint Opinion that we thought upon the whole that an unconnected support of Government would then have more weight and efficacy than if we were to take a share in any part of the administration. I added that my opinion still continued on that subject pretty much the same, and that, instead of having seen anything to alter it since, I found it rather confirmed by circumstances that had happened. He answered that he was very glad I had mentioned the subject as it would give him an opportunity of saying a word or two upon it, though he should not have mentioned it first himself, because at the present moment there was no opening that would enable him to make any proposal of the kind; he, however, hoped that I should still allow the matter to remain open, and in case any occasion offered such as to put it in his power to make any such proposal, that he might have my leave to communicate again with me upon the Subject. This is as near as I can recollect the substance of what passed between us in private; or this latter part of our conversation.

I particularly noticed that he treated the Idea of a possibility of our coming into office only on the Supposition of our doing it jointly, and I took the more particular Notice of this, because in the conversation I had at Lord Lucan's with Lord Bayham, which gave rise to this meeting, he had thrown out something like a hint, which at the same time he assured me he was not commissioned to do, but which I think he never could have mentioned if it had not been concerted, that his Father, Lord Camden [1] now found it impossible for him to con-

---

[1] Sir Charles Pratt, first Earl Camden (1714-1794); Lord Chancellor,

tinue in Office, and that he had no doubt but that if that Situation would be agreable to me, the members of the Administration would be very glad it should be filled by me, but that at the same time there was not *at present* an opening for any other Cabinet Office. My immediate Answer to this was, first generally, the same sort of answer which I afterwards gave to Pitt, but besides that even if I did think the occasion called for my coming into Office, I could not for a moment entertain an Idea of doing so unaccompanied by you. He again repeated that he had no Commission to mention the matter to me, and that he did not know whether Pitt would mention it in the Interview we were to have ; but I have myself very little doubt but that he was employed to feel the ground a little before that Interview, and that, finding me so clearly determined on the subject, Pitt took the Line I have already described to you, in our conversation. I took occasion to express in the course of what I said my decided purpose of supporting government in a vigorous prosecution of the War ; and, indeed, I do not now see what other possible track we can pursue in order to arrive at a desirable termination of it, for any appearance of relaxation in our efforts now must unquestionably not only encourage the Enemy, but tend to discourage and disunite all our Allies, whom, it certainly is of essential consequence, if possible, to keep together. I understand from Pitt that the last private accounts they have from the Prince of Coburg mention his having received positive Orders from Vienna to do everything in his Power to force the Enemy to a general Action, It is, therefore, a most anxious moment for he had begun to take measures accordingly, and the very next accounts may very possibly contain something of infinite importance. The Accounts in yesterday's Extra-ordinary Gazette from Toulon are, I think, very satisfactory, as they seem to

1766–1770 ; President of the Council, 1782–1783, and again from 1784 until shortly before his death.

indicate a great deal of Spirit, and a very cordial union among the different troops of the Garrison, which, from all the reinforcements they have lately received, appears to be very equal to the defence of the Place ; there have also been some very great dissensions between the French and Americans, which may very probably turn to good account.   Upon the whole, notwithstanding the unfavourable circumstances which in the course of this very long letter I have alluded to, I feel inclined to be in pretty good spirits and if we should happen to gain anything like a brilliant advantage to close the Campaign in Flanders it may have a surprising effect in making people forget the former miscarriages, and join heartily in the maintenance of what every day becomes more and more the general cause of all that is good or estimable under the Law. Pitt has promised to send me word if any important Event should take place, and, of course, you shall certainly hear from me again, if I should have anything worth communicating.

I am quite ashamed of having been so long winded, but I did not well know how to abridge what I had to tell you, though after all I believe you will not think there is much in it.   I go down to Althorp to-morrow and shall stay there till the beginning of January.   Parliament, I understand, is to meet a few days before the Birthday.[1]

WILLIAM WINDHAM *to* JAMES WYATT [2]

Felbrigg : November 23, 1793

I shall no longer insist upon a right which I have no means of enforcing, nor complain of injuries, which it is not in my power to redress.   It is near two years since you undertook a business for me neither requiring, nor

---

[1] Add. MSS. 37845 f. 119.

[2] James Wyatt (1746–1813), architect, adapted the Pantheon in Oxford Street for dramatic performances ; restored Salisbury, Lincoln, Hereford and Lichfield Cathedrals ; from Græco-Italian style he developed into Gothic.

admitting of, delay ; and which you have not done yet. I have written to you no less than five letters desiring to know, whether you meant to do this, or not : and you have returned no answer.

You may think perhaps that this is a mark of genius, and the privelege of a man eminent in his profession : But you must give me leave to say, that it must be a profession higher than that of an Architect, and eminence greater than that of Mr. Wyatt, that can make one see in this proceeding anything but great impertinence, and a degree of neglect, that may well be called dishonest.

It is dishonest to make engagements, which you are either not able or not willing to fullfil : It is in the highest degree uncivil to receive letter after letter, containing a question which the writer is entitled to ask : and to send no answer.

Pray, Sir, who are you, upon whom engagements are to be of no force ; and who are to set aside all the forms of civility established between man and man ? Had the most private Gentleman of the country written to the first minister of the country, he would have received an answer in a quarter of the time. And what is this privelege denied to persons in that station, which you suppose to be possessed by you ? A privelege not allowed to a man's betters may be expected to be one of which he has no great reason to boast. But of this I leave you to judge. There is one privelege which you shall not possess, that of acting with rudeness and contumely without being told of your conduct. If you are fond of placing yourself in a situation, in which you must hear these charges without the power of refuting them, I wish you joy of your choice, and with that reflexion shall take my leave of you.

P.S. Am I to expect, that the metal frames, which you ordered at Sheffield, will come at last, when they are no longer wanted : or am I to understand only, that what you told me, is not true, and that no such order was given ? [1]

---

[1] Add. MSS. 37914 f. 67

EDMUND BURKE *to* WILLIAM WINDHAM

November 25, 1793

Since I wrote last, the outside of affairs is a good deal
mended, but they will not bear inspection. Our politics
want directness and simplicity. A spirit of chicane, or
something very like it, predominates in all that is done,
either by our allies or by ourselves. Westminster-Hall has
ruined Whitehall ; and there are many things in which
we proceed more like lawyers than statesmen. If this
distemper is not cured, I undertake to say, with the
more positive assurance, that nothing but shame and
destruction can be the result of all our operations in the
field and in the cabinet. All the misfortunes of the
war have arisen from this very intricacy and ambiguity
in our politics ; and yet, though this is as visible as I think
it is real, I do not find the smallest disposition to make
any alteration in the system. I have the greatest possible
desire of talking with you on this subject. I think something ought to be done, and I know that I cannot act
alone. If I had not always felt this, all that has happened
within these three months would have convinced me of it.
The very existence of human affairs, in their ancient and
happy order, depends upon the existence of this ministry ;
but it does not depend upon their existence only in their
ministerial situation and capacity, but on their doing
their duty in it. They are certainly bewildered in the
labyrinth of their own politics. What you observe is
most true ; they think they can defend themselves the
better by taking part of the ground of their adversary.
But that is a woful mistake. He is consistent and they
are not. He is strengthened by their concessions. He
avails himself of what they yield, and contends with
advantage for the rest. As to the affairs of France, into
which they have entered at last, it is plain to me that
they are wholly confounded by their magnitude. The
crimes that accumulated on each other astonish them.

These crimes produce the effects which their authors propose by them. They fill our ministers, and I believe the ministers of other courts, not with indignation and manly resentment, but with an abject terror. They are oppressed by these crimes—they cry quarter—and then they talk a feeling language of mercy ; but it is not mercy to the innocent and virtuous sufferers, but to base, cruel and relentless tyrants. I shall explain myself more fully when we meet. People talk of the cruelty of punishing a revolutionary tribunal, and the authors of the denunciation of an infant king, concerning offences that the voice of humanity cannot utter, in order to criminate his own mother, at the very moment, (this very moment) when they turn out of the house, which they have given them in the king's name and taken credit for it, six hundred and eighty virtuous and religious men, in the beginning of a winter, which threatens no small rigour, without a place to hide their heads in.

I am mortified at all this, and I believe I express myself with some confusion about it. But we must endeavour to make our complaints rather effectual than loud. The other faction is dreadful indeed. It consists of two parts ; one of which is feebly and unsystematically right, the other regularly, uniformly, and actively wrong ; and, what is natural, that which is the most steady and energetic, gives the law to that which is lax and wavering. The entire unfolding of the Jacobin system has made no change in them whatsoever. Not one of them has been converted ; no, nor even shaken ; and those who coincide with us in the absolute necessity of this war (to which, however, they give but a very trimming and ambiguous support), are become far more attached than ever to their Jacobin friends, are animated with much greater rage than ever against the ministers, and are become not much less irritated against those of their old friends who act decidedly and honestly in favour of their principles. This state of things requires to be handled according to its true nature. If you and I take the steps we ought to take, there is yet a chance that all may be right. For God's sake come, and come speedily, for no time is to be lost.[1]

EARL SPENCER *to* WILLIAM WINDHAM

Althorp : December 8, 1793

Lord Lucan tells us that you and Burke will be in Town. If I thought that my presence there at this moment could be of any possible good Effect, your Wish should not long remain unaccomplished, but as I do not foresee that any useful Purpose can be answered by my being there at present, I shall, I believe, prefer staying here till the beginning of next Month, when I shall certainly come to Town, as I think it will be very desirable that those who think alike on the present State of Politicks should have some Communication, and Concert at least for a few days previous to the meeting of Parliament. I have of late much wished for you here, more especially when Tom Grenville[2] was with me, as we had at that time a great deal of conversation on these matters, the purport and tendency of which, though it is much too extensive for the compass of a Letter I am extremely desirous for you to be acquainted with. I wish I could prevail upon you to come down here in the course of this Month, but if that is impossible, I hope I may depend on finding you in London in the first week in January. The Period which is to produce something of rather a more decisive Nature in our Conduct is now fast approaching, and not to have well weighed and naturally considered all its bearings before we are to act, will be of very bad consequence. I, in my own Mind, not only remain of the same Opinion on the general Nature of what that Line of Conduct ought

[1] Burke, " Correspondence," iv. 201.
[2] Thomas Grenville (1755–1846), younger brother of Lord Grenville, diplomatist and statesman. He bequeathed his books to the British Museum, where his collection is known as The Grenville Library.

to be, but are much confirmed in it, by several Circumstances, which may best be explained when we meet. In
general terms, the Line of Conduct which the present
Situation of the Country loudly calls upon us to pursue
appears to me to be, the most vigorous, determined, and
declared Support of the War (and, of course, of Government), unconnected, however, by Office with Administration, and not only unconnected, but avowedly hostile to
the views and Measures of the Party who call themselves
the Friends of the People ; unconnected with Administration, because we shall by that means establish our Claim to
the Confidence of every independent Man in the Country;
and convince the People if they are open to Conviction;
that there are Men who can adopt a Line of publick
Conduct solely because they think it right, and not as
being the old hackneyed Road to high Situations or great
Emoluments; and openly hostile to the views of the violent
Party, because we shall thereby cut off all Idea of any
lingering after the old Opposition as it used to be formed;
which in truth consisted of such a Medley of discordant
and absolutely contradictory Principles, as could not but
extinguish all hopes of its being either useful to the
Publick, or creditable to those who composed it. On
Principles like these I am inclined now to be more sanguine than I was when we last talked on these Subjects,
as to the Chance of our being able to collect a body
sufficiently respectable both as to number and character
to make a considerable and that a very desirable impression on the Publick, and to have a really efficient Weight
with Ministry and Parliament ; and if I am not too
sanguine in this Hope, I think you will agree with me
that the chance of doing it is worth the tryal ; the more
particular details of this Idea, which I allow is not yet
sufficiently matured for me to state them fully, will be
the subject of the Conversations which we *must* have
before the 21st of next Month, and my principal Reason
for troubling you with this Letter now, was to endeavour,

if possible, to have as early an opportunity of entering with you into these Details, as the nature of your other Engagements will allow.

I am much afraid, from the present Complexion of our military Operations both by Sea and Land, that to all our other difficulties, we shall have an addition of a great deal of ill humour to struggle with on the subject of the Conduct of the War, but the Objects that we have to contend for, are much too important for us to hesitate in taking our Share of that difficulty.

Pray let me have a Line at least to tell me, when I am likely to see you and whether here or in Town.[1]

LORD MALMESBURY [2] *to* WILLIAM WINDHAM

Frankfort : December 13, 1793

Altho' I have been in the way of armies I have had no military event come in my way, which you have not heard and seen from the newspapers—you should otherwise have received a letter from me and been thanked for the very kind one you wrote me just as I was leaving England. I have, indeed, no inducement of news, to write to you now, but one which I flatter myself you will not think either an uninteresting or useless one.

The Duke of York was so good as to meet me at Alost about a week ago and to talk to me in a very confidential manner. I cannot trust the particulars of his conversation to the post. The result, as far as it related to himself, went to confirm me in the good opinion I was always disposed to have of him, and in general not to alter that I had, that many mistakes and missions had in the course of the summer defeated the effect of his exertions and rendered the end of the campaign less brilliant than the beginning. He was not insensible to those neglects,

---

[1] Add. MSS. 37845 f. 124.

[2] Lord Malmesbury had been sent by Pitt to Berlin to give a necessary reminder to King Frederick William of his treaty obligations to support England in the war with France.

but he expressed a very anxious and earnest desire that if any of the more violent members of opposition should, in their wishes to harass and criminate Government, affect a sollicitude about him and a compassion for his situation, or even if they should join him in the common censure *about Dunkirk* or any other military operation, I say, that in either of these cases, the Duke expressed his anxious and earnest desire, that, none of his friends out of zeal or regard for him should say anything which might raise a clamour against administration or weaken their measures by defending him at their expense : that such a defence, however grateful he should feel for it, would necessarily go to diminish the strength of Government and in its effect militate directly against a cause the support of which he felt as a duty before which any personal consideration ought to give way. That it would be impossible to separate in the minds *of the many* the partial blame of any one specifick measure in the course of the war from a general disapprobation of the principle on which it was begun and going on, and that the very worst of consequences would attend such an idea being attributed to those he was happy to call his friends. He named you and Pelham and expressly directed me to write to you both, which I do, I am sure without altering his sense, if I have altered his words.

The only case in which he hoped to be supported and defended was if any gross and notoriously abusive attack should be made upon him, and even then he only wished (as it would be evidently made with a view to provoke) that the defence should rest on general grounds, and all particular details and *personalities* be avoided. I am the more anxious to write to you on this subject, as I am sure you will feel the Duke to be as right and judicious in his advice as he is temperate and forbearing in his character, and admit the extreme importance that Parliament should open with the greatest appearance of concord and unanimity, and that England should give an impression to Europe, which may perhaps as much contribute to the success of the great cause in which we are struggling as victories or successful negotiations.

I have written to the same effect, nearly in the same words to Pelham. I shall be happy to hear from you at your leisure and promise you that my next letter shall be more entertaining.

I leave this place for Berlin to morrow. I see nothing but insurmountable difficultys there ; and if I am absurd for undertaking them I trust my friends will at least vouch for my not having accepted a sinecure office.[1]

WILLIAM WINDHAM *to* WILLIAM PITT

December 16, 1793

The only point in which it is material that I should trouble you is that which relates to the communication with the Princes. On this I would wish to state such portions as I have happened to hear, without repeating opinions with which you are already acquainted.

The Princes, I understand, are full of jealousy of this conference which they understand is to precede any recognition of their title. Their jealousy turns principally upon these points :

A fear lest the purpose of this country should be to limit their authority in order to keep France henceafter in a feeble and depressed state.

A fear lest the ideas of the Constitutionalists should be suffered to prevail too much, in which apprehension they are confirmed by the terms of the agreement at Toulon.

A fear lest views of indemnification should operate too far, and sacrifices be required of them, inconsistent with their duty and character.

A general apprehension growing out of all the former, that the Cabinet here is not in earnest in wishing to see

[1] Add. MSS. 37873 f. 243.

them for the present at the head of the Royalist party ; but would rather that the cause should, to a certain length, be carried on without them.

These seem to be the principal heads of uneasiness which, whether reasonable or not, must be considered as very excuseable in their situation.

The danger is that in the state of ferment in which their minds must be, and stimulated in particular as the Comte D'Artois [1] is by every feeling of duty and honour, he should take some rash step, and without consulting anything but his sentiments and feelings, should throw himself upon the Coast of Brittany, in the first vessel that he can procure.

The person from whom I hear this principally; and who, though standing in an inferior station to the Duc D'Harcourt, [2] is still secretly much in their secrets, is persuaded nevertheless that they are much disposed to be tractable, and would be quieted by any general assurance relative to the above points, conveyed to them by a person in whose sincerity he could confide.

I know not that I can add anything to the simple exposition of the fact, coupled with those opinions which I took the liberty of stating to you the other day. I am obliged at present to write rather in a hurry, as I wish to leave Town to-day. I regret now rather that I missed the occasion of discoursing on any such points more at leisure which you and Mr. Dundas were so obliging as to offer. [3]

WILLIAM WINDHAM *to* MRS. CREWE

Felbrigg : December 26, 1793

I have just got a letter from you, which might serve to whet my purpose had it been before almost blunted,

---

[1] Charles Philippe de France, Comte d'Artois (1757–1836), succeeded his brother to the throne in 1824 as Charles X ; abdicated, 1830.

[2] Duc D'Harcourt, son of Marshal D'Harcourt, sometime Governor of Normandy.

[3] Add. MSS. 37844 f. 15.

which it was not, of writing to you by this post. Don't feel any immediate fear of the machinations of the Jacobins; notwithstanding the bad news which this Gazette has brought from Toulon ; [1] and still less suffer yourself to be perplext or shaken by their reasoning. Those who can stand all these effects of their blessed system must have good stomachs indeed. It is in vain for them to try to lead off the attention to other objects, or to seek for evasions or subterfuges. The experiment is full and flat in their faces. There is a full exemplification of the state to which they wished, and endeavoured, and are endeavouring, to bring the world-robbery, murder, atheism, universal profligacy of manners, contempt of every law divine and human. Much of this is what many of the leaders of this sect have no objection to. It is, indeed, to them its recommendation. It serves to cover what good-nature and softness may otherwise make them shrink from.· What others' intentions may be I know not ; but my determination is open, steady war against the whole Jacobin faction ; and junction for that purpose with whomever it may be necessary to join. That it will be necessary to join anybody in office I do not mean to say. You need not fear my doing it alone ; first, because I do not think it will be advantageous to the general cause to do it in that way ; and next, because whenever the time comes that that question shall arise, there will be others, I hope, disposed to do it with me. These are my ideas upon the subject, and which there is no necessity to make any secret of. The sum of the opinion is, that I am a determined foe to the new system, and that I shall oppose that, either in or out of office, according as circumstances shall show that one or other mode is most effectual.

Your correspondent from Buxton; as well as the other who talks about Lord Howe, both provoke me ; but I think the last the most ; as he is perfectly foolish, while

[1] Toulon was regained by the French on December 20.

the other may only be wicked : and folly, though less odious, is more provoking than wickedness. These clamours against the Duke of York are for the most part utterly without foundation ; and in all very nearly so. They originate in the mere licentiousness of the office part of the army. The Duke of York is, I believe, a most respectable character ; his conduct is, I am sure, in many respects perfectly exemplary. Nothing material in the campaign has suffered from him, if anything at all has ; and all the latter part has been of a sort to do him the highest honour. Both the court of Vienna and the Austrian army are full of his praises. The charges against Lord Howe are so perfectly senseless, that one wonders how rational creatures can be found to utter them. I wish your correspondent, who thinks that Lord Howe is so careful of himself, was bound to stand by Lord Howe in all the danger to which he would be willing to expose himself. If I were to guess at your correspondent from his language on this occasion, I should set him down as some Tory clergyman, who had learnt to abuse the Howes because they did not conquer America. Pray let me know if I am right.

I was going to say that I had nothing more to say, but I have upon recollection what I should be sorry to omit. It is to recommend a book, which, for soundness of thinking as well as eloquence of stile, has had no fellows since the commencement of the controversy about the French Revolution. It is of great bulk, and has a great deal of foppery in it, enough to destroy a work of less powerful merits. But it is full of proofs of the most uncommon genius, and has a charm and grace in the midst of its fopperies that has led me on like a novel, and puts me in mind, in some respects, of the attraction which every one finds in Montaigne. It is written by a Mr. Wylde, an advocate of Edinburgh, and a friend of Mackintosh ; but a man of more genius and of not less acuteness ; there is no doubt of his being a better man,

I

and that conviction of the author's character is one of the graces of his book.   The Jacobins, who may laugh at it, can neither answer it nor equal it.

Farewell! till we meet.   The hour of attack approaches, and I am beginning to throw off my weeds of peace, and furbish up my armour.   I am luckily, too, at present in much better health than I have been through the greatest part of the summer.[1]

---

[1] The Crewe Papers : Windham Section, p. 23 (" Miscellanies " of the Philobiblon Society, vol. ix.).

SECTION IV

SECRETARY-AT-WAR IN THE PITT ADMINISTRATION, 1794–1801

SECTION IV

SECRETARY-AT-WAR IN THE PITT
ADMINISTRATION, 1794–1801

CHAPTER I

1794

The state of parties : Windham's position among the leaders
of the Opposition : His personal charm : His merits and
defects as a speaker : The Duke of Portland clearly defines his
position at the beginning of the year : His reluctance to accept
office under Pitt : The Norfolk Militia : The Emigrant Bill :
Martinico : The acquittal of Warren Hastings : The managers
of the trial thanked by the House of Commons : The retirement of Burke from the Parliament : He is granted a pension :
His wish for a peerage : The coalition of the Portland party
with the Government : The Duke, Lord Spencer, and Lord
Fitzwilliam accept office : Windham becomes Secretary-at-War
with a seat in the Cabinet : Irish affairs : Lord Spencer's
mission to Vienna : Sir Sidney Smith's plan of attack on the
French fleet : His dissatisfaction with the treatment he has
received at the hand of his country : The Prince of Coburg
resigns the command of the Austrian army : He is succeeded
by General Clerfayt : The loss of Valenciennes and Condé :
Windham goes abroad, and stays at the head-quarters of the
English army : The operations on the Scheldt : Windham, in
a private letter to Pitt, recommends the removal of the Duke
of York from the command of the British army abroad : The
delicacy of the position : Pitt's embarrassment : The controversy concerning the appointment of Lord Fitzwilliam to the
viceroyalty of Ireland : The Duke of Portland and his friends
threaten to resign : Pitt at last consents to make the appointment.

THE political situation has already been defined
in the foregoing letters. The breach between
the followers of Fox and those of the Duke of
Portland had, naturally, weakened the Opposition. On the other hand, the Government was far from

strong, and Pitt was desirous to strengthen it by a coalition with the Portland party ; but the Duke of Portland, while well aware of the gravity of the situation, and considering it his duty to support the measures introduced to allay the unrest produced in this country by the spirit of the French Revolution, was unwilling to take office under Pitt.

Windham now occupied a position of no little importance among the leaders of his party. It is a little difficult to understand how, within eight years of his taking his seat in Parliament, he was within an ace of becoming the head of the Opposition (as he confessed he might have done, had he been ambitious) when the dissension between Fox and Portland was in danger of destroying it altogether as a striking force.

The position he thus early secured was, apparently, less the result of great parliamentary talents than of personal popularity and the respect in which he was held. As a friend of Fox and Burke, he had, of course, been a marked man from the time he took his seat as member for Norwich, and these men had naturally put him in the way of making himself a power in the House. With this excellent start, he had done the rest himself, and without apparent effort. He was not a great orator, and he had the defect of a somewhat shrill voice that did not carry far ; but on all the subjects that he took for his own he spoke well. " In his parliamentary speeches his principal object always was to convince the understanding by irrefragable argument, which he at the same time enlivened with a profusion of imagery, drawn sometimes from the most abstruse parts of science, but oftener from the most familiar objects of common life. . . . His language, both in writing and speaking, was always simple, and he was always fond of idiomatic phrases; which he thought contributed greatly to preserve the purity of our language." [1] Thus wrote Malone; who; is, however, careful to add that Windham was never "what is called a thorough party-man." This last; regarded from the point of view of parliamentary leaders; was a sad defect ; but Windham was never disloyal to his political associates, though at times rather a dangerous as well as a candid friend. To all affairs, whether of public or private life, he brought a chivalrous sense of honour; and when he changed his views, as change them he did on more than one occasion, no one ever doubted his sincerity.

The Duke of Portland *to* William Windham
Bulstrode: January 11, 1794

When I look at the date of your Letter and recollect the sort of engagement I entered into at the time I returned you my thanks for it, I feel it quite impossible to attempt to justify my silence. It is very certain that the subject, on which I undertook to give you my sentiments more at length, abounds with so many unpleasant vexations and distressing considerations that I can not but say I was always ready to avail myself of a pretext to lay it aside ; and I will say with no less truth, that although the temper and habit of your mind appeared to me necessarily to suggest to you many questions and many uses of conscience respecting our publick conduct, the line which it became and behoved us to follow in the present crisis seemed to me so plain and distinct, that even the jealousy of my friendship for you did not give me a minute's apprehension of any difference in our ultimate decision.

After all that has been said and written upon the subject, the question for our present determination reduces itself to the consideration of what our Duty to

[1] *Gentleman's Magazine*, June 1810, xxx, 590

the Publick requires us to do as Whigs; that is; as members of a Party, or, as unconnected Individuals— or, in other words, what are the most effectual means that can be taken by *US* for the support of the Government and Constitution of our Country, and the general preservation and maintenance of Religion, Law, Good Order, in short, of the principles and purposes of Civil Society.

I know it has been very strongly urged, and by some for whose judgement and disinterestedness I have the highest respect, that our Duty calls upon us at this moment not only to cooperate or act in conjunction with ministers, but to make so perfectly a common cause with them as to become members of their Administration by accepting certain offices which there is very good reason to believe are ready to be offered to us. That every mode of support other than this demonstrates a distrust and diffidence on the part of the Giver, which cannot but be injurious to the existing Government, be the hands what they may, by which it is administered : that support to be effectual must be given completely and indiscriminately, and cannot be dealt out by apportionment or measure ; that if given partially, it betrays an undecision and unsteadiness of character in the Givers, which in as much as it is prejudicial to them, equally diminishes and weakens the effect, even of that portion of assistance which it is intended to be Given, so as to render it doubtful whether it is not rather of disservice than of any ability or benefit to the Publick. This subject has also been treated with ridicule as well as with good and powerful arguments, but it is an abuse of your time to take more notice of them, knowing as I do that there is not a medium through which this subject would be seen in which it has not been prescribed to your view, that friendship, affection, partiality, admiration for you, Integrity and artifice have all been exerted to the utmost to induce you to adopt this opinion ; and I only state them to show you, that I am not unmindful of the arguments which have been used on this side of the question.

As I have long been in the habit of believing that certain obligations or conditions or Duties are respectively attached to every station or rank of life, I have no difficulty in admitting that the acceptance of office under certain conditions is one of those to which persons of our description are liable; but then I contend that the judgement of those conditions, under, what I shall call, his innate responsibility rests with every individual. I am also decidedly of opinion that the existence of a Whig Party is essential to the well being of this Country, as well as to the preservation of its Constitution, and allow me, my dear Windham, when the name of Whig has been so prostituted and counterfeited, as we have seen it, to deposit with you in a very few words my definition of the Whig Party, which I have always understood to be: an Union of any number of persons of independent minds and fortunes formed and connected together by their belief in the principles upon which the Revolution of 1688 was founded and perfected; and by the attachment to the present form of our Government to all its Establishments and Orders Religious and Civil; and the test of whose conduct as a Party, must consist in their never supporting, proposing or resisting, any measure, in or out of Parliament, to which, if they were possessed of power, if they were the Ministers of the Country, they would not give equally the same treatment.

Considering these positions as the standard or scale by which I am to try the propriety of the Conduct I am to hold upon all publick occasions, it is certainly not from envy and I hope as little from resentment that I feel myself under the necessity of adverting to the present Administration. Whenever I have thought their measures right I have supported them, and as often as I think so I will support them, in the Conduct of the present War. Though there are years in which I may have thought them injudicious, and some which have been unfortunate, they will not, in the present moment, be arraigned or blamed by me ; nor shall any encouragement be wanting on my part to bring the War to a successful, a safe and honorable termination. I shall advert to the conduct of the present Administration no further, nor desire the principles of their formation or conduct to be remembered, no otherwise, than as they may be necessary to justify the opinion I mean to submit to you. It will not be denied to me that the characteristick feature of the present Reign has been its uniform and almost unremitting attention and study to debase and vilify the natural aristocracy of the Country, and, under the proper pretence of abolishing all party distinctions, to annihilate, if possible, The Whig Party. For these express purposes the present Ministry was formed ; and that they have most religiously adhered to and most exemplarily fulfilled the purposes of their creation every year of their existence would furnish us with abundant instances; but this conduct at the time of the Regency would of itself be sufficient and I would be satisfied to confine myself to that measure only, could I forget what passed no longer ago than the latter end of the last Session with regard to the Election of the 16 Peers of Scotland. But to compress what occurs to me upon this subject into the smallest possible compass, I will not insist at all upon the objections which arise out of the circumstances I have just alluded to, and I will endeavour in the further consideration of this question to make the interest of the publick the main and sole ground upon which my opinion shall be formed.

If the case could permit of any exception, I should insist that there never was a crisis, in which it was of so much importance, as the present, that the Character of those, who are admitted to responsible situations in Government should be exempt from all suspicion of being influenced by motives of interest, that, considering the

predicament in which we have so long stood in opposition
or contradistinction to the present Ministers, it would be
almost impossible, for any of us, under any circumstances
which have as yet come to my knowledge to accede to;
and suffer ourselves to, be incorporated into the present
Administration without making ourselves obnoxious to
such suspicions ; from whence I conclude; that it is
inconsistent with the uniform tenor of our Conduct and
incompatible with our duty to the Publick to accept any
offer which there is any reason to imagine will be made to
us. The conversations which passed about the time of
the late Chancellor's[1] removal from His Office, the *Glass*
which Lord Loughborough was desired by Dundas and
authorised by Pitt, to hold up to us, the overtures which
have been since made to you, and the intimation of such
a weight, of so many seats, in Cabinet as might be sufficient to ensure an honourable support to Lord S[pencer]
if he could be prevailed upon to undertake the Lieutenancy of Ireland are proofs to demonstration to me,
that no intention has ever been entertained or perhaps
conceived of forming an Administration upon such a
Basis as would comprehend the collective strength of the
Country ; that the ideas of strengthening Government
have not originated out of a wish or hope of Union, but;
as I fear, out of a desire to take advantage of the differences
which have unhappily arisen among us, and with a view
to make those divisions, which have been the consequence
of them, irreconcilable and irreparable. This at least has
been evidently the object of all the new Proselytes.
When a conduct has been pursued so very reverse from
that which I should have thought the peculiarity and
magnitude of the present Crisis required, and which the
Duty of Persons in Ministerial situations imposed upon
them, I own myself at a loss to give them credit for that
sincerity or for any one of those motives which will

---

[1] Lord Thurlow was succeeded as Lord Chancellor by Lord Loughborough, January 1793.

warrant me to suppose that any such inclination has ever been felt by Pitt as can secure Us, were We to consent to listen to his overtures, from the reproach of having made a sacrifice of our principles, or can give us admission to the publick service in such a way as to ensure to Government the full benefit of the Influence We derive from our characters. If it was worth while to advert to the circumstances of the offer of the Marquisate of Rockingham to Lord Fitzwilliam and of the Garter to myself, there would appear in these trifles a want of sincerity, so perfectly unnecessary that one cannot help wondering at—but which it can not help discovering itself on such very trivial occasions. You will allow that it must create an impression not very favorable to the idea of trusting what ought to be most dear to one, to the keeping of so inattentive and careless a Manager. So much then for the sincerity which We are to look for in these offers, one word now for the Candor, and to you and me, who each of us know a little of Ireland, it requires a measure of Zeal for the publick service which I confess I am not possessed of, to admit the state of that country to be brought forward, to be set in the front of all their arguments by the *present Ministers* as the inducement, the justification, the unanswerable reason for our inlisting into their Corps, for our not hesitating to accede to their administration : and is it impossible to refuse one's hand to Sylvester Douglas [1] and declare the honor of being led by him through ranks of Renunciation, Commercial Propositions, Regency Measures, encouragements and discouragements to Catholics, and Reformers, alternate submissions and resistances, new Jobs, new Boards, and the whole Battle array of temporary expedients to the Head of the Council Table in Ireland ? But here I will leave this part of the subject, a very serious and important one most assuredly, and one, which in my more

---

[1] Sylvester Douglas (1743–1823), Member of the Irish Parliament, afterwards created Baron Glenbervie.

enthusiastic moments, I have looked to as one of the
earliest and most certain instruments by which, it might
be hoped, that, the salvation of this Country as well as
that, might be permanently effected.   But in considering
the question of our acceding to the present administration,
it is not the expediency or prosperity of the measure as it
concerns any of us personally that I trouble my head
about : it is solely the effect which it would have upon the
publick mind, and its tendency through that Organ to
render Government more or less respectable, concerning
which I feel any way interested.   It must be allowed that
there are several persons known by the name of the
Opposition or Whig Party who, from the responsibility
of their characters, possess a considerable share of the
good opinion and esteem of the Publick.   Some of them
certainly owe this to their Talents and Abilities, but all of
them are at least as much indebted for it to the ingenuous-
ness, the integrity, and disinterestedness of their Conduct.
As long as they preserve this title to the publick esteem, so
long will they have it in their power either as Individuals
or as Party men to give very great assistance and strength
to Government by their avowed sanction and support
of the measures which Ministers may have formed in
their private Situations ; they can give energy to measures
which want force ; they can Control and suppress others
before they can have risen to a state to be obnoxious,
they can in many cases counteract popular prejudices,
and engage and insure popular favor, from the confidence
they possess from the supposition of any jealousy or
suspicion attaching to them, they can give the tone to the
publick mind, and very nearly be able to place every
measure of administration in the light in which they wish
to be seen.   But let them accede to the present
administration, let them take offices under Mr. Pitt, and
from that moment their weight, their consideration, their
very names are lost.   Will it ever from that moment be
a question what may be the opinion of Mr. Windham, Lord

Spencer, Lord Fitzwilliam, or any other person of that description ?   Whether suspicion or distrust shall follow that step, I don't here inquire—I will even suppose that the publick will do you all perfect justice—But You become involved in the mass of administration, you become the adherents and followers of Pitt.   You may be of some use in Council, but your Station in publick opinion is gone, it is lost, and, as far as I am able to judge, can not in the present moment be compensated by any good which may be done by your obtaining Seats in the Cabinet. As upon the Party, the effects of this conduct can not but be productive of very material injury ; and to one, devoted to Party as I was, for the reasons which I have stated in the former part of this Letter, it can not but appear certain to produce the most serious injuries to the interests of the Publick.   It has of late been specially convenient to some persons, to whom it has at other times been as convenient to be thought to be attached to the Whig Party, to suppose, and to endeavour to make it generally believed, that the Party was broken to pieces, that it was dissolved, that it had not any longer even the means of existence ; and I am sorry to say, but with too much success.   But according to my ideas of several of those who have professed themselves members of it according to my idea of its vital Principle, I shall deny the possibility of its dissolution.   It must be consistent with the principles of Right and Wrong.   That it has suffered, that some of its most precious and most lovely Ornaments have been torn from it, I admit and lament—the wound it received last year in one of its most capital Branches, is an event which affects me with the deepest concern and affliction ; that no support can be now, at this moment, expected from that Branch I can not deny ; but let us hope, that time may restore it to its Parent Trunk, and that it may again strengthen and invigorate its native Stock.   If the existence of a Whig Party is as essential, as I contend it to be, to the well being and prosperity of the

State and that the inlisting with the present Ministers
is productive of discredit and weakness to that Party, I
conceive that it can not well be denied, under the actual
circumstances of this Country, that a greater injury could
befall *the Cause of Government*, than would ensue by the
principal members of that Party being induced to accept
any offers which can be held out to them by the present
Ministry. I have already said enough, and perhaps more
than enough, upon this subject; and yet I can not pass over
an argument arising, as I understand, out of the plans of
the present opposition and the irreconcileable difference
which is likely to continue for a very long period of time
between us and that description of persons. Because a
certain number of Gentlemen, who have been in the
habit of acting with us for several years, happen now
to differ from us so essentially upon points of very great
and high moment and importance, so as to have occasioned
a complete separation or breach between us ; and Because upon these points a perfect uniformity of sentiment
and Conduct has prevailed between the Whigs and the
present Ministers, it is urged that the Whigs ought to
accept offices (seats in the Cabinet, I understand) if such
should be offered them by the present Ministers. For
my own part, I must say that no such obligation can be
admitted by me, any more than that a conclusion is
warranted by the promises I have stated. I should easily
conceive a proposal on the part of administration to that
effect to be particularly ill timed and in all respects very
injudicious and ill imagined. It would seem on this part
an admission of weakness which our Conduct is intended
to render unnecessary and would be a disregard or aban-
donment of an advantage which the liberality of that
conduct would alone hold out to them. In another
light it can not be considered but as liable to particular
objection in the present moment, in as much as it would
subject them to the imputation with which they have
been so often charged, of availing themselves with eager-

ness of these unhappy differences to prejudice the characters of that Party and of those very persons whom it is their interest to hold out to the publick view as disposed to give them a disinterested and consequently the most effectual support. So far with respect to the offer, now as to the acceptance of it ; I can not discover, with all the attention I am master of, any one inducement or justification which this unhappy schism affords for it : in my view of it (the schism) it operates the direct contrary way. I should infer that it rendered it necessary for us to be more reserved and guarded in our conduct towards administration, and to be more than ordinarily cautious in not giving ground for suspicious jealousies of an interested nature. That it being but too probable that opposition, even to *this War*, would not be an unpopular conduct, and considering of whom that Opposition would be principally composed, comparisons would naturally be made of their conduct with that of the Friends they had guided; and that this consideration ought to be an additional argument against our listening to any offer that could give colour to suspicions which I am very sure the factious spirit which animates and actuates some of those who compose that opposition will not let them be backward in raising and propagating. I therefore must be allowed to say that to the best of my poor judgement I can not but rank this argument on the side of those which I should urge for depreciating any such offer in the present circumstances. There now remains, as I believe, and as you must hope, only one more subject for consideration, and on that I mean to say but a very few words, as I conceive I have already in a great measure, anticipated what would be applicable to it. But it having been asked, if a sincere disposition to form an administration upon what we consider its true bottom should really exist, whether it should be frustrated ? I will acknowledge to you, to whom I wish to speak without any reserve, that it is a question which under the present circumstances would require the most cool and serious consideration, and to which I am certainly not prepared to give an answer. It does not however seem to me to be an embarrassment of which we are immediately likely to feel the weight, and in the meantime I have not the least hesitation in declaring, that considering the proofs I have had of the sincerity and candour of the present Ministers; and the judgement I have been able to form of the habits of their minds and their general track of sentiments, it is my clear and decided opinion that the disposition, such as it appears to me, ought most certainly to be frustrated; and if possible the idea of it not suffered to exist, because it seems to me incapable of producing any other effects, than the ruin of those who suffer themselves to be deluded by it, the inflicting a deeper wound on the cause of Whiggism than it has ever yet suffered, and preparing a severer blow for the cause of Government than it has yet been exposed to.

You are now possessed of my sentiments respecting the conduct which it appears to me it would become us to hold in the present crisis. I have laid them very fully before you, and without any reserve. Should they be fortunate enough to meet your concurrence, and that of any other person (I mean Lord Spencer in particular) or persons to whom you may think proper to communicate them, I shall be extremely happy, and very ready to concert with you the best means of giving them effect. You cannot be more anxious than I am to give the most effectual support to the War, to reestablish the Reign of Order; and to vindicate the cause of Whiggism. I shall be in town on Tuesday, and hope to find you there.[1]

FREDERICK NORTH [2] *to* WILLIAM WINDHAM

January 28, 1794

I am truly sensible of your kindness in communicating to me the Step you have taken in Regard to that of

[1] Add. MSS. 37845 f. 17.
[2] Frederick North (1766–1827), afterwards fifth Earl of Guilford

I   O

Portland and rejoice most sincerely in its Success. Though I have no personal Connection in that Quarter; the being able to form an independent Party under so very respectable a Head, in this Critical Moment, is what has long appeared to me the most desireable political Event that could take Place ; and I hope that Lord Spencer, Charles Townshend and Cholmondely have already told you how much I wished it, though I doubted of its taking Place. At present I wish you Joy of it most sincerely, and request you to believe that no one coincides with you more sincerely in that and every other Opinion, than,

My dear William,

Your most affectionate and faithful Servant,

FREDERICK NORTH [1]

WILLIAM WINDHAM *to* CAPTAIN LUKIN

Hill Street, March 22, 1794

The papers of yesterday announced your return to the Downs with some Danish vessels; arrested in consequence of the late orders. I hope it may turn out that they will be made prizes. The conduct of these Swedes and Danes is so perfectly rascally, that I have no sort of compassion for them, and none, I dare say, will be felt by those who will find such good account in this kind of neutral war. The only danger is, that they may be driven at last to join themselves openly to those to whom they are now giving every kind of clandestine assistance. Though they will find their own destruction in this, they may, in the main, considerably embarrass our operations.

No great stroke has yet been struck by any of the armies on the continent. Our campaign here too, in the Houses of Parliament, is pretty quiet. If it was not for the trial of Mr. Hastings, and the delay which his friends create, by insisting on the presence of the judges, and

[1] Add. MSS. 37874 f. 6.

adjourning the proceedings in consequence, till after the circuit, he might be set at liberty in a few weeks ; and I should then be tempted to make an excursion towards the coast, and to meet you probably either at the Downs or at Portsmouth.

There is another business indeed that may call me towards Norfolk. With a view to the possibility of a descent, troops of different sorts are proposed to be raised in aid of the Militia ; one class of which will be volunteer cavalry, composed of persons who are in a state to furnish their own horses, and till they are called out of their own county (which is to be only in the case of actual invasion) are to receive no pay; nor any thing from government, but their saddles and arms. What think you of the possibility of my raising a troop of fifty such persons, including such as part of those concerned may be willing to hire or bring with them, in addition to themselves ? Should the occasion not arise in which their services will be really wanted, the trouble will be very little, as I should not propose their meeting more than once a week ; and the expence would be no more nor so much as attends their weekly meetings at market. For a uniform, I would have nothing but a plain coat, such as they might wear at other times, or no more ornamented than might make them a little proud of it. I believe something of this sort I must attempt, and if it could be settled without the necessity of more attention on my part than I ought to allow myself to spare from other objects, I should not dislike to have such a troop established under my direction.

Mr. Courtenay (the member) who dined with me yesterday, shewed me a letter which he had received from a Mr. Hayes, one of the Lieutenants, I conceive, on board the *Boston*, in which an interesting account is given of some of the principal circumstances of the action. It appears; by his account; that the *Boston* had only 200 hands, not above 30 of whom had

ever before been on board, while the *Ambuscade* had
450. This difference I suppose must have told considerably : much more than the difference of four guns
which the French frigate had beyond ours.   The conduct
of one of the Lieutenants, Mr. Kerr, seems to have been
singularly gallant. He staid on deck, after he had
received a cannister shot through his shoulder, and till
a splinter striking him on the face altogether blinded him.
The first Lieutenant too, a Mr. Edwards, though wounded
badly in the hand, came up again after the Captain's
death, to take command of the ship.   In a former account,
it was said, I think, that he had fainted from loss of blood.
It is said in this letter, that there was a French fleet in
sight at the time when the *Boston* bore up.[1]

THE DUKE OF PORTLAND *to* WILLIAM WINDHAM

London : April 16, 1794

By wishing to do too much I have the mortification of
having done nothing—to own the Truth.   I had a great
desire to be authorized to say that your presence would
be necessary in the course of the Emigrant Bill, and for
that reason postponed my thanks and congratulations
which I have the most satisfactory assurances are both
equally and most amply due to you for the event of
Saturday at Norwich,—and in the mean time the Bill has
escaped, notwithstanding all the obstructions with which
it was threatened, and will get into our House to-day.
From what I hear of it, you have had a very great loss
indeed, in missing Burke's speech upon it on last Friday.
There is not a Jacobine who pretends to taste who dares
for his own sake to withhold from it his full tribute of
applause, and I understand it was given in Burke's best
manner.   You had also another loss of a similar kind in
not hearing Lord Mansfield in answer to Lord Lauderdale's
motion for overhauling the sentence against Muir and

[1] Amyot, " Memoir of Windham," p. 32

Palmer.[1] He completely overset all Lauderdale's facts, his Law, his arguments and his Inferences, and the best proof I can give you of its effect is that it appeared to be spoken as *fast* as any one could wish and that he was; after the first 5 minutes, as completely in possession of the attention of his audience as any Speaker ever was upon any occasion.

Accounts have been received to-day from Sir Charles Grey, dated the 15th March, from the Camp before Cape Bourbon, in which he says that the whole Island of Martinico is in his possession, excepting the Forts Bourbon and Royal, the *latter* it was in his power to take whenever he judged it necessary, but wishing to preserve the former he should be sorry to be obliged to proceed to that extremity—since his landing he has lost in killed 71 and in wounded 193—and 3 missing. I suppose long before this the English flag flies every where in that Island. Would to God I could see the *true French* Colours hoisted in Nantes, St. Malo's, or in any town in old France. This wish leads me naturally to represent to you that during your absence from hence the poor Royalists will not have a friend, at least not one that can say a word for them to Ministers, or who can support the only cause that can be successfull; for sure I am that neither the capture of Martinico nor of all the French Possessions in the W. Indies will have any effect here; or do one hundredth part of the service which the Common Cause would derive from the *real French Army* in the Vendée. Pray hold yourself engaged to dine with me the first Trial Day [of Warren Hastings] after the Holidays and I will ask some true Royalists to meet you. The Clock strikes six.[2]

---

[1] Muir and Palmer sentenced for sedition. *See* Howell's *State Trials*, xxiii, 117, 237

[2] Add. MSS. 37845 f 39.

RICHARD BURKE *to* WILLIAM WINDHAM

June 19, 1794

I am much obliged to you for your communication of the intentions of Government with regard to my father; which, as far as the pecuniary consideration goes, are fully adequate to my wishes.[1]   But I cannot help expressing my surprise, that there should be anything like a demur with regard to the peerage.   It is not that I lay much stress on what Sir G. Elliot conveyed to him from the Ministers on that subject.   I think his pretensions stand upon grounds much stronger than any promises actual or implied.   The terms used to Sir G. Elliot might have been general, tho' he seem'd to attach a particular sense to them.   They were certainly, however, not such as to imply that the Ministers had very mean ideas with regard to my father, and I did not conceive that what was considered as a debt due from the country, due to the opinion of Europe at large, could be less than the peerage. However, it is for the Ministers to judge what they will do or not do.   It is a matter absolutely in their own breasts.   It would be as ridiculous for my father at this time of day to haggle about the recompence for his services, as it would have been absurd in the Ministers to chaffer with him about the price before those services were rendered ; services which if the effects of them could have been foreseen or could have been bargained for (if he was a man capable of bargaining) I do not believe any rewards the country has to bestow would have been thought too much.   But in the retrospect, things have

---

[1] Burke on June 16 concluded his famous nine days' speech, wherein he sought to justify the impeachment of Hastings.   Four days later he and the other managers of the trial received the thanks of the House of Commons.   At the prorogation in July he retired from Parliament. He was granted a Civil List pension of £1200 on the lives of himself and his wife, and a few months later Pitt secured him a further annuity of £25(). Lord Fitzwilliam returned his old friend's son, Richard, the writer of the above letter, for the borough of Malton.

a different appearance, especially when impressions are
no longer fresh and when the man is going off the stage
and can be of use no farther. It is, therefore, not un-
natural that difficulties should be made. I confess that
if the thing was to be judged of in the abstract, if my
mother was not concerned, and if the arrangement of his
affairs did not imply the sale of his place in the country
(in which so much of his as well as my mother's satis-
factions are involved), I should certainly agree with you,
that it would be more becoming the place and character
my father sustains in the world—foregoing all expectations from the public to cut himself down to the measure
of his means (which, however moderate, are more than
human necessities require) than to consent to have his
services, which now stand in the first order, set down by
a secondary reward, at a secondary standard. As matters
stand however, some sacrifice of dignity must be made
to ease. And tho' I think he might expect an *otium
cum dignitate* and that the peerage is not more than his
due and, if I may say, the specific reward appropriate to
his peculiar services, Yet if the Ministers think otherwise and think that services like his can be paid in money
—as far as my vote goes, I shall advise him to submit;
and I see nothing else for him to do, but to take what is
given him with thankfulness, and with as good a grace as
he can.

I cannot think that the Ministers have sufficiently considered or that it can be their intention that what they
do should lose so much of its grace and effect with regard
to the public, by what they withhold ; or that they have
reflected what will be thought when it comes to be known
that this was an object to my father and that it was
refused on any grounds whatever. If they do not give
it to him, for God's sake for what kind of services is it
reserved, unless it is determined that it should never be
given to civil service, or only follow in the common line of
official promotion ? Who do they mean to make peers

in future ?   I say nothing with regard to the past, tho' I believe some might be found on the list whose services are not more brilliant or their fortune more ample than his.   Indeed; if it was a subject fit for me to discuss, I might compare his services for effect and public benefit, with those of any single man, since the Restoration.   However this may end, I shall never forget your active friendship on the occasion.   And depend upon it that he is sufficiently a philosopher not only to bear the want of any reward at all, but perhaps what is more difficult cheerfully to acquiesce in that which does not come to his ideas.[1]

THE DUKE OF PORTLAND *to* WILLIAM WINDHAM

July 3, 1794

My company had separated just before your letter arrived, as you may probably know already, by having seen Lord Spencer and Grenville who intended to call upon you in their way home.   I now regret your absence much more than I could have imagined I could have had any reason to do, because, from what I learn'd from Grenville, I concluded that your mind was made up to become a member of Cabinet and that the mode was become to you a very secondary consideration.   I can not but wish you to reconsider this question and to recollect that I may be under the necessity of bringing your doubts forward to-morrow in a place where I should be very sorry that any ground could be given for suspicion or apprehension of backwardness in any, and more particularly in so conspicuous a Leader on our side as you certainly are.   It would be idle to attempt to refute arguments of which I am ignorant.   But I can not help

---

[1] Add. MSS. 37843 f. 41   It was decided to make Burke a peer. The title was to be Lord Beaconsfield, and an income for three lives was to be attached to it.   The patent was being prepared, when the death of Richard Burke on August 2, 1794, made his father no longer desirous of the dignity

asking whether the Opponent to your coming into administration considered that measure in its bearings upon the general credit and character and Interests of the Cause, and did give and was *capable* of giving its due weight and appretiating the difference of the Office of Secretary of War as merely ministerial, or being a real efficient Cabinet employment, upon which my opinion of the propriety of your acceptance of it, principally, if not wholly, rests and depends.   There are persons very wise; and virtuous friends of ours, and most active and zealous supporters of the Cause of Government, who endeavoured to make Lord Fitzwilliam refuse to take an active part in administration.   But they could not succeed—and I devoutly pray that further reflection will make them equally unsuccessful in your case.[1]

At last the question of joining the Pitt Administration was settled, to the great relief of all concerned.   " The continuance of the negotiation occupied a good deal of my time and thoughts, and prevented my engaging in any regular employment," Windham wrote on July 2, in his Diary.   Neither the Duke of Portland nor Windham was anxious to take office, and, when pressed to do so, urged that they could give greater support to the Government by remaining independent members.   Burke, however, convinced Windham that this point of view was erroneous, and that it was useless to have the best intentions in the world without the power to give them effect.

To accommodate the members of the Portland party various changes had to be made in the Ministry.   The Duke became Secretary of State for the Home Department in place of Dundas, who went to the War Office ; Lord Spencer accepted, for the time being, the position of Lord

[1] Add. MSS. 37845 f. 41.

Privy Seal; and, Lord Camden retiring, Lord Fitz-william became Lord President; on the understanding that he was presently to be appointed Lord-Lieutenant of Ireland. A Secretaryship of State was at first proposed for Windham, but, to facilitate the Ministerial arrangements, he took the place of Sir George Yonge (who became Master of the Mint), as Secretary-at-War, with a seat in the Cabinet. His patent as Secretary-at-War, countersigned by Dundas; bears the date July 11, 1794.[1] Five days later he was sworn in as Privy Councillor.

It may here be mentioned that one of the conditions imposed upon Pitt by the Duke of Portland was an alteration in the government of Ireland at the time of the juncture of the two parties. Lord Westmorland[2] was Lord-Lieutenant. The Duke of Portland wished to go there himself, and was only dissuaded, with great difficulty, by Lord Mansfield and others,[3] who pointed out that it was his duty to take responsible office in the Cabinet. The Duke then decided that Lord Fitzwilliam must go to Ireland. Though Pitt did not approve this choice, he did not refuse his assent, but contented himself with saying that Fitzwilliam could not be appointed until a suitable office at home was found for Westmorland. Fitzwilliam at once began his preparations for his new position. He communicated with Grattan and Ponsonby, which indicated that under his administration many changes

---

[1] Having accepted office, Windham had to offer himself for re-election at Norwich. His constituents were not well pleased with the change in his political views, and Mingay, a lawyer, who offered himself as a candidate, received some support. Windham, however, was returned to Parliament.

[2] John Fane, tenth Earl of Westmorland (1759–1841).

[3] See Lord Mansfield's letter, October 1?, 1794 (vol. i. p. 259 of this work).

desired by the Irish would be made. Fitzwilliam did not observe or enjoin secrecy, so it is not surprising that it was generally reported in the summer that he had already been appointed Lord-Lieutenant. The statement was accepted as authentic, and travelled far, reaching the Duke of York in Flanders at the end of August.[1] Pitt, however, was in no hurry to remove Westmorland ; and only in October, when the Portland party gave him the choice between sending Fitzwilliam to Ireland, and their resignation, did he appoint Westmorland Master of the Horse. Fitzwilliam then became Lord-Lieutenant, and was succeeded as Lord President by the Earl of Mansfield.

DR. CHARLES BURNEY *to* WILLIAM WINDHAM

Churchfield, Margate : July 14, 1794

The *Gazette*, which announces your having honoured Administration by joining them, has just reached me at Margate. Amidst the congratulations, with which you must be surrounded, on this occasion, permit me to venture offering mine : not, however, so much to you, as to the Country !

YOU have accepted a Post :—the honours of it cannot greatly have influenced you :—the emoluments of it cannot, in the slightest degree, have biassed you.—Even those justly merited honours will not escape the breath of slander ; and those emoluments will be dearly earned by the labours, which must be necessary to give them security. That *Amor Patriæ*, however, which has inspirited your decision, fails not in conferring a due reward. A reward, which Treachery cannot violate, and Wealth cannot purchase !

Our COUNTRY has insured your services ;—Attacked by an infuriate Enemy abroad ; endangered by an insidious

---

[1] *See* the Duke of York's letter to Windham, August 31, 1794.

foe at home; the very vitals of her Constitution under-
mined, avowedly by one Party, and secretly by another;
united with allies, lukewarm, I fear, if not inclined to
treachery :—to our COUNTRY then permit me to offer my
congratulations !—To our COUNTRY, which can still
boast herself supported by the 'Οι καλοὶ καὶ ἀγαθοί, and
may still hope to be preserved by the exertions of talents
scarcely rivalled, aided by virtues undaunted, and integrity
unimpeachable !

Pardon the intrusion !—Your engagements must be too
numerous and too constant, well to allow it ;—but as
my distance from town prevents my *wishing you joy* in
person, I really feel too strongly, on the present occasion,
not to venture taking the liberty of doing it, by letter.[1]

H.R.H. THE DUKE OF YORK *to* WILLIAM WINDHAM

Head Quarters at Rosendael

August 1, 1794

I have many thanks to return you for your most
obliging letter which was delivered to me by Lord Spencer,
and am not half expressing to you how sincerely happy
I am at you and your friends having stood forward in
so Handsome a Manner, and accepted office and
responsibility at a moment when it is so peculiarly
necessary to strengthen the Hands of Governments.
I am likewise exceedingly glad that everything went off
so well at Norwich.[2]

I am exceedingly impatient to hear the result of Lord
Spencer's negotiation.[3] I am sure it can not be in better
Hands, and I never saw people so eager so anxious
to succeed as both His Lordship and Mr. Grenville. I
confess I am exceedingly sanguine in my expectations
particularly since I saw the day before yesterday Letters

---

[1] Add. MSS. 37914 f. 105.

[2] Windham had secured re-election as member for Norwich.

[3] Lord Spencer had gone in June to Vienna as Ambassador Extraordinary. He returned to England in December.

DR. BURNEY

from the Prince of Coburg to the Hereditary Prince of
Orange written quite in a different stile from one which
he had received from Him only two days before, and
holding out a probability of His moving forwards again
soon with His Army.[1]

EARL SPENCER *to* WILLIAM WINDHAM

Vienna : August 12, 1794

I ought to have written to you a long while ago, but
my journey so entirely turned my head, and the occupation I have had since I have been here has filled up
so much of my time that I have not been able till this
moment ; and in choosing this moment for the purpose,
I do not treat you very well, for I am more than half
asleep, having been the whole evening plodding over
the long letter [2] which you will have the reading of from
us in the Cabinet, which will very probably produce
something of the like effect on the Readers as it has on
the writers of it at least I am sure if you read it as we
wrote it at one o'clock in the morning, it cannot fail
to do so.

You will see by the contents of it what a long way we
are come, to do, as far as it seems, very little, and you will
not fail, I dare say, to observe that, as we have been
driving for nothing, we are.determined you shall have
at least a long reading for nothing. However, as I am
sure you will have had enough of our dispatch already;
I will not give you a bad hash of it in my letter.

I promised Sir Sidney Smith,[3] to write to you something
about what he calls his Ideas, but my own Ideas have

---

[1] Add. MSS 37842 f. 67.

[2] Regarding a project for an English descent upon the French coast
to aid the Royalists against the Revolutionists, which was to end in the
disastrous Quiberon Bay expedition.

[3] William Sidney Smith, generally known as Sidney Smith (1764–
1840), entered the navy 1777, and fought at the battle of St. Vincent
and in other actions. He was sent home with despatches after the
evacuation of Toulon in 1793.

really been so turned and twisted and jumbled about ever since, that I protest his have been pretty nearly shaken out of my head; in general, however; I remember he said a good deal about the French coasting ships which, by their being very flat bottomed, can run into shoal water where none of our Ships-of-War can follow them, and of course he is very desirous of having a fleet of flat-bottomed Vessels at his Command to go and break them all to pieces. He does not seem to think much of the Scheme about Calais, but he has an Idea that something might be done at Havre; he is certainly an odd excentrick man, but he is very clever, and has a great deal of contrivance about him, and if he could any how be put into activity without giving offence to more regular and orderly sort of Geniuses, who I believe all look upon him as a Fellow of the College of Physicians does upon a Quack Doctor, he might be of great service.

I cannot write this without telling how very much both Lady Spencer and myself are obliged to you for your very kind and friendly offer which she tells me you made her the other day of an Ensigncy in the Guards; we are both as much obliged to you as if we had been in the way of availing ourselves of it, and I am very glad it happened so, as it gave you an opportunity of multiplying your satisfaction, by obliging some body else besides us, on the occasion.

Adieu, dear Windham, I wish much to be at home again and among you all : I feel quite out of my Element here, and though I don't know how much I might be in my Element if I were at home in my new situation there; yet I cannot help thinking I should be rather less of a Bear in a Boat than I feel myself in this still newer Character of a Negotiator.[1]

[1] Add. MSS 37845 f. 127.

CAPTAIN SIR W. SIDNEY SMITH *to* WILLIAM WINDHAM
Private   *Diamond, at Plymouth*
                                              August 13; 1794

Your letter of the 3rd inst.; Franked the 7th, and sent
to Deal, has followed me here.   Lord Spencer and I had
some conversation on the subject in question during the
passage to Holland and it was settled that I should communicate the purport of it, direct to you, on my return
to England.   The Labour of beating to the westward
against strong contrary winds from Flushing to Plymouth,
and the necessary repairs of the Ship since my arrival,
have so taken up my time as scarcely to allow me any
for rest or refreshment, much less to set down quietly
and give you a digested and detailed opinion of the
Duc de Levis's[1] " crude " proposition.   I am sorry my
distance from town and the orders I am under to go to sea
immediately will prevent my having an opportunity of
making the communication verbally.

The Duc de Levis called on me (by introduction from
Lord Warwick), I believe previous to his waiting on you.
I gave him a patient hearing and think with you that
the Idea should not be wholly abandon'd, though it may
not be immediately practicable to carry it into effect in
the mode he suggests.

I agree with him entirely that the best way of acting
against France, either in order to make a diversion to
save Holland, to ward off a threaten'd attack on this
country, or to make an impression on the centre of the
enemy's country so as to effectuate the great object of
the war, is by a *descent on their coasts*.   The *point of
attack* must depend on intelligence to be obtained, and
the extent of the force that may be destined to carry the

---

[1] Pierre Marc Garton, Duc de Levis (died 1830), left Paris in 1792
and joined the army of the Princes, in which he served as a private
soldier.   He was wounded in the Quiberon expedition, and came to
England.

plan into effect. I am of opinion that the coast must be destitute of sufficient strength to defend it by the concentration of their forces in the formation of their great armies; but I am by no means of opinion that they are so liable to be surprised as the Duc de Levis seems to apprehend, for their intelligence is so good and their establishment of COAST SIGNALS is so perfectly well arranged and so well attended to that that intelligence is quickly conveyed from one point to another. The *attempt* might be made to surprise, but it should be with such a force as would be equal to proceeding by open assault when discovered, which is not impracticable on the very gates of a place inadequately garrisoned and irregularly fortified on some one side.

A Ruler laid on the map, from London to Paris shews the strait line of *shortest distance* to be by way of Dieppe or Havre de Grace and Rouen, and it is to be remember'd that there is no chain of fortified places requiring regular sieges by that route.

Having received the latter part of my education at Caen in Normandy, I have had opportunity of being acquainted with the Normans, and I am inclined to give credit to the Duc de Levis's assertion that Normandy and the Southern part of Picardy are disaffected to the convention, or at least to the Jacobin System; and consequently that they might be induced to shew themselves if a sufficient force was at hand, as a central point round which to rally; but my experience at Toulon has proved to me that this never can be expected if the *white flag*[1] is shewn to them as an earnest of the return of the antient System in its full extent. A *Constitution* is the desire of every thinking man in France, I am persuaded; they have seen the bad effects of unlimited power in the two extremes of absolute and popular government too often and too recently not to be averse to placing it anywhere; and cannot (I think) be inclined to place it in the *same*

---

[1] The flag of the deposed French monarchy.

hands who misused it before; and who would be likely to govern with a heavy hand in revenge for the persecution they have endured. There can be little doubt that there exists a party in France, and even in Paris itself, of the moderate kind, impatient under the present Tyranny which puts their persons and property in such an irksome state of insecurity. This party might be induced to shew itself if support were near, and such support cannot be so quickly convey'd as by the *shortest route* and that on which there are the fewest barriers, viz. that above named.

Calais from its position does not seem to come into this line, or to be of any use as an insulated possession now that the Netherlands are evacuated. Dieppe and Havre I think would be valuable acquisitions. An Army on the two Banks of the River Seine, using that river as its line of communication, having its baggage; battering train and magazines *afloat* under the protection of Gunboats and consequently being unencumbered but with horses and forage might move with facility and be less liable to total discomfiture in case of failure, having a *floating fortress* to rally to.

I am persuaded that an expedition of this kind, if it did not succeed to the full extent of the object, might still do essential service ; it would cut off one channel by which Paris is supplied with provisions ; it would enable government to form a positive judgment of the real disposition of the people and finally in case of being obliged to fall back by the arrival of the Northern army on the East bank of the Seine, the [*illegible*] would afford our army a secure position with its flanks towards the sea communicating *on each side* with its floating Magazines by Carentan and La Hogue on the East, and the little ports opposite Jersey on the west. Cherbourg would by this position be cut off from the possibility of receiving succour and as the high land behind the town overlooks it, as Faron does Toulon, it must fall in the same way ; and thus, in case of ultimate relinquishment of the enterprise, we should have destroy'd the two ports of Havre and Cherbourg, from whence we have otherwise everything to apprehend if the enemy are left quietly at liberty to realise their project of invading and "revolutionising" this country. I speak from local knowledge of the coasts and ports in question, having examined the ground at leisure during the peace when on a visit to the Duc D'Harcourt, then Governor of Normandy, and I recommend his being consulted on the enterprise, his local knowledge and military experience, together with his name and influence in the country, would go a great way towards ensuring the success of it. I beg to be understood to be very far from volunteering it myself. I see my *way* clearly but I do not see my *means*. Long legged frigates cannot approach the shore to cooperate with or cover an army. Gun boats alone can do it, but it is not a boat with a Gun that answers to my Idea of a Gun boat. I have acquitted my conscience towards my country by having given my Ideas distinctly to Lord St. Helens on the form of vessel I consider as adapted to this service as well at home as in Holland; where the species actually exists and requires only to be fitted. I have thus enabled whoever may be destined for that service to act as my peculiar experience would enable me, but I hope I may stand excused from stepping forward myself, which I am disinclined to do considering the little encouragement I meet with for such voluntary exertions. Besides, no man can serve in a situation of any degree of eminence without hurting his private fortune, and I have unfortunately none to supply the demands incident to such a situation. If I had I would most willingly sacrifice that as I do my time and my health ; these with a daring spirit and as much military experience as I could acquire by going wherever it was to the obtained; being all I can call my own, I devote them to my country's service; though I confess to you not so cheerfully as I have done hitherto. I have suffered such pecuniary embarrassment and distress since my return from Toulon as makes me; though reluctantly, impeach my country's Justice ; an Englishman never works the free horse to the utmost of his powers without seeing that he is well fed when he comes home, and yet collectively they can suffer an officer who has served them to the best of his ability to starve in their streets. I do not say this in any ill temper. I am ready to do what I am *ordered* as a military man ought to be, but when a man has suffered much and worked hard without having in the least mended his situation or even *his prospects in life*, his feelings must be wounded at seeing that he is working to little purpose. If a service which is denominated from the Throne and acknowledged by Parliament of great national importance be left unrequited, what hope is there that any future service will be more consider'd ? I content myself at present with a cruise in a frigate; the object of which; as it cannot affect the success of the war, does not afford even the prospect of that satisfaction which is the only repayment I can look to under the certainty of a lodging in the King's Bench prison as my ultimate retreat when the service is ended. I hope, my dear Sir; you will excuse the freedom with which I speak; but an honest man may, nay ought to, speak out to *another*.[1]

EDMUND BURKE *to* WILLIAM WINDHAM

Beaconsfield : August 17; 1794

I always knew you to have a mind formed for generosity and friendship—and I now experience it in the way of all others most acceptable to me, that is in your protection of Woodford.[2] My Richard was very sollicitous for his establishment ; and the employment which you have so very kindly bestowed upon him entitling him to half-pay

[1] Add MSS 37852 f 32.
[2] Colonel E. J. A. Woodford, appointed by Windham Inspector-General of Foreign Corps in the pay of Great Britain.

puts him out of anxiety for the future. It will be a satis-faction for you to know, that besides giving to my Mind, and poor Mrs. Burke's, a solid comfort, you serve a young man of very great honour, and great good-nature, as well as of excellent Talents and much activity. There will appear in nothing you have done, any the least trace of blind partiality. It is, too, the Son of an excellent father (of whom, however, I have not much personal knowledge), who is, I believe, of remarkable ability in his profession, I mean Col. Woodford. If he is what I hear of him he is a sort of man to be looked to ; for I fear we are not overrich in soldiership. Again a thousand thanks for what you have done for his son.

I have been talking with our excellent Dr. Walker King, (who, having been several times in Ireland with his father, the Dean of Raphoe, has very just notions concerning that country), about the University. He tells me, indeed concurrently with the universal opinion, that Dr. Murray has, for several years, governed the College as Vice-Provost, with the greatest credit, and indeed saved it from utter Ruin ; and that he is in the highest Esteem with the whole body. Now, he is in the order of Gradation, and would possess no power, but what in effect, he has long exercised. This would cut off all Cabal, all bickering, and be a plain and simple answer to every kind of unstatutable applications from without and to all intrigues from within ; not but that I believe, if the place were elective, they would choose of themselves this respectable Divine. Be sure, my dear friend, that I do not meddle in this affair from any predilection to persons : I do not know Dr. Murray personally. If I have anything personal in it, it is my earnest desire that everything done in the Duke of Portland's department should be done to his honour.[1]

---

[1] Add. MSS. 37843 f. 43.

H.R.H. THE DUKE OF YORK *to* WILLIAM WINDHAM

Head Quarters
August 31, 1794

I have many thanks to return you for your very obliging letter which was delivered to me the day before yesterday by Mr. Gunning, the Surgeon-General. I am exceedingly sensible of your attention to my representation in having sent Him, and have no doubt of his being able after a thorough examination to put the Hospitals here in a good train, which I am sorry to say they want very much. I will take care that he shall receive every information, which can be given Him, and he must afterwards visit the different Hospitals and examine Himself into the different disputes which subsist between the Gentlemen of the Medical Departments and which I am afraid have been very detrimental to His Majesty's service, as well as to the Health of many of His brave Soldiers.

I am sincerely rejoiced at Lord Fitzwilliam's having accepted of the Lord Lieutenancy of Ireland. His appointment can not but give the greatest satisfaction to both countries.[1]

The Death of Count [*illegible*] is certainly very unfortunate at this moment. I trust, however, that it will not cause any essential delay in the negotiations. Lord Spencer and Mr. Grenville appear to me to have succeeded thus far perfectly well in theirs, as I have already received a letter from the Prince of Cobourg notifying to me his having resigned the Command of the Austrian Army to General Clerfayt, and this morning I have received a letter from General Beaulieu acquainting me of his being arrived at Grave, and being charged with a commission for me. I shall do every thing in my power to persuade him to press General Clerfayt to move forwards as soon as possible as particularly at this time of the year every moment is pretious.

[1] *S e a it.*, p. 219.

I have at last taken up yesterday the position which I had determined upon ever since our retreats with the Prince of Orange; but which he has under different protests delayed me for these last four weeks from occupying. My right is covered by the Inundations of the river Aa; my front by the Fortress of Bois-le-duc, and my left is at present secured by its connection with the Austrian Post at Vechel. Should the Austrians however not be able to keep that Post, which I trust now will not be the case, by throwing it back a little it will be compleatly covered by a Great Morass called the Peel.

From this position I can move forwards to the Assistance of any of the Dutch Forteresses which may be attacked, I effectually cover the only passage into Holland which is not defended with Forteresses, and I keep up my communication with the Austrian Army.

Before I finish my letter I can not help troubling you in your official capacity concerning the Bat and Forage Money for the officers of Cavalry. While I was in England last winter I made an application for leave to give it to them, to which I did not get an answer for some time, when Lord Amherst informed me that it was settled, and that I should receive the official instructions to issue it by the next mail, which good piece of intelligence I lost no time in communicating to the officers. Since that time I have never received the orders which I was led to expect and naturally have not issued it. The Cavalry officers now complain bitterly, and certainly, if I may be allowed to give my opinion, with some reason. I should therefore be infinitely obliged to you if you would enquire into this Business, and if possible attain it for them as really their courage and good conduct is very exemplary and their necessary expenses are very great.[1]

[1] Add. MSS. 37842 f. 71.

WILLIAM PITT *to* WILLIAM WINDHAM[1]

Wimbledon : September 10, 1794

The unfortunate Loss of Valenciennes and Condé,[2] and the opinion you appear to have of the little Dependence to be placed on the Exertions of Austria (in which our Letters from Vienna concur) change much the Situation of Affairs since We parted. The Suggestions which you state relative to the Command, are such as to shake in some degree (coupled with the other Circumstances) my Opinion of the Advantage of sending Lord Cornwallis ;[3] but how this may finally be arranged for next Campaign, cannot now be determined. It must depend partly on what has passed at Vienna and on many other Considerations. In the mean Time there is no doubt that the Duke of York's Command must continue while the operations now in Contemplation last. It is equally clear that the Force destined to serve under Lord Moira can neither be withdrawn nor exchanged during the Course of those Operations. If the operations should be soon concluded, the Exchange might still take place ; but I incline to think it would be too late for any Attempt on the Coast, and on the whole I am more and more inclined to the Opinion that any Attempt in that Quarter (except sending in Supplies) ought to be deferred till next Spring, when it may be attempted with a very formidable Force.

The Projected Attack upon Antwerp, and the forward movement is, I think, clearly right, if Clerfayt will enter into it heartily. From what is understood here of his Instructions, compared with his Letter to the Duke of York, I cannot help having some doubt whether he will

[1] Windham had left England at the end of August and was at this time at Berlkom, where the Duke of York had quartered his army.

[2] Valenciennes, which had surrendered to the Allies under the Duke of York on July 28, 1793, was retaken with Condé by the French on August 30, 1794.

[3] Charles Cornwallis, first Marquis and second Earl Cornwallis (1738–1805), General, Commander-in-chief in India, 1786–1793.

not find reasons for declining the Attempt. Supposing Him not to do so, My chief Reason for thinking the Measure useful is that a Victory on our part will at least check the Operations of the Enemy, damp their spirits and raise those of our Army. I am not competent to judge how far it can enable our Armies to take a Position which they can improve or which they can maintain for the Winter. The Beating the Enemy (if there is a fair Chance of it) is itself a great object (independent of Consequences) in the present Circumstances. If the Consequence should be to dislodge them from Flanders, or to drive them beyond the Scheld, it would be infinitely better. But I cannot help fearing that it will be very doubtful whether We can take secure Winter Quarters in Flanders. Our Situation was not thought good last Year, even when We had Valenciens and Condé. I do not mention this as a reason against the attempt, which it certainly is not, provided there is a good chance of immediate Success; But I wish it to be considered beforehand, whether in case of Success, a Safe Position for Winter Quarters can be established, except under Cover of the Dutch Fortresses.

The Manner in which the Duke of York has treated these discussions certainly does him infinite Credit. The King has sent me a Letter from H.R.H., which has struck me very much, both from its Manliness and Liberality. In my own Mind I consider the Expedition to the Coast as over for this Year, except for the Purpose of Supplies. We have sent to our Friend Tinténiac and shall probably send him over immediately to explain why nothing can be done now and to say that much will be done hereafter. If Lord Spencer has not closed already on the Terms we proposed, I think our Plan will now be, to give no Subsidy either to Austria or Prussia, but to employ 2,000,000*l.* in getting Troops where We can. Poland is so distant, that even if Measures are taken immediately *and quickly*, I doubt whether We can have the Use of them early next

Campaign. But you will have the Means of collecting much useful Information on these Points; and it will be very material to ascertain, as far as possible; what subsidised Force can be obtained exclusive of Austria and Prussia.

I hope you will be enabled to send us an Account particularly of what is the Plan for Winter Quarters in Flanders. Till the attack on Antwerp is over, I reckon We have no Chance of seeing you, and I am sure you will be of infinite Use while you remain where You are.[1]

WILLIAM WINDHAM *to* MRS. LUKIN

Berlikom, near Bois le Duc
September 12, 1794

The ways of a camp life are so idle, that all the habits of business which I may be supposed to have acquired in the last two months, seem to give way before them; And I am in danger of finding myself a worse correspondent here, when I have so much to tell, and so much more time for telling it, than I was in London, when occupied from morning till night; and when my occupations would leave me but little else to talk of. In fact, the pleasures of moving about in a scene so full of interest, the fatigue that is apt to follow, and the want of a comfortable room to retire to, are the causes that prove so fatal to my correspondence; and the reasons why, for want of a little occasional respite, my pleasure in this situation is less than it shouldbe.

We are, as you will have learned from one of my former letters, near Bois le Duc, which is rather a large town; and a strong fortress belonging to the Dutch. About three miles from this place are the Duke's headquarters, and at four or five miles further is the camp. The immediate place of my residence is the village where headquarters are, and I am lodged in the house of a

[1] Add. MSS. 37844 f. 34.

Dutch attorney. The country about is light and sandy, affording very pleasant rides, which are not the less so from your occasionally meeting bodies of troops, of different dresses, establishments, and countries. The variety in this respect is not so great as it was last year, nor, from a number of circumstances, is the scene so interesting, after allowing even for the difference of its not being seen, as that was, for the first time. The relief which all this gives, after confinement during the summer to London, and to such business as that of the war-office, is more than you can conceive. It has given me a new stock of health ; and the beauty of the autumn mornings, joined to the general idleness in which one lives by necessity, and therefore without self-reproach, has given me a feeling of youthful enjoyment, such as I now but rarely know. You cannot conceive how you would like a ride here, with the idea that if you wandered too far, and went beyond the out-posts, you might be carried off by a French patrole. It is the enjoyment that George Faulknor was supposed to describe, of a scene near Dublin; where " the delighted spectator expects every moment to be crushed by the impending rocks." Were public business out of the question, I should stay here probably for a week or two longer ; but, as it is, my stay must be regulated by other considerations, and it is probable that the messenger whom we are waiting for impatiently may occasion my departure immediately. The general state of things is as bad as need be. The shooters in your part of the world must not suppose that they have all the sport themselves. So strong is the love of mischief among men, that all the shooting of one another that is going on here, does not prevent their filling up their intervals by a little murder of partridges.[1]

---

[1] Amyot, " Memoir of Windham," p. 36.

WILLIAM WINDHAM *to* WILLIAM PITT

Grave : September 16; 1794

I will not trouble you with a detail of events; which; however important, you will learn so much more satisfactorily from the dispatch of his Royal Highness the Duke of York ; but only say, that however unpleasant another retrograde movement may be, and whatever opinion may be entertained of our present position, with the objections to which no one is so much impressed as his R.H. himself ; the measure was wholly unavoidable ; and if his R.H. wanted in any instance the concurrence of every officer of consideration in the Army, it was in endeavouring to maintain his position so long, as He did. The evils, however, that might have been apprehended from such an endeavour have not been felt. The retreat was effected in the most perfect order, and without even being molested ; and the previous loss, except in a part of the foreign troops, and where it seems too to have proceeded from causes which no skill or prudence of the Commander could prevent, has been altogether inconsiderable. It was plainly desirable to continue to maintain the position; till it should be known whether the movements of the Enemy, were merely intended to alarm; or were likely to be followed with his whole force.

On the subject of the past, therefore, no more need be said. Enough will remain in the consideration of what should be done in future, with a view to which the Duke will send off this day an aide-de-camp, to General Clerfayt, and who will be accompanied, I believe, by Mr. Pelham. The principal points to be considered will, no doubt, long since have engaged your attention : and will be stated probably more particularly in the Duke's letter. The Question; I presume, is pretty much of establishing the Austrians in the Country, where they are; including in that idea the recovery of Treves :—of preserving the frontier of Holland; and recovering; if possible, in whole or in part, the possession of the Scheldt.

The Duke of York seems to be of opinion, that from the direction of the River in this part, His movements must become so circuitous, as to require a greater force to render them effectual, than if He had not the benefit of the protection of the River : But I should hope, that He rather overrated the disadvantages of his situation in that respect ; and that a corps less considerable even than that which He has, might by being kept in a moveable state, and applied with address to the movements of the Enemy, make it impossible for them to pass the River ; and might afford to his R.H. means far from being ineffectual both for a co-operation with Gen. Clerfayt and for all the other objects of the Campaign. These objects for some time past have been confined very much, in my apprehension, to the assistance of the Austrians in maintaining their present position, and in the protection of the Dutch Frontier.

The recovery of the Scheldt, though in the highest degree desirable, has been for a great while very much out of my hopes ; and it was very much from that consideration, that I shared less, than I should otherwise have done, in the desire of the Duke to maintain his late position, and to take the chance of an action. It seemed to me, that even a complete victory, attended with as great slaughter and as great dispersion of the Enemy, as could possibly be looked to, would have given us after all no very confident hope of being able to effect a great deal in that quarter. At present with the Enemy not beat, and with this Army at a greater distance, this prospect must of course become very faint indeed.—I shall be very well satisfied, therefore, dating from my last hopes, if we secure the other two points, namely, the establishing completely the Austrians, and the preserving entire the frontier of Holland. This, I should think, may very well be done; with the chance too of something better, if every power concerned; will fairly play their part : But this will as certainly not be done, (at least great doubt may be entertained of it) if the Dutch are to go on, as they do; throwing the whole business of their defence upon us, and never seeming to entertain an idea; that they are to contribute anything to the support of their own cause; or not to cheat and obstruct us, who have been willing to undertake it, by every means in their power.   There is really such a brutish insensibility; a base selfishness in the conduct of this people, so far as I have had an opportunity of knowing it, that I cannot but think, that nothing will have any effect, but a direct menace to abandon them to their fate ; and to make them sensible, that when the means of safety are in their own hands, if they will not make use of them; they will be left to perish.   Whatever they can hope to get done by another, they are perfectly certain not to do themselves.   The Duke of York is of opinion that the loss of the Lys is to be ascribed wholly to the measures which we took to assist them in its relief.

Finding that we were willing to do what we could, they hoped that we should do everything ; and of consequence abandoned immediately the measures, which they had before intended, and which were then practicable, for the relief of the place.   As a Specimen of their exertions; the Garrison of this place consists of a few companies of very ordinary troops, with a General of 80 years of age; so helpless and infirm, that the Bailiff of the Town, begged; that whatever was necessary to be done for the mere military police of the Town, might be done by our troops, and under the direction of our officers.

The first thing, therefore, I should think, which Government will be desirous of attending to, will be the impressing the States with the absolute necessity of coming forward fairly in their own defence.   Representations of a Similar sort will probably not be thought superfluous with respect to Austria ; and with respect to objects not capable of waiting for the effect of such communications; provision will be made; as far as circumstances admit, by the Communication; which as I mentioned above, the Duke is about to have with Gen. Clerfayt. Till the result of this is known, it does not occur that I have anything more to state or to suggest. It does not appear, either, that after that time my presence here can be of any particular use : I shall therefore, if nothing new presents itself, continue in the intention; which I wrote word of sometime since to Chatham; and repeat the request, which I then made, of having a frigate; if he can spare one; to meet me at Helvoetsluys about the 20th. Should it appear to you; however; that my presence here can be useful in any respect, I shall be at your service, for a longer period.

[P.S.] Though the Duke of York's opinion seems at present to be, that his situation at present may require even a larger force than was necessary in that which he quitted, yet it is possible; that further inquiry and information may alter his opinion in that respect, and that the Course of events may enable him to spare, as His own inclination will prompt him to do, whenever He can; a sufficient change to enable you to set up again; the expedition to the Coast of France. You will forgive; therefore, my urging to your consideration the importance of keeping everything in readiness for such an event; that no chance may be lost of what is so infinitely to be wished as a successful attempt in that quarter.[1]

The affairs in Flanders had been growing steadily worse. After the defeat by Pichegru at Tournay (May 18), when the ability of Generals Abercromby and Fox alone saved the English army from disaster, the outlook became more gloomy each week. Even the reinforcement of 7000 men, sent out in June under the Earl of Moira, had failed to stem the tide of retreat. The suspicion in men's

---

[1] Add. MSS. 37844 f. 40.

H. Dawe, sculpt.

THE DUKE OF YORK

minds that the Duke of York was not a leader likely to achieve success had slowly been crystallised into a conviction. The situation, however, was one full of difficulty, and it was left to Windham to make that courageous move, which resulted in the Duke's recall.

WILLIAM WINDHAM *to* WILLIAM PITT

Most private   *Grave : September* 16, 1794

I am now to write to you upon a subject, which I feel to be at once so delicate and important, that nothing but a sense of that extreme importance, would induce me to speak upon it, even under that seal of secrecy and confidence, under which I wish you to consider it as being delivered. My last letter to Mr. Dundas betrayed; probably, an opinion, which, if the distinction might be admitted, I should be better satisfied to have betrayed; than declared ; but which, if it does exist, must be made known in some way or another, however it may go to my heart to do anything unfavourable to the hopes and wishes of a person, for whom I feel the most genuine respect and attachment. There is something too, that has an appearance of treachery,—though certainly in this instance an appearance only—in secretly frustrating the views of any one, from whom one is receiving daily marks of confidence and kindness, and whom one is anxious to impress with an opinion of ones being warmly attached to them. Such undoubtedly is my situation with respect to the Duke of York. I really respect and love him more and more, the more I see of him : I am glad that He should be persuaded that I do so ; But certainly no attachment that I have ever expressed or meant to convey, can be supposed to be carried to that length as that I should prefer his personal wishes or interests to what may be capable of affecting the fate of the country and of the world in a crisis like the present. My opinion, therefore, on any point of this sort, where its being known may be useful; must be declared; whatever effect it may have, on those, whose wishes I should be happy to promote, or whatever painful consequences it may in the end draw upon myself. To avoid those consequences I would take all legitimate means ; one of which is to communicate my opinions in all possible confidence. My motives are such (and can be no other) as I should be ready to have manifested to all the world, but it may be naturally wished not to have the fact known; where the motive and the reason do not appear at the same time.

Let me give you; therefore; freely but confidentially my opinion, that the operations of this Army will, I fear; never go on well, while the present Commander remains at the head of it. This is my present opinion, nor do I foresee any probability of change. It is, I am sure, so true at present as to make me bless myself at our escape from our late difficulties, and to alter my whole views of what it may be proper to do, in the remaining part of the campaign. It is from this latter consideration; that I think it right, not only that you should know my opinion; but that you should know it immediately. The reasons of it may come afterwards :—the first of them is, that the Army certainly has not that opinion of the Duke of York as to act under him with confidence. Though the licentiousness of one class of Officers is kept within somewhat better bounds : though the unpopularity of the Duke is abated ; though his virtues, and his other amiable qualities, are gradually making their way, yet a confidence is not felt in his capacity to conduct an Army ; nor can I fairly say, that; judging less from the merits of the case than from collateral circumstances, I think it likely, that it should be so. The consequences are, in the mean time, most pernicious, and show themselves in ways not immediately obvious. But the great consequence is the effect which this feeling in the Army may have in circumstances such as those which we have lately been in : and the force of this is so great, joined to a chance always that the feeling may be well founded, and to more than a chance that it *is* well founded to a certain degree, that I must confess I shall tremble for every step which they will have to make when left to their own direction.

What remedy is to be applied in this state of things I cannot undertake to point out. I show you the difficulty, but can say but little as to the way out of it. To remove the Duke at this instant, would certainly be cruel ; for it would appear to be the consequence of a step, right in itself, and in which He yielded more to the opinions of others, than followed his own. The King, too, is delighted with his Decision, respecting the question of Lord Cornwallis ; and will consider the whole as a manœuvre to get rid of the Duke, which not having succeeded by stratagem, must now be effected by force. I stick, however, to my opinion, that some great change must be made, or the Army will be undone, and our affairs in this quarter never succeed, but by what may be considered as chance. A thoroughly able man, like such as the Austrians chose for their Quarter-Master General, might set all right : but where is such a one in our service to be found ? I do not now think, that even the plan, which I caught at so eagerly, of the Archduke[1] commanding the whole, would by any means answer all the purpose. The evil lyes, as much as in anything, in the domestick Economy, and discipline of this particular Army. What, therefore, is to be done, I do not know. As a preliminary step, having in the first place the recommendation of justice, and being calculated afterwards to reconcile to the Duke's mind and to the King's, whatever measure of change may, now or hereafter, be adopted, no symptom of disapprobation should appear or be suspected of the last movement ; but on the contrary the clearest approbation be expressed of it ; at least, (which is all that I am intent upon) the clearest acquittal of the Duke. I am doubly

---

[1] Archduke Charles of Austria (1771-1847).

bound to say this, as I certainly took all pains to make him adopt that resolution ; nor could such censure upon him be countenanced by any of those persons about him, whom I had the opportunity of consulting.   Perhaps when every idea of censure or dissatisfaction was removed, the offer of some principal situation at home, connected with Military service, and including great Patronage, which no one would discharge more uprightly, and ably (I mean, distinctly, Commander-in-Chief, or Master-General of the Ordnance, or both together) might serve to reconcile the loss of the command of the Army here ; and would be an arrangement good in my opinion, both in the Offices, which it gave, as it will in those, which it took away.   If by adding the Ordnance to the situation of Commander-in-Chief, under some general denomination, or half a dozen Offices besides, the removal might be affected for this Campaign, supposing that much is to be done in it, I should think the advantage of the change, cheaply purchased.   If from the answer of Clerfayt, or your decisions at home, the Campaign is likely soon to end, or not to be very critical, it may be better to let it run out, as it is.

With respect to what I said at the beginning, of the confidence, in which this is written, I shall leave it to your discretion to whom you may wish to communicate the contents, observing only as I have already done, that I should be sorry to be known, as the author of the advice, though I shall certainly never dissemble the opinion. Should the measure be taken, I shall not fail to have my full share in the resentment, which it may possibly excite in one quarter, and what I shall feel more sensibly, in the emotions of wounded kindness, which it may produce in another.   All, however, must give way before the considerations, which ought to govern on such an occasion. Should Mr. Dundas be among the persons to whom you may communicate what I have mentioned, He will not take it ill, if I suggest the expediency of a little more guard than his general frankness sometimes suffers him to observe.[1]

WILLIAM WINDHAM *to* WILLIAM PITT

Most private   *Head Quarters, near Grave*

September 19, 1794

I pursue shortly the same topick, that made the subject of my private letter to you the day before yesterday.—I now know for certain, what I before only conjectured, that one of the situations, which I mentioned, that namely of Commander-in-Chief, is one so perfectly consonant to the wishes of the party in question, that it would go a great way towards curing any mortification, that would be felt, at losing the present command. I have little doubt, therefore, that by the aid of this compensation, the affair might easily be arranged for another year : and it is certainly much better, that it should, if possible, be deferred till then ; not only as such delay will render it more easy, but as it may give time for the consideration of such further changes in the distribution of offices, as I hinted at in my last letter, and as I am persuaded, would be of infinite advantage to the publick service. It is a question, however, how far the Army can be trusted in its present state for the execution of the short, but critical service with which it is at present charged. Nothing can be conceived more important, nor at the same time more delicate, than the services, which it has at this time to perform. It is one of the nicest operations of war, I conceive, either to pass an army over a river in the face of an enemy, or to prevent an enemy from passing. It is a game of great skill on either side. If I could by wishing set down the general of my choice, I should certainly choose, as the player of that game, my Lord Cornwallis. His authority would do more to correct the abuses of the Army ; his Experience would conduct it

[1] Add. MSS. 37844 f. 44.

better : should an action be brought on, the army under him would infallibly act with a degree of confidence more, I am sorry to say, than it does under the Duke of York. The hope is, that the Enemy may not attempt to pass the River, or that if they do, the action may not be of a sort, to require any very nice and regular movement, or anything more, than that which the mere valour of the troops will perform, whether they feel confidence in the skill of their commander, or not.

One step to make the hazard less of leaving it as it is till the end of the campaign, will be to furnish it with those aids, which it ought to have had long since, and the want of which is really a subject of very serious complaint. When the line was drawn out the other day, in circumstances as critical as an army ever stood in ; where nothing but uncommon exertions could have ensured its success, and where the ruin of the world must have been the consequence of defeat, there was but one Major-General from one end of the line to the other, and most of the Brigades were commanded by men, too young both in age and in service to be properly entrusted with the care of a company. There is, besides, as I mentioned before, a terrible want of many articles of the utmost importance to the movements of an army. The single circumstance of a bad supply of drivers for the Artillery may easily lead to consequences involving the fate of a campaign   Their want of proper care will ruin the horses ; their want of skill will be the cause perpetually of guns overturning, of their being lost in consequence, and, what is worse, of their stopping a whole line of march. These are things, which I heard stated, when I was abroad last year ; The same are of some consequence now, when the business, which the army has to perform, depends above all things upon a prompt movement of Artillery.

One sits at home quietly and overlooks such particulars ; but the fate of armies and of Kingdoms is decided often by nothing else Every such defect must, therefore, speedily be supplied ; and I will endeavour for that purpose to obtain from the Duke a more correct and detailed account of them. I mentioned in one of my former letters, that Cavalry would be of use. At present, in some respects, their want is less ; yet in others they are still desireable : observing only that the number should not be so considerable, as make the necessity of their being encamped ; which would come under the objections before made, to putting troops to take the field at this season of the year. Upon my stating that objection the answer given was, that part of the Cavalry might be used as a reserve, and be suffered to remain in Cantonments. A Regiment, therefore, of light horse would be very useful.

The conduct of the Dutch is such as to create every day new resentment. Anything so brutish, stupid, and selfish, was never seen. I am quite persuaded, that the only way to deal with them, is to make them know, that what they can do for themselves will not be done for them ; and that if they should choose by leaving it undone, to let their country be ruined, it is their affair much more; than it is ours. The Duke of York in a conference last night with Prince Frederick, entered into some engagements, of which I did not see much the necessity ; but not having known of the intention before, I could do little more than suggest some changes. I do not much see, why the Duke should be called upon to bind himself by engagements to the defence of Holland, when all that they had to offer in return ; and which they did not do without some difficulty ; was an engagement to defend themselves. They seemed to consider that; as the valuable consideration, which was to make the bargain on our side binding. The danger most to be apprehended at this moment is the reduction of Crèvecœur ; and this danger arises almost wholly from their having no garrison in it.

I find it happen so continually, that beginning to

write you a few lines I am drawn in to write a long letter; that I fear you will dread the sight of my hand, and will be happy to hear, that at the return of Mr. Pelham, I purpose to set off on my way home.[1]

WILLIAM PITT to WILLIAM WINDHAM

Private   *Downing Street*
                                  September 21, 1794

The Messenger arrived this afternoon with the Duke's dispatches of the 17th and with your two letters of the 16th. You will easily conceive how much their Contents add to the Embarrassment of a Situation, before sufficiently discouraging. It is, however, one of the Peculiarities of that Situation, that there is no Sense of difficulty which it does not oblige us to encounter. With respect to the Events which are Public, I have very little doubt, from the Considerations you have mentioned, of the Propriety and Necessity of the Retreat. Even if I thought otherwise, I should consider it as one of those Measures, which Persons not on the Spot are not at Liberty to criticise ; and I have had no Hesitation (in the Absence of Mr. Dundas who has left his Pen in my Hands) in sending a dispatch to the Duke of York in terms of express Approbation. With respect to what is to follow, I own it is quite as much as I expect if We can succeed in maintaining in the first Instance our own Position and that of the Austrians, and in putting ourselves and them in a state to Move, as Circumstances may require, for the actual Protection of the Dutch Frontier. It would however, be impossible to think of sending any decisive Instructions from home, at least till We hear what has passed with Gen. Clerfayt.—I distrust extremely any Ideas of my own on Military Subjects ; but on the very superficial Grounds, on which I can proceed, I confess I am inclined to fear that the Length of River which the

---

[1] Add. MSS. 37844 f. 50.

Duke has to guard is more than His Force will be equal to, if the Enemy turn their chief Attention to forcing a Passage.—However, with this Impression, and from observing the doubts which you mention The Duke of York himself to entertain on this Subject, I have thought it best to insert a Paragraph in the dispatch which may strengthen his hand in enforcing any demand of Reinforcement which He may on due Consideration find it necessary to make on Gen. Clerfayt.

There is another Alternative to which I have also pointed very generally in the dispatch, but which I suggest for your Consideration, with a degree less of diffidence, because it was in part suggested to me by a Conversation which I had yesterday with Mulgrave.[1] He seemed to think that possibly one object in crossing the Meuse (of which We had then had only a general Account from The Hague) might be to concenter our Force with the Austrians, in order the better to ensure their Compleating the operations at Treves and securing the Left of their Army; that, altho' this might leave the Fortresses on the Dutch Frontier more exposed for a Time, It would be impossible, considering the Inundations, for the Enemy to make immediately any serious Impression, supposing them to be tolerably garrisoned and supplied; and that, after compleating the Business on the Side of Treves, a concerted Movement, might be made in greater Force and with more Security, by the Austrian Force in conjunction with ours, in Time to relieve the Fortresses, and perhaps to attack the Enemy, when their operations had proceeded just far enough to entangle them in additional difficulties. I am not sure whether I state his Idea correctly, but this is what arose in my mind from conversing with Him. If it is worth thinking of at all, the Whole would depend upon the certainty of the Fortresses holding out for a given Time,

---

[1] Henry Phipps, third Baron Mulgrave (1755-1831), afterwards first Earl of Mulgrave.

of the Operations at Treves being compleated in that Interval; and of the Subsequent Movement being conducted vigorously and with a hearty Concert.

Independent of these Conditions there may be a Thousand Objections which put the thing absolutely out of the Question; but the Worst which will then have happened is the giving you the trouble of reading three useless Pages.

I come now to your Private Letter, on which, however, I will not venture to say much, because I think it will not be possible to take any final decision on the Subject till after seeing you, and because, in the Uncertainty whether you may not have proceeded to Helvoetsluys, I do not like to run any unnecessary risk from this Letter falling into other Hands. I feel in its fullest Extent the Sacrifice you make to Public Duty, as well as the unreserved Confidence you have been so good as to place in Me. The Subject is *every Way* so full of difficulties that I hardly know what Opinion to incline to.—Perhaps if Abercromby [1] could be taken *voluntarily*, into *real and full Confidence*, It would give the best Chance for the Remainder of this Campaign, which I think must be an important Period, because the Enemy will probably be active if We are not. But if the Idea does not arise almost spontaneously I hardly know how it can be suggested without losing its full Chance of Success.

A total Change, even if we could make up our Minds to it, I believe impracticable at this moment, because the only Person whom We could think of as a Successor, would not, I am Convinced, accept under such Circumstances. For another Campaign, perhaps the Course of Events might of itself point to employing so much of the *British* Force in other Quarters, as to leave only a less considerable Auxiliary Army in Flanders, and so

---

[1] General Ralph Abercromby (1734-1801), in command of a brigade under the Duke of York. He greatly distinguished himself in the war, and on his return to England in 1795 was created K.B.

avoid the difficulty. To this, however, there are obvious objections from the Impression in Holland and the Want of Reliance on Austria. I feel that I am saying more on the Subject than I intended to do, and yet I am only stating difficulties without making any Progress towards a Solution of them. I have as yet communicated your Letter only to The Duke of Portland, who was with me when I received it, and with whom I am persuaded its Contents are safe. I shall venture to send it to Dundas (who is for a few days at Walmer), with whom your Caution at the End will I am sure have its full effect. And I know that I may mention it with the most absolute safety to Grenville, whose Opinion I shall be very anxious to know. The Duke of Portland was as unable as myself to find any satisfactory Way out of the difficulty. We both agreed in the opinion that it would be very desirable to see you as soon as possible.

From the Absence of my Brother and Mr. C. Middleton, I have not been able to ascertain with positive Certainty which Measures have been taken to secure a Frigate for you at Helvoetsluys, but I think it is pretty clear that *the Jason* must be there before this Time. I shall know, however, with certainty to-morrow, and will take care that one shall be provided immediately, if it has not been done already.[1]

WILLIAM WINDHAM *to* WILLIAM PITT

Most private   *Head Quarters*
                                        September 21, 1794

You may be tolerably secure of not receiving a long letter from me to-night, if I would not run the risk of writing part of it in my sleep.

I have only to say, that I think the Duke is not unprepared to acquiesce in his recall at any moment, provided such a reception could be ready for him as I hinted in my last letter, and that no idea should be

[1] Add. MSS 3; 844 f. 60.

conveyed of dissatisfaction at his conduct during his command. I am not quite sure, whether what he said in this respect, related to the measure of Lord Cornwallis being appointed to the command of the whole, agreeably to the first proposal ; or to his being appointed to the command of the British (or troops in British pay) only : and I did not think it expedient, in the instant, to press for an explanation ; But, I believe, it would in the event prove true of either. I rather think, that if the Duke were recalled at this moment, to be appointed to the situation, which I have suggested, and that every possible pains were taken, as they ought to be, to obviate every idea of imputation upon him for any failure in the campaign, that his recall might be effected, without pain to his feelings, and without injury to his reputation.

At the same time I don't say, that the measure would be desirable, if the Army was at this moment in the most difficult situation. You will receive from the Duke an account of the last news from Gen. Clerfayt. On every supposition of what may happen in consequence, nice operations may be necessary, and an action possibly take place. I cannot dissemble my opinion, that I should think the army in either of those cases safer under the conduct of Lord Cornwallis than under the Duke. Though the Duke is exerting himself with great activity and very considerable address, though his conduct has been hitherto very judicious and his views perfectly just, He has failed by some means or other, of obtaining the confidence of the Army, and I tremble for the effect, which, in critical circumstances, the want of that confidence may produce.

This is the best exposition perhaps, that I can give of the state of the case, as it appears to me. The appointment of Lord Cornwallis, if it should be thought desireable, and if it should be possible, at the present moment, must appear rather as the consequence of this new position of the Austrians, or of reasons existing, when I came over;

rather than of the last movement of the Duke of York. With them indeed it must not appear (as it could not without great injustice,) to be connected at all.

[P.S.] It would be very desireable, in the opinion, of Mr. Gunning, if a quantity of porter could be sent out for the use of the convalescents in the Hospitals, in lieu of the wine or spirits, which they now have. The principal Hospital at present, to which this could be sent, is at Dordrecht.

Nothing can equal the examples of stupidity and brutality, that occur among the Dutch. It is with the utmost difficulty, that a place of reception has been procured to day for some hundred sick, who, if not received at Nimeguen, must have been left in the open air ; and Maestricht is confessedly without anything like an adequate supply of ammunition.—They are Chicaning about the return of the British troops borrowed for a short time for Bergen-op-Zoom, &c., and Crèvecœur, when our troops are withdrawn, will hardly be secure against a coup-de-main. There is no other way, however, I am convinced, than by showing them, that if they will not strive to keep themselves above water, they will be left to sink.[1]

EARL SPENCER *to* WILLIAM WINDHAM

Vienna : September 22, 1794

I should have answered your letter of the 5th from Bois-le-Duc by our last Messenger, if you had not appeared to be on the Point of returning home, in which case I knew you would receive the Dispatch he carried, which will have contained the completest Answer to it.

You will have seen, before this reaches you, in the several Dispatches we have sent from hence, the impossibility of adopting the Plan respecting the Command of the Army suggested in your letter to H.R.H., which

---

[1] Add. MSS. 37844 f. 66.

Plan we had already been charged to propose here, but had found that it was perfectly out of the Question from the Age and Infirmities of Marshal Lacy, the extreme ill health of General Brown, and the absolute refusal on the part of this Government to consent to an Arrangement which should place the Archduke nominally at the Head of the Army and give the real Command to General Mack. If, therefore, we had had an Option of proposing either of these Plans to the Consideration of this Government the Impracticability of that mentioned in your Letter would have at once decided that question; but the Instruction we received from London by the same Messenger left us in fact no Option upon the Subject. They represented Lord Cornwallis's Appointment as having actually taken place; and it consequently became a part of the most urgent necessity to obtain Orders from hence to General Clerfayt to guard against any Misunderstanding which might arise from such a Change in the Command for the present Campaign, even though they should not consent to the arrangement proposed for the next. We, therefore, did not think ourselves justified in delaying an Application for this purpose a single day, more especially as we were not certain that Lord Cornwallis might not have actually joined the Army before the Return of the Messenger, and as we knew at the same time that the other expedient which had been thought of could not be carried into execution.

What the Event of our Negotiation on this Point has been, you will perceive from our last dispatches, in which it is described more at length than I have time to do in this letter; I can only say generally, that though we have certainly no great reason to be much better satisfied with the dispositions we find in the Ministers here than you had with the Account you received of the proceedings of their Generals in the Low Countries, I still hope that it may be possible to find some means or other of attaching them sufficiently to our Interest, which is at the same time their own, without making Sacrifices to them for which it would be difficult to find a justification in reasoning beforehand, and which would not promise such consequences as even to furnish a good defence for them in future. To carry into execution a System of this Description must be the Business of a longer Residence here than I flatter myself is to be my lot ; as I hope and trust that before you receive this, our *Congé* will have been sent to us. I need not say with how much Impatience I look forward to that period, nor how much satisfaction I shall feel at being with you again in England. Grenville meant to write a line or two to you by this Messenger to thank you for your letter, if he had had time, but as he is obliged to write a private letter to his brother, and we wish to send the Messenger off without delay, he desires me to make his kindest remembrances to you.[1]

WILLIAM PITT *to* WILLIAM WINDHAM

Private   *Downing Street*
                                            September 25, 1794

As in your Letter of the 21st, which I received this morning, you do not say when you should quit head-Quarters, I take the chance of a Letter still finding you there or at least meeting you in Holland.

The account of the last Austrian Retreat[2] in addition to all the other Circumstances which were before us, seems to press for an almost instant decision. Whatever is the further Plan of this Campaign, I am clear, and all whom I could consult on such a subject agree with me, that we must change as soon as we can the Command of our Army in Flanders, taking care to do it with every possible Attention to the Duke of York; and to avoid any Imputation on his Retreat. That Point, I hope, is secured already. The next Question is whether,

---

[1] Add. MSS. 37845 f. 129.
[2] General Clerfayt was defeated by Marshal Jourdan on Sept. 18.

supposing the Duke of York to quit, Lord Cornwallis can
be induced to take the Command. This is at least doubtful,
but I think it will be possible to ascertain that Point
before I can hear from you again.—I cannot, on various
Accounts, undertake to say positively that we could open
the situation of Commander-in-Chief here for the Duke
of York.—That and the Master General of the Ordnance
can never, I think, be joined in one Person, supposing
we could vacate both without difficulty. I am not sure,
however, how far the King would like a Prince of the
Blood (*even* the Duke of York) at the Head of the Army
at home. And I own I am not without an apprehension
how far any one who has commanded an Army abroad,
can make it his chief Object at home to assist in bringing
forward troops to be sent under the Command of his
Successor. The Mode of stating to the King the Necessity
of recalling the Duke of York is one of the Points on which
I have thought a great deal. I am persuaded there is no
way of doing it so good as letting him see it exactly as it
has arisen. It would be impossible to state it to him under
the Cover of general circumstances, without his guessing
that the Representation came from you ; and if he does
not know the whole, he will fancy every sort of intrigue
the Reverse of the Truth. I wish, therefore, your permission to send to the King your letters on the Subject.
The manner in which they are written will best prove the
Sincerity and Fairness of the whole Transaction. They
will shew that they were not written in order to be shewn,
and they will shew, too, in a way which must strike the
King's mind, the attachment to the Duke of York, which
mixes itself so strongly with what you feel necessary
for the Public Service. I feel, nevertheless, that this is
proposing to you to have your name brought before the
King in a way that is not pleasing. I scruple it the less
because I must take at least my share with you in so unpleasant a Task, and because I am sure he is as much interested in the grounds which lead to the Measure as we are.—

As you probably could have no copies of your Letters on this Subject and may wish to look at them again before you give me an answer, I send them enclosed. I must, however, say that I think no *second thoughts* could render them more adapted to the Purpose than they are at present.

It seems a little unreasonable to multiply disagreeable Commissions ; but I believe there is nothing will want a recommendation to your Mind which can be of use in the present Crisis. Nothing I believe could be so useful, as your going (for as many days as you can spare) when you leave head-Quarters, to The Hague, in order to try whether Courage or Shame or Fear can be enough roused among the Dutch to give themselves and us some Benefit from their Exertions. Even our Ambassador, Lord St. Helens, tho' sensible and full of many good Qualities, is not made to animate a sleeping Country, and would be the better for being a little electrified. It is impossible but that Holland could still do much, and knowing all the Points where their efforts can be best directed, in the present moment, you can, I am sure, be of more use there than any one. I believe you know Lord St. Helens, who will be most thankful for your assistance. Lord Grenville writes to him to prepare him for your stopping in your Way thro' The Hague, in order to assist in concocting what may be necessary in the Present Crisis. To shew you how things stand with Holland, I enclose a Copy of the Dispatch which Lord Grenville writes to-night to Lord St. Helens. The Duke of Portland is writing to General Bentinck to enforce the same sort of language in a less Official Way.

As to the plan for the rest of the Campaign, little can be said till one knows who are to be Generals, and what may be expected from Allies. But I still cannot persuade myself that it is possible for such a place as Maestricht to be taken in the presence of 140,000 Men, of the best Troops in Europe.[1] Perhaps, if Vigor could at last be

---

[1] Maestricht was taken by Jourdan before the close of the year.

given to the Combined Armies, the Attempt on the Part of the Enemy might lead to good. On the Side of Brittany there seems an opening, which has the peculiar Advantage belonging to it (if it turns out as stated) that it need not be made use of till nearly the close of active Operations in Flanders. I am not yet sure that the Accounts can be relied on, but if they can they are favourable enough to give more than a gleam of hope, even under the Succession of Bad News from Flanders.[1]

THE DUKE OF PORTLAND *to* WILLIAM WINDHAM

Bulstrode : October 8, 1794

I have had a short but very decisive conversation with Lord Fitzwilliam. He is determined to resign the Presidency unless he is declared Lord Lieutenant of Ireland the first time the King comes to town, or that he is authorized to name the day on which that declaration is to be made. You already know my sentiments and determination could He be prevailed upon to retain the Presidency. Perhaps I have waited too long already for Lord Fitzwilliam's appointment, but I cannot forget myself so far or be so unmindful of one of the principal inducements for my accepting office as to suffer the Government of Ireland to continue to be administered by any person in whom I have not an implicit confidence. My reason for wishing to convey this determination to Pitt through *You* is to avoid every expression that might sound rash or that would be construed as implying a doubt of his good intentions and good faith. Pray, bring this business to a speedy issue.[2]

THE DUKE OF PORTLAND *to* WILLIAM WINDHAM

October 11, 1794

I have seen Lord Fitzwilliam and he has written already to Ponsonby and Grattan to inform them of his deter-

---

[1] Add. MSS. 37844 f. 70.   [2] Add. MSS. 37845 f. 45.

mination; or at least to appoint them to meet him for that
purpose to-morrow.   To crown the whole, when I came
home, I found a letter from Douglas to King, desiring
to know what progress the King's letters were in, which
appointed *him Secretary of State and the Bishop of
Cloyne Provost*, and urging King to forward them as he
(Douglas) intended setting out for Ireland on Monday or
Tuesday if the *above* should permit.   The whole of this
must be stopped and given up and the other conditions
so arranged as to ensure their being complied with in a
reasonable time, or I must see Pitt to-morrow or make
an appointment with him for the next day, to desire him
to apprize the King that I think it my duty to lay the
Seals at His Majesty's feet the first time he comes to
town.   I am very sorry for it—and devoutly wish I had
never come into office.[1]

Pitt now undertook to appoint Lord Fitzwilliam to the
office of Lord-Lieutenant of Ireland at the end of the year.
The men met to discuss the question of Administration;
and the Prime Minister expressed his wish that no
important changes in the Staff should be made, and, while
stating that he was in favour of Catholic emancipation,
said that he could not entertain any such measure during
the war.

EARL FITZWILLIAM *to* WILLIAM WINDHAM

October 11; 1794

As we enter'd into Administration together and professedly as members of one corps, I must not take the very
important step of retiring from Administration without
giving you the earliest notice of my intentions and my
reasons for doing so.   Stripp'd of the history of other
transactions which led to my suppos'd destination to
Ireland, all the particulars of which you are full as

---

[1] Add. MSS. 37845 f. 47

R

intimately acquainted with as I am, nay, better, so much of the previous negociation having pass'd through your hands, the story is not very long.   I believe (but I am not quite sure) that I may be permitted to go to Ireland, but this permission is under conditions : and the conditions are in substance, that I step into Lord Westmoreland's old Shoes—that I put on the old trappings, and submit to the old chains,—the men, and, of consequence, the system of measures to remain the same, with or without my approbation, and without any consideration for my responsibility to the King, the Country, and my own reputation—these are now the terms.

Will any man say, would any man have presum'd to have said last July, that at that time, when upon negociation the management of Ireland was transfer'd to the care of the Duke of Portland, these were the terms or the spirit of the terms? For the safety and general good of Ireland, in my humble opinion they should not be insisted on ; for the honor of the individual they must be rejected by me : and looking upon the proposal as a mark of indignity offer'd to me, it would be fit for me to mark my sense of it. But still what affects myself does not weigh now with me.   In consequence of the certainty I entertain'd of going to Ireland, I thought it a duty to look forward to the management of the country, and therefore invited the most respectable persons of the Kingdom to communicate confidentially with me, and upon the credit of the situation I held myself out as intended to fill, I found them willing to let me into many of their private thoughts and opinions upon such things as I think they would not have open'd themselves upon under other circumstances. To them I feel myself bound in honor to atone for having misled them : to my own character I am bound to make clear in the most unequivocal and most overt manner, that if I have misled and duped, I have done so because I was misled and duped myself ; no act will be so overt, none will so unequivocally mark a sense of indignity and resentment, as a retreat from that Government which I charge with having duped me. In these sentiments and for these purposes I mean to take the earliest opportunity of entreating his Majesty's permission to give in my resignation. The Duke of Portland and Lord Mansfield are both acquainted with my intention. Lord Spencer's great distance prevents my communicating it to him.[1]

THE EARL OF MANSFIELD *to* WILLIAM WINDHAM

Private   *Kenwood : October* 12, 1794

I will make no apology for troubling you upon a subject that is equally interesting to us both. I see, with infinite concern, that we are upon the brink of a Rupture, the evil consequences of which are such as I am sure no man living can calculate ; a few words of explanation at the time would have prevented a great part of the mischief. I knew from the Duke of Portland from time to time every thing that passed, and can safely venture to assert that, had he conceived it possible that he was not to have the entire and perfect management of all Irish business, the negotiation would have instantly stopped. The prospect of being of use in Ireland was his great inducement. He wished himself to go thither, which I for one combated to the utmost of my power, being persuaded that it was essential to the success of the arrangement which you will remember I had so much at heart, that he should hold a great, responsible situation in the Cabinet. His desire of going to Ireland is irrefragable evidence of the light in which he considered what had passed upon the subject. Had he imagined that he was to follow the same plan that had been followed by Lord Westmoreland, and was to work with the same instruments, he would no more have accepted the Lieutenancy of Ireland than he would have taken the Government of Botany Bay. In

[1] Add. MSS. 37874 f. 83.

consequence of the repeated sollicitations to him not to think of Ireland for himself, he relinquished that idea, and then thought of Lord Fitzwilliam, who, if it had not been for a delicacy to Lady Fitzwilliam, would have accepted instantly, and all this mischief would have been prevented.

It was perfectly understood that Lord Westmoreland was to be properly provided for, that is, that, the moment an opportunity offer'd of providing for him properly in any department, that opportunity was to be seized and he was to be considered as having a prior claim to any other person to a situation similar to that which he formerly enjoyed. With respect to the Chancellor of Ireland, I always understood that it was a thing perfectly settled that the Duke of Portland was to have the entire management of all Irish business, that it was not to be merely nominally in his department, but that the real management was to be in him. It followed, of necessary consequence, that the Lord Lieutenant he named was not to use the Irish in the land, but was to make use of other means ; was, in a word, to connect himself with the Ponsonbys and their friends. Of all this I could give such evidence as would be received in a Court of Justice. The fair and manly manner in which Mr. Pitt seems determined to support the war makes me regret this misunderstanding the more. I say it with heartfelt anguish. My clear opinion is that, if there be a rupture at present, the country is undone.[1]

WILLIAM WINDHAM *to* EARL FITZWILLIAM

October 12, 1794

I hope that in pursuit of a purpose, pregnant with consequences so very serious, you will not suffer yourself to act from any impulse of passion, nor under any misapprehension of the merits of the case. Is the embarrass-

[1] Add. MSS. 37874 f. 88.

ment that has arisen, fairly to be charged to the account of Pitt; and are the means of relieving it, such, in all their parts, as He can properly be expected to furnish?

The first consideration simply is, did Pitt or did He not say from the beginning, that He could not open the situation of Ireland till he had provided for Lord Westmoreland another at his return, as good as that which he held before his appointment? The second is, can Pitt without dishonour suffer a proscription of those, who are principally marked out to enmity, (and will be represented as being wholly so) in consequence of their support of his former measures, and has not He some colour for saying that if a measure so strong as the removal of the C[hancellor] was intended, it ought to have been signified, when the terms of the arrangement were first settled.

The evil has been, that things have been suffered to lye under a supposed General understanding, which ought to have been distinctly brought forward, and which were not of that sort, that an agreement to them should have been preserved. I really think, to speak in fairness, that Pitt could hardly have been expected, when he was augmenting his administration by a junction with another party, to give up at one stroke all his friends on the other side of the water, to the mercy of those, with whom he was connecting himself. Should you in similar circumstances have thought such a conduct warrantable in yourself? We must consider them not according to their actual merits, but according to their merits, as they appear to him, or at least as He is bound to consider them.

What I wish is that it should be considered fairly, how much change is absolutely necessary for carrying on the Government, according to your own, and the Duke of Portland's ideas (for such a change only can in anywise be insisted on); and then what means may be desired for effecting that, without violating the protection which Pitt is called upon to give to those, who have supported uniformly his former government. The question of Lord

Mansfield is a separate consideration, and must be decided by inquiring which of the two, He or Lord Westmorland, should in reason be expected to give way.

If, after every endeavour used, these opposite considerations must at last remain irreconcilable, there will at least be the consolation of thinking, that the ruin which will ensue, and of which it is difficult to foretell the extent, will not have happened but by the unhappy course of things and not for want of the exertions of those, whose duty it was to prevent it.[1]

EDMUND BURKE *to* WILLIAM WINDHAM

October 16, 1794

My state of mind was not the most enviable before the present unhappy misunderstanding. I cannot think without horror on the effects of a breach in the Ministry in this state of our affairs, and just before the meeting of Parliament   It will complete our ruin ! Every honest man in every country in Europe will by this event be cast into dismay and despair. It looks as if the hand of God was in this, as it is strongly marked in all the rest. However, we must still use our poor human prudence, and our feeble human efforts, as if things were not, what I greatly fear they are, predetermined. I am out of action, but not out of anxiety. I feel deeply for yourself —I feel for my other friends—I feel for the general cause. Ireland, the country in which I was born, is the immediate cause of the dispute : Lord Fitzwilliam, the man in the world I am most obliged to, is the party chiefly concerned in it. To Mr. Pitt—the other party—I have strong and recent obligations. Before I had any such, I was clearly of opinion that his power, and all the chance we have for the rescue of Europe, were inseparably connected. You know that, though I had no part in the actual formation of the present system of a coalesced Ministry, that no pains

---

[1] Add. MSS. 37874 f. 85.

were wanting on my part to produce the dispositions
which led to it.   You, of all men, therefore, are the best
judge how much I am in earnest that this horrible breach
should not be made.   How to prevent it I know not ;   I
cannot advise.   I can only make statements, which I
submit entirely to your judgment.   I do not write to
any one else, because you alone have desired to hear my
sentiments on this subject.   I will trouble you with no
other view of the matter than as it concerns the interest,
the stability, perhaps the existence, of Mr. Pitt's power.
I was one of those who were of opinion that he could have
stood merely on his own basis ;   but this was my private
speculation, and hardly justified, I fear, by the experience of mankind in cases any way similar.   But to have
gone on without this new connection, and to bear the
loss of it, are two very different things.   The accession
of a great mass of reputation taken out of a state of very
perilous and critical neutrality, and brought to the decided
support of the Crown, and an actual participation in the
responsibility of measures rendered questionable by very
great misfortunes, were the advantages which Mr. Pitt
derived from a coalition with you and your friends.

I say nothing just now of your weight in the country,
and the abilities which, in your several ways, you possess.
I rest only on your character and reputation for integrity,
independence, and dignity of mind.   This is everything at
a moment, when opinion (never without its effect) has
obtained a greater dominion over human affairs than
ever it possessed ;   and which must grow just in proportion as the implicit reverence for old institutions is found
to decline.   They who will say that the very name which
you and the Duke of Portland and Lord Fitzwilliam and
Lord Spencer have as men of unblemished honour and
great public spirit, is of no use to the Crown at this time,
talk like flatterers who despise the understandings of
those whose favour they court.   It is as much Mr.
Pitt's interest, as a faithful and zealous servant of the

Crown (as I am sure he is), to hold high your honour and estimation with the public, as it is your own.   Can it be preserved, if Lord Fitzwilliam continues in office after all that has happened, consistently with the reputation he has obtained ; and which, as a sacred trust for the King and country, he is bound to keep, as well as for his own inward satisfaction ?   I will not say that Lord Fitzwilliam has not, in some respects, acted with a degree of indiscretion.   The question is, whether Mr. Pitt can or ought to take advantage of it to his own material prejudice ?

You are better acquainted than I am with the terms, actual or understood, upon which the Duke of Portland, acting for himself and others, has accepted office.   I know nothing of them, but by a single conversation with him. From thence I learned that (whether authorised or not) he considered without a doubt that the administration of Ireland was left wholly to him, and without any other reserves than what are supposed in every wise and sober servant of the Crown.   Lord Fitzwilliam, I know, conceived things exactly in that manner, and proceeded as if there was no controversy whatever on the subject.   He hesitated a long time whether he should take the station ; but when he agreed to it, he thought he had obliged the Ministry, and done what was pleasant to the King, in going into an office of great difficulty and heavy responsibility.   He foresaw no other obstacles than what were found in his own inclinations, the nature of the employment, and the circumstances in which Ireland stands. He, therefore, invited several persons to converse with him in all the confidence with which men ought to open themselves to a person of honour, who, though not actually, was virtually in office.   Whether the Duke of Portland and Lord Fitzwilliam had reason for this entire security, you are better able to judge than I am.   I am sure they conceived things in the light I state them, though I really think that they never can reconcile it to the rigid rules of prudence with regard to their own safety, or to an entire decorum with regard to the other Cabinet Ministers, to go so far into detail as has been done until all the circumstances of the appointment were settled in a more distinct and specific manner than they had been.   But I am sure they thought that a very large discretion was committed to them ; and I am equally sure that their general places (so far as I know them) were perfectly upright and perfectly well understood for the King's service and the good of his empire.   I admit, and lament, the error into which they have fallen.   It must be very great, as it seems Mr. Pitt had no thought at all of a change in the Irish Government ;   or, if he had, it was dependent on Lord Westmoreland's sense of the fitness of some other office to accommodate him on his resignation of the great place which, for five or six years, he has held.   This puts off the business *sine die*.   These are some of the mischiefs which arise from a want of clear explanation on the first digestion of any political system.

If an agreement is wished, criminations and recriminations, charges and defences, are not the way to it.   If the communication hitherto has not been as full and as confidential as it ought to have been, let it be so now. Let it be such as becomes men engaged in the same cause, with the interest and with the same sense of the arduous trust which, in the most critical of all times, has been delivered over to them by their King and country.   In this dreadful situation of things, is it not clearly Mr. Pitt's interest, without considering whether he has a case as against his colleagues or not, to keep up the reputation of those who came to his aid under circumstances liable to misconstruction ;   liable to the exaggerated imputations of men, able, dexterous, and eloquent ;   and who came to him when the whole of the affairs under his administration bore the worst aspect that can be imagined ? I am well aware that there is a sort of politicians who would tell Mr. Pitt that this disgracing his colleagues would be to him a signal triumph, and that it would be to the public a splendid mark of his power and superiority. But alas ! it would be a triumph over his own force. His paramount power is well understood. His power is an object rather of envy and terror, than of contempt. I am no great dealer in general maxims. I am sensible how much the best of them are controlled by circumstances. But I am satisfied, that where the most real and solid power exists, there it is the most necessary, every now and then, to yield, not only from the real advantages of practicability, but from the advantages which attend the very appearance of it. What is given up by power, is a mark of moderation ; what is given up because it cannot be kept, is a mark of servility and meanness. What coffee-house politician is so grossly ignorant as not to know that the real seat of power is in Mr. Pitt, and in none of you who by the courtesy of England are called Ministers. Whatever *he* gives up will be manifestly for the King's service ; whatever *they* yield will be thought to flow from a mean desire of office, to be held without respect or consideration. If he yields any point he will be sure to put out his concessions, to be repaid to him with usury. All this unfortunate notion of triumph, on the one part and the other, arises from the idea, that Ministry is not *one* thing, but composed of separate and independent parties—a ruinous idea, which I have done everything in my power to discourage, and with a growing success. I can say almost with assurance, that if Mr. Pitt can contrive (and it is worth his while to contrive it) to keep his new acquisition of friends in good humour for six months more, he will find them as much of his party, and in my opinion, more surely to be depended upon, than any which he has hitherto considered as his own. It is of infinite importance to him to have it *thought* that he is well connected with others besides those who are believed to *depend* on him.

If it is once laid down, that it is true policy in Mr. Pitt to

uphold the credit of his colleagues in administration, even
under some difference in opinion, the question will be,
Whether the present is not a case of too much importance
to be included in that general policy, and that Lord Fitzwilliam may very well give up the lieutenancy, and yet
hold his office, without any disgrace ?   On that, I think,
there can be little difference in opinion.   He must, to be
sure, resign ; and resign with every sentiment of dis-
pleasure and discontent.   This I have not advised him
to do ; for, most certainly, I have had no conversation
with him on the subject ; and I am very glad I have not
had any such discourse.   But the thing speaks for itself.
He has consulted with many people from Ireland, of
all descriptions, as if he were virtually Lord-Lieutenant.
The Duke of Portland has acted upon that supposition as a fundamental part of his arrangement.   Lord
Fitzwilliam cannot shrink into his shell again, without
being thought a light man, in whom no person can place
any confidence.   If, on the other hand, he takes the
sword, not only without power, but with a direct negative
put upon his power, he is a Lord-Lieutenant disgraced
and degraded.   With infinite sorrow I say it—with
sorrow inexpressible—he must resign.   If he does, the
Duke of Portland must resign too.   In fact, they will both
consider themselves turned out ; and I know it will be
represented to them, because I know it has been predicted
to them that their being brought into office was no more
than a stratagem, to make them break with their friends
and original natural connections, to make them lose all
credit with the independent part of the country, and then
to turn them out as objects of universal scorn and derision
without party or adherents to resort to !   I believe Lord
Fitzwilliam has in his bureau one letter to this effect—I
well recollect that he was much affected by it, and indeed
doubtful of accepting—perhaps more than one.   I am
certain, that whether they stay in under a state of degra-
dation, or are turned out, their situation will be terrible ;

and such as will be apt to fill men with rage and desperate resolutions. Both their coming in and their going out will be reviled ; and they will be ridiculed and insulted on both by the Opposition. They will affect to pity them. They will even offer to pardon them. Amongst Mr. Pitt's old adherents, as perhaps you know as well as I do, there were many who liked your coming in as little as Mr. Fox or Mr. Sheridan could do. They considered Mr. Pitt's enlarging his bottom as an interloping on their monopoly. They will join the halloo of the others. If they can persuade Mr. Pitt that this is a triumph, he will have it. But may God in His goodness avert the consequences from him and all of us !

' But why,' will some say, ' should not Lord Fitzwilliam take the Lord-Lieutenancy, and let the Chancellor remain where he is ? He will be good-humoured and subservient, and let the Lord-Lieutenant do as he pleases.' But, after what has passed, the true question is, which of these two is to govern Ireland ? I think I know what a Lord-Lieutenant of Ireland is, or I know nothing. Without a hearty and effectual support of the Minister here, he is much worse than a mere pageant. A man in the pillory is in a post of honour in comparison of such a Lord-Lieutenant. ' But Lord Westmoreland goes on very quietly.' He does so. He has no discussions with the junto who have annihilated English government. Be his abilities and his spirit what they may, he has no desire of governing. He is a Basha of Egypt, who is content to let the Beys act as they think proper. Lord Fitzwilliam is a high-minded man, a man of very great parts, and a man of very quick feelings. He cannot be the instrument of the junto, with the name of the King's representative, if he would. If Lord Fitzwilliam was to be sent to Ireland, to be exactly as Lord Westmoreland is, I undertake to affirm, that a worse choice for that purpose could not be made. If he has nothing to do but what Lord Westmoreland does, neither ought Lord Westmoreland to be removed, nor the Chancellor, no, nor the Chancellor's Train-bearer. Lord Fitzwilliam has no business there at all. He has fortune enough. He has rank enough. Here he is infinitely more at his ease, and he is of infinitely more use here than he can be there, where his desire of really doing business, and his desire of being the real representative of the Crown, would only cause to him infinite trouble and distress. For it is not to know Ireland to say, that what is called opposition is what will give trouble to a real Viceroy. His embarrassments are upon the part of those who ought to be the supports of English government ; but who have formed themselves into a cabal to destroy the King's authority, and to divide the country as a spoil amongst one another. *Non regnum sed magnum latrocinium :* the motto which ought to be put under the harp. This is not talk. I can put my hand on the instances, and not a doubt would remain on your mind of the fact. His Majesty has the patronage to the Pashalic, as the Grand Seignior has to that of Egypt, and that is all. Such is the state of things. I think matters recoverable in some degree ; but the attempt is to be made.

If Ireland be well enough, and safe enough, as it is ; if the Chancellor and the Government of the junto is good for the King, the country, and the empire, God forbid that a stone in that edifice should be picked out to gratify Lord Fitzwilliam, or anybody else. But if that kingdom; by the meditated and systematic corruption (private, personal, not politic corruption) of some, and the head-long violence and tyrannical spirit of others, totally destitute of wisdom, and the more incurably so, as not being destitute of some flashy parts, is brought into a very perilous situation, then I say, at a time like this, there is no making questions about it mere discussions between one branch and the other of administration, either in England or Ireland. The state of Ireland is not like a thing without intrinsic merits, and on which it may be

safe to make a trial of skill, or a trial of strength. It is
no longer an obscure dependency of this kingdom. What
is done there vitally affects the whole system of Europe.
Whether you regard it offensively or defensively, Ireland
is known in France. Communications have been opened,
and more will be opened. Ireland will be a strong digue
to keep out Jacobinism, or a broken bank to let it in.
The junto have weathered the old European system of
government there, and brought it into utter discredit. I
look in this affair to Ireland, and in Ireland to Great
Britain, and in Great Britain to Europe. The little
cliques there are to me as nothing. They have never done
me a favour nor an injury. But that kingdom is of great
importance indeed. I regard, in this point, all descriptions of men with great comparative indifference.
I love Lord Fitzwilliam very well ; but so convinced am
I, on the maturest reflection, of the perilous state into
which the present junto have brought that kingdom (on
which, in reality, this kingdom, at this juncture, is dependent), that if he were to go with a resolution to support
it, I would, on my knees, entreat him not to have a share in
the ruin of his country under the poor pretence of governing a part of it. Oh ! my dear friend, I write with a sick
heart, and a wearied hand. If you can, pluck Ireland out
of the unwise and corrupt hands that are destroying us !
If they say, they will mend their manners, I tell you, they
cannot mend them ; and if they could, this mode of doing
and undoing, saying and unsaying, inflaming the people
with voluntary violence, and appeasing them with forced
concession ; their keeping the ' word of promise to their
ear and breaking it to their hope ; ' their wanton expenses,
and their fraudulent economy ;—all these, and ten times
more than these, but all of the same sort, are the very
things which have brought government in that country
to the state of contempt and incurable distrust under
which it labours. It cannot have its very distemper for
its cure. You know me, I think, enough to be quite sure;

that in giving you an opinion concerning Mr. Pitt's interest and honour, I have not an oblique regard, at his expense, to the honour and interest of others. No! I always thought advice the most sacred of all things, and that it always ought to be given for the benefit of the advised. I am now endeavouring to make up my accounts with my Creator. I am, almost literally, a dying man. I speak with all the freedom, and with all the clearness of that situation. I speak as a man under a strong sense of obligation to Mr. Pitt, when I assure him, under the solemn sanction of that awful situation, that my firm opinion is, that by getting rid of the new accessions to his strength, and especially upon the ground of protection to certain Irish politicians (at what distance of time I cannot say), he is preparing his certain ruin, with all the consequences of that ruin, which I tremble to think on. God bless you all, and direct you for the best.[1]

EDMUND BURKE *to* WILLIAM WINDHAM

Beaconsfield : October 16, 1794

What I enclose to you with this is to yourself principally ; but if you enter into my ideas, it is ostensible to Mr. Pitt and Mr. Dundas ; and, if you will, to the Chancellor. This I don't desire, because, in case of our agreement the arguments will come with far more authority from yourself. But if you think that my opinions would tend in any way to strengthen yours, you have my permission to show them to any of the three upon whom you conceive they are the most likely to make an impression. Mr. Pitt is surprised that your friends should think of breaking the Ministry at such a time as this ; sure it is equally surprising that he should do so by putting them out of their offices, for it is plain they cannot stay in them under the present circumstances. It is he who is chiefly responsible (almost, indeed, wholly

---

[1] Windham's " Diary," p. 321

so) for carrying on the public business in this dreadful
season. It is his system and his power that are to be
supported ; and I never knew a minister that would not
do a thousand things to gain, and to keep, men convenient,
at least, to the support of his power and reputation,
especially when the greatest interests ever staked were
depending. When he will do no one earthly thing to
keep them, they must think, and the world must think,
he wants to get rid of them. I wish you to speak fully to
Dundas on this business. I conceive all others ought to
be postponed to it. I don't know what part he has in the
intrigue. But if he is clear of that, he is open to reason;
and is not without influence. You mistook me about
Grattan. I did not wish Mr. Pitt to reason him into a
dereliction of opposition to Lord Westmoreland, for I
well knew that a dread of that opposition would be a
principal inducement to Mr. Pitt to be reconciled to your
friends ; I wished you to get the Duke of Portland and
Lord Fitzwilliam, with whom he was in confidence, and
to whom he came over in order to destroy the system of
the junto, and to pledge himself to support them in
opposition to it ; to consult with him what it was best for
that purpose to do, whether to resign or not, or what other
course to take. I should have made a great scruple of
conscience to do anything whatever for the support,
directly or indirectly, of a set of men in Ireland, who,
that conscience well informed tells me, by their innumer-
able corruptions, frauds, oppressions, and follies, are
opening a back door for Jacobinism, to rush in expenses,
and to take us in the rear. As surely as you and I exist,
so surely this will be the consequence of their persisting
in their system. As to yourself, you have my most ardent
prayers that God would direct you, through your reason,
to the best course. I am glad that neither the Duke
of Portland, nor Lord Fitzwilliam, nor you, have called
on me for my opinions on your conduct. Whatever you
do will be well intended and well advised. You will then

smile, and ask me, why I am so free in my advice to Mr.
Pitt through you, who has asked it as little as the rest ?
Why, because the whole depends on him.   If he mistakes,
so as to let this Ministry go to pieces, we shall, along with
him, be all undone.   The Lieutenancy of Ireland is an
arrangement subservient to the reformation, or to the
continuance, of the abuses reigning in the country, and
he who is the real minister can alone support or destroy
them.   I ought to have sent my packet earlier.   But I
have been oppressed with such sinkings and dejection of
spirits, that in adding, after the coming of your messenger,
to what I wrote the night before, I have been obliged to
go into the open air from time to time, to refresh myself,
and thus the time went away.   This is dreadful ! dreadful ! beyond the loss of a general battle.   I now despair
completely.   I begin to think that God, who most surely
regards the least of His creatures as well as the greatest,
took what was dearest to me to Himself in a good time.
Adieu ! [1]

WILLIAM WINDHAM *to* WILLIAM PITT

October 16, 1794

I also have talked to Mr. Gr[attan] since your conversation with him, and with an opening of better prospects.   A
very little would I am persuaded content them, I mean
Mr. Gr[attan] and his friends, if the matter could be fairly
brought as a question to their moderation.   What might
give an unfavourable appearance to Mr. Gr[attan]'s conversation, was a suspicion in his mind that more was meant
than was declared, and that it was rather an objection
to the system than a tenderness about particular persons.
I am persuaded that if the Chancellor could be given up;
he might be saved.   But I don't know, nor should I think,
that there could be a secret article about that ; and any
understanding upon the subject would be a matter too
delicate and dangerous.—If you cannot make up your

---

[1] Windham's " Diary," p. 328.

I   S mind to exposing the Ch[ancellor] to the risk, the thing is, I fear, desperate : and with it I should also fear all hope of quiet or safety in Ireland. An acquiescence of persons in the situation of Gr[attan], and his friend, is an effort of virtue too great to be long continued, should it even be attempted.

I ought not to disguise to you either what are likely to be the effects here. Great or small, it is proper they should be before you. Though I could say nothing positive respecting myself, till Lord Spencer's return, yet it does not appear to me that I could stay on the grounds on which the Duke of Portland and Lord Spencer are likely to go out ; nor do I conceive that Lord Spencer with respect to himself will be of a different opinion.

I need not say, I am persuaded, how much I deprecate on the publick account such an extremity ; and I assure you, I hardly do so less on account of the perfect satisfaction which I have found in the conviction, as it has hitherto subsisted.[1]

WILLIAM PITT *to* WILLIAM WINDHAM

Private   *Downing Street : October* 16, 1794

The more I consider every part of this unfortunate Subject, the more I am confirmed in the impossibility either of consenting to the Chancellor's Removal, or of leaving either him or any of the Supporters of Government exposed to the Risk of the new System. What you say with respect to yourself embitters the Regret, which, even without it, I should feel at the probable consequences of what has passed. My Consolation under all the Difficulties will be that I have nothing to reproach myself with, in what has led to this misunderstanding ; and I must struggle as well as I can with a distress which no means are left me to avoid, without a sacrifice both of Character and Duty.

---

[1] Add. MSS. 37844 f. 78.

Allow me only to add, that before you finally decide on your own line of conduct, I trust you will give me an opportunity of discussing with you without reserve, the great Public Considerations, which at this moment are involved in it.[1]

WILLIAM PITT *to* WILLIAM WINDHAM

Downing Street : October 16, 1794

Strongly as I have stated to you my Feelings in my last letter, I fear on looking at your Letter again, that I have stated them in one respect imperfectly.

Besides the Impossibility of sacrificing any Supporters of Government, or exposing them to the Risk of a new System, I ought to add that the very Idea of a *new System* (as far as I understand what is meant by that Term) and especially one formed without previous Communication or Concert with the rest of the King's Servants here, or with the Friends of Government in Ireland, is in itself what I feel it utterly impossible to accede to ; and it appears to me to be directly contrary to the General Principles on which our Junction was formed and has hitherto subsisted. Painful as the whole Subject is, I feel nevertheless that [it] is material to leave no Part of it liable to be misunderstood, and I, therefore, give you this additional Trouble.[2]

THE DUKE OF PORTLAND *to* WILLIAM WINDHAM

October 18, 1794

You need not be under any apprehension upon the subject of concessions—but, notwithstanding, I shall be much disappointed if I don't see you to-morrow morning and I wish you could come soon after ten. Grattan is to be here at 12 and he is always punctual.—I find from Dr. Laurence[3] that Burke has been all this morning

---

[1] Add. MSS 37844 f. 80.   [2] Add. MSS. 37844 f. 82.
[3] French Laurence (1757 1809), the friend and executor of Burke.

writing to the Chancellor and Laurence also tells me that Burke has been more agitated and that his spirits have been more affected and harried within these two last days than for some weeks past, and Laurence supposes that it is to be entirely attributed to paragraphs which have appeared in the papers respecting the Government of Ireland.[1]

EDMUND BURKE *to* WILLIAM WINDHAM

Beaconsfield : October 20, 1794

I had your letter. Everything is undone, if the matter is put upon private and personal ground. If it be a question of men and of favour, it is quite clear what men and what favour must prevail ; and, as to the public opinion, it will be clamorously against those who come in and go out lightly in the most critical seasons. I have thought this matter over and over. I have looked back at our former experience : and I have considered the genius of the new times. I have considered the character of the men you are come to act with, and your own character ; as well as the character of the Opposition and the bystanders. I have compared all these with the situation of England, and of Poland, and of Europe. I never gave anything in my life so thorough a sifting. The result is, that I am clearly and decidedly of opinion that [neither] the Duke of Portland, nor Lord Fitzwilliam, nor yourself, ought to resign ; but to wait—for what I foresee will be the case of some of you—to be turned out. You are in a post of strength, if you know how to defend yourselves. Whereas nothing but obloquy, unpopularity, disfavours above and below, and complete impotence, will follow you, if you are once out ; and never can you come in again but on the ruins of your country. But when I say the resignations ought not now to be thought of, I do not say that the matters for which you contend ought to be abandoned ; but the

[1] Add. MSS. 37845 f. 59

very reverse. You are where you are; only to act with
rectitude, firmness, and disinterestedness, and particularly to resist, *ad internecionem*, the corrupt system of
Ireland, which goes directly to the ruin of the whole
empire. I seemed to think, in my last letter, of the
resignation of the Duke of Portland and Lord Fitzwilliam
as inevitable. That letter was the result of my second
thought. You know that in my first, to which I am now
come back, I stated this position to you as a thing between
the two alternatives. In substance, perhaps, my opinions
are the same : go out they must. I believe it is a thing
that does not depend on them to avoid—the question is
on the manner of it. Clearly, the most reputable thing
in every point of view is, that they should not commit
suicide ; but be slain on their post in a battle against this
Irish corruption, which is another thing than the mis-
application of so much money. If, indeed, my opinion
was wholly changed on reflection, why should I be
ashamed of it in one of the most difficult questions that
ever was ? Whatever is done, I am against all squab
proceedings, such as seem rather the effect of temper
than principle. They are very ill-used—very ill indeed ;
but their own conduct has been such that they have put
themselves in the wrong ; and it is not by base yielding;
or by a stubborn perverseness, they can get right, but by
producing such a body of principle as really *actuates* them;
and which will make their mode of proceeding, however
irregular, a thing of very subordinate importance. The
closet must be resorted to, with all sort of gentleness and
attention ; the matter stated, the substance given in;
in writing ; opinion and direction rather asked than
resolution declared on their part ; lamentation rather
than blame. Honour and principle are never the worse
for being conducted with address. Two things—not to
resign, not to abandon the ground of dispute. With good
conduct the whole may yet be gained—points, office, all.
But then, the temper to be used, in my mind, ought not

to extend to the Irish job system. You can only defend yourselves by open, avowed unappeasable war, against that, as long as no temperaments of any kind are held out ; when they are, their value will be considered. I shall write, I think, a note to this purpose to Lord Fitzwilliam and the Duke of Portland. I wrote, last night, a *threnodia* to the Chancellor ; but I did not enter into any particular whatever : it would have been quite useless. He is a very able, good-humoured, friendly man ; and for himself, truly, no great jobber; but where a job of patronage occurs, ' *quanquam ipsâ in morte tenetur.*' For in the article of death, he would cry, ' Bring the job ! ' Good God ! to think of jobs in such a moment as this ! Why, it is not vice any longer : it is corruption run mad. Thank you for the account of the few saved at Bois-le-Duc—Pichegru [1] has more humanity than we have. Why are any of these people put into garrison places ? It is pre-meditated and treacherous murder. If an emigrant governor was, indeed, appointed, a better thing could not be done. Then we should hear of a defence : it would, indeed, be a novelty; and one would think, for that reason; would be recommended. But cowardice and treachery seem qualifications ; and punishment is amongst the *artes perditæ* in the old governments. I am very miserable —tossed by public upon private griefs, and by private upon public. Oh ! have pity on yourselves ! and may the God, whose counsels are so mysterious in the moral world (even more than in the natural), guide you through all these labyrinths. Do not despair ! if you do work in despair. Feel as little and think as much as you can ; correct your natural constitutions, but don't attempt to force them. Adieu, adieu ! [2]

---

[1] Charles Pichegru (1761–1804), French general ; conquered Holland, 1794–95 ; entered into negotiation with the Royalists for the restoration of the Bourbons ; found guilty of conspiracy, and sentenced to transportation, escaped to England ; returning to France in 1804, was cast into prison, where on April 6 he was found strangled.

[2] Windham's " Diary," p. 330.

EDMUND BURKE *to* WILLIAM WINDHAM

October 28, 1794

I am in a state of mind as near complete despair as a man can be in ; yet whilst there remains the faintest possibility of doing good, I think you whose duty it is to act, and who have vigour of body and mind sufficient to that duty, ought to omit no rational means of removing the evil which presses the most nearly, and is the most within your reach.   A mediator is wanted in this business. I doubt whether you are exactly in that situation.   I think the Chancellor is.   I feared he might be too much influenced by the jobbery of his Irish connections, particularly that of Douglas   But I rather think I wronged him. I have heard from him, and by the strain he writes in, I am sure he wishes this rupture to be made up in some proper way, as you and I do.   Now I apprehend he may be a little crippled in this business of a useful go-between, if there be not some confidence shown to him by our friends.   I just throw out this hint, not being able to say much more than what I have already troubled you with at great length.   How comes it that I have heard nothing of Dundas in this business, no more than if no such thing existed ?   and yet he must certainly tell for a great deal in it.   I know this affair can never come to any sort of amicable conclusion whilst they treat the matter in dispute exactly in the spirit and upon the principles of ministers of adverse courts (and very adverse courts too), debating on a matter in negotiation and not as members of the same Cabinet Council and servants of the same King. The order of the questions and all this fencing, tends to keep alive the hostility.   There is something of the worst tendency imaginable in the whole mode of their carrying on business.   God bless you ! [1]

[1] Windham's " Diary," p. 333.

CHAPTER II

1795

Windham's belief that a Royalist force should be organised
against the Republicans : The negotiations entrusted to him
by the Cabinet : Quiberon Bay expedition : Correspondence
with Lord Grenville : The Duke of York gazetted Field-Marshal:
Lord Fitzwilliam, as Lord-Lieutenant of Ireland, acts in
defiance of his instructions : He is recalled by the Ministry :
And is succeeded by Lord Camden : The state of Corsica :
Sir Gilbert Elliot appointed Governor : Paoli : Lord Hood : Sir
Hyde Parker : Joseph Gerrald : Dr. Parr's plea for him : The
Prince of Wales's debts : Burke suggests a remedy for the
future : England and the French Royalists : The Treasonable
Practices Bill : Correspondence with Malone, Mrs. Crewe,
Lord Grenville, and others.

WINDHAM held the view that if the Royalists in the west of France were assisted with money and munitions by the British Government they could raise a force that might be used effectively against the Republican army. The management of these difficult negotiations was entrusted to him by the Cabinet, and his enormous correspondence on this matter, including letters from the Royalist chiefs, Puisaye,[1] Georges Cadoudal,[2] and Tinténiac, provides material for a history of the war in Brittany and La Vendée. Windham was the person most responsible for the disastrous Quiberon Bay expedition in July 1795,

---

[1] Count Joseph Puisaye (1754?–1827), French Royalist general, took an active part in the insurrection of La Vendée and in the Quiberon Bay expedition.

[2] Georges Cadoudal (1769–1804), Chouan chief. The Vendean Royalists were named *Chouans*, a corruption of *chat-huant*, screech owl, whose cry was used as a signal cry of a band of smugglers.

though, in fairness to him, it must be said that the failure was attributable not to the design, but to the execution; with which, of course, he was not directly concerned.

WILLIAM WINDHAM *to* LORD GRENVILLE

London : January 1, 1795

The time for preparation is slipping away very fast; and after some examples that we have seen, we have no reason to hope that the opportunities of repairing what may now be lost will be numerous or long continued. If we wait for the conclusion of these necessarily tedious negotiations with the Court of Vienna, on a subject, too, where they are not pressed to decision by any very strong wish or necessity, we shall lose the season for raising any considerable force under the Prince of Condé [1] on that side of France.

My idea is that we should directly send a M. D'Artez, who is here and has been long marked out for the station we are speaking of both by the Duc D'Harcourt and others, with a commission to the Prince de Condé empowering him immediately to raise a regiment, naming the officers himself, and giving to M. D'Artez, who is already known to him, such commission as he may think fit and as his former rank in the army may entitle him to. I would then send M. Lambertye, whom his Majesty has been graciously pleased to favour us with, to concert with Wyndham at Florence about raising a regiment in those parts; and if any place besides the dominions of the King of Sardinia can be found as a depot for that regiment, would send the Marquis de Miran to Turin to open there a rendezvous for all the well affected who either are already out of the

---

[1] Louis Henri Joseph de Bourbon, Duc de Bourbon and Prince de Condé (1756–1830), the son of Louis Joseph (died 1818). He married, April 1770, Marie Thérèse d'Orléans, and was the father of the ill-fated Duc d'Enghien. The Duke left France in 1789, and eleven years later accompanied his father to England, where they resided at Wanstead House

country, or may be drawn from the provinces in that neighbourhood. There is every reason to hasten these measures, not only because the time now remaining to us is barely sufficient for the purpose, but because the effects of the present milder system will be to call back many into France who might be well contented still to remain out if they were furnished with the means of subsistence. My reason for proposing the Marquis de Miran is that he commanded in Provence for 15 years ending with the Revolution, and gave, in the last crisis, the most distinguished proofs of zeal and good conduct. This consideration is sufficient for giving him a preference over others that may have been on the Duc D'Harcourt's list. and for departing from a rule hitherto not uniformly observed, and certainly not necesssary to be observed, of excluding from the command of regiments all above the rank of Maréchal de Camp. If there should be any objection to giving the corps to M. de Miran, he might be stationed at Turin as Lieutenant General to superintend the formation of M. Lambertye's corps, and any other corps that it might be found practicable and expedient to raise there. M. Lambertye, too, who makes more difficulties than he ought to do considering his good fortune in getting a corps at all, may be sent with letters to the Prince de Condé, desiring the Prince either to keep M. Lambertye with him, and to send an officer of his own into Italy, or to let M. Lambertye go on as proposed, and keep his own officer for the quarter nearest him. Some measures of this sort are absolutely and immediately necessary. For besides that we must have the force, Italy is in the most immediate danger, being so completely defenceless that there is nothing, I apprehend, to prevent the merest handful of French that should once pass the frontier from marching to the further extremity. The emigrant French, now dispersed in Italy, are in perfect despair on that account, and are driven by that despair to join in a wish which nothing else could dictate, namely; a wish for peace. At the same time that country may certainly, under proper management; be made to yield great means, not only for its own defence, but for that which may be very necessary for general success, offensive operations on that side of France. The first step is to begin raising there some force in our pay, and I know of no better way of doing so than those which I have pointed out. I reflect with great regret, and some shame, that steps for this purpose have not been taken sooner. One idea by the way occurs to me at this moment not unworthy of being considered, namely the landing there the Duc de FitzJames,[1] with his officers, and possibly even another of the Franco-Irish regiments who have, I fear, but little prospect of speedy success in Ireland, and who would not find the same ill-dispositions towards them that may be apprehended in some parts of Italy against the emigrants. No objection would probably be made to them in the Pope's States ; and we need have no jealousy of them, any more than the Corsicans would have if employed, where they will be sufficiently wanted, for the defence of Corsica.

This is connected with the question of more direct communication with the Pope, which I cannot but wish to see effected, and speedily though possibly not through the medium of the person who has so earnestly recommended it. Why should not Frederick North in his way to Corsica be directed to pass through Rome, with some letters of civility to the Pope ? It will be a good opening of communication, and connected with the idea of it which you entertain.

At all events I would send two of the Irish Colonels to fill up their regiments with French, Italians, and Corsicans, instead of attempting only to fill them up, as I fear will be the case, with Irish, whom they cannot get either without encroaching upon the success of other corps.

Postcript.—I wish you could concert with Mr. Pitt a

---

[1] Edou - 1, fourth Duc de Fitz-Jame (1776 1821).

short letter to be sent to the coalition in Normandy by a person whom I have here ready to go, and who waits only for these credentials.   A general assurance vouching for the person, and quieting them as to any views of conquest, is all that is wanted.[1]

WILLIAM WINDHAM *to* LORD GRENVILLE

Hill Street :   February 13; 1795

I send you a letter of M. D'Artez containing a proposal of his which, upon discoursing it over with him, I cannot but think deserving of some attention.   He means it only as an experiment, the continuance of which, if successful; should be left to the Austrians.   If would certainly be their business to begin it, but if they will not begin it, as is probably the case, is it not better that it should be begun by us ?   M. D'Artez is of opinion (and his opinions seem so temperate and well formed that I feel a great disposition always to agree with them) that in the present state of thinking in France, a large defection in their armies might be effected by the use of the means which he proposes.   At all events the cost could be but inconsiderable ; and as soon as any considerable body should be raised as much as might amount to a regiment, it might be transferred to the army of the Prince de Condé.

Upon the subject of this army I feel great uneasiness. I have no idea that the Austrians, if left to themselves, will ever put that army in a state, or employ it in a manner, to make it produce its proper effect.   Would it be impossible, though now it is rather too late, to make some stipulation in its favour, so as to require that, as part of the Austrian contribution of force, the Prince of Condé's army should be put on a proper footing, and be kept up to a certain amount.   The proper footing will be; besides that of regular pay and clothing, the changing

[1] Fortescue MSS. iii. 1.

that shocking and prodigal system of using officers as common soldiers, and stopping the dreadful consumption which that system has made, and continues to make, of the flower of French nobility. This would be done by enlarging that army to its proper dimensions, and filling up the vacant spaces by those whom there may be hopes of drawing from the enemy's army and from the interior. To part of this purpose, indeed, the Chevalier D'Artez's present plan is in some degree adverse ; inasmuch as by giving commissions to officers from the other side, he lessens the number that would remain for those now serving. The only question is whether you do not gain by the increase of the army, and consequent increase of commissions, more than you lose in that view in the increase of the number of persons to be provided for. There are, I confess, great difficulties. It would be a heart-breaking thing to see a Republican officer, newly come over, confirmed in his commission, while hundreds of the old chevaliers were still serving as common soldiers, and liable to be commanded by him. It must be left to the judgment of the Prince of Condé ; but, if he thinks the experiment may be made, I should be inclined to be at the expense of beginning it. The fatal adherence of Austria to her views of acquisition, which has hitherto ruined everything, and will but too probably do so in the end, it is in vain to say anything to. I suppose it is impossible to do anything even to mitigate that system. Our mouths are unfortunately stopped by our own proceedings in the West and East Indies. Is it impossible, however, to make them lay them aside for the time, and feel that even the purpose of acquisition will be better attained by not being pursued directly ? [1]

[1] Fortescue MSS. iii. 18/9.

GEORGE III. *to* WILLIAM WINDHAM

Queen's House : February 10, 1795

Mr. Windham is to notify my Son the Duke of York[1] as Field Marshal and insert it in this night's *Gazette* besides sending the usual Notification to the Secretary of State's Office.

At the Same time he is to have a letter of Service placing him on the Home Staff, which will give him naturally the command, which has till now been entrusted to Lord Amherst.[2]

I suppose Lord Amherst's Situation ceasing, it will be proper that [it] should be notified to him by Mr. Windham, who, I am persuaded, will express it in terms of my approbation of his Services, both when commanding in North America and since I have called him into Succession to the head of the British Staff.

GEORGE R.[3]

The trouble that had preceded Fitzwilliam's appointment as Lord-Lieutenant continued after he had arrived at Dublin on January 4, 1795. The whole business indeed, was a tangle of misunderstandings that has not yet been satisfactorily unravelled. On January 7 the new Viceroy, careless of Pitt's expressed wishes, dismissed John Beresford, Commissioner of the Customs, Edward Cooke, the Military Secretary, Wolfe, the Attorney-General, and Toler, the Solicitor-General. Beresford, without delay, appealed to the Cabinet, which not only ordered his reinstatement, but declined to confirm the

---

[1] The Duke of York had returned to England in the previous December.

[2] Jeffery Amherst (1717–1797), created Baron Amherst 1776. Commander-in-Chief 1778 ; resigned in favour of the Duke of York, 1795 ; Field-Marshal 1796.

[3] Add MSS. 37842 f. 3.

dismissal of Wolfe and Toler. Fitzwilliam, for his part, informed the Cabinet that the Catholic question must be dealt with at once. After some correspondence the Cabinet took the only course open to it : on February 23 it recalled Fitzwilliam. He left Ireland on March 25, and it is recorded that, " The day of his departure was one of general gloom ; the shops were shut ; no business of any kind was transacted ; and the greater part of the citizens put on mourning, while some of the most respectable among them drew his coach down to the waterside." [1] Fitzwilliam was succeeded by Lord Camden.[2]

EARL FITZWILLIAM *to* WILLIAM WINDHAM
Dublin Castle : March 1, 1795

I had the honor of receiving your letter of the 29th ult : expressing your wish for Mr. Grattan's presence in England, but not specifying that of any other member of that cabinet, which has unanimously reprobated generally the measures of my administration, and on that account has recall'd me. I have not recommended to Mr. Grattan to take the journey, but to wait till it is made the unanimous request of that cabinet that he should do so.[3]

WILLIAM WINDHAM *to* LORD FITZWILLIAM
March 5, 1795

I have received your Excellency's letter of the 1st inst and am sorry to find, that by an act of zeal, hasty perhaps, and injudicious, but certainly well-intended, I have exposed myself to a reception, which acts of that sort are apt at times to meet with.

---

[1] Stanhope, " Life of Pitt," ii. 236.
[2] John Jeffreys Pratt, second Earl of Camden (1759–1840), created Marquis of Camden, 1812.
[3] Add. MSS. 37875 f. 1.

With respect to disapprobation of measures, I know of none, to which your Excellency can allude, except an opinion, which I cannot but distinctly avow, that a great part of your Excellency's measures have been in direct opposition to what I had understood to have been agreed upon, either directly or by implication, in the conversation which took place in Downing Street, a little previous to your Excellency's departure ; I mean particularly in the appointment of Mr. W. Ponsonby, the appointment of Mr. G. Ponsonby, the removal of Mr. Beresford, and in the bringing forward the Catholick question, so far as your Excellency approved of, or was concerned in that measure, before a communication could be had with this country.

If in this opinion I have the misfortune to differ with your Excellency, I have the consolation, I believe, of agreeing with every other person, who was present at that conversation.[1]

SIR GILBERT ELLIOT[2] *to* WILLIAM WINDHAM

Private   *Bastia : April* 2, 1795

I cannot easily tell you how much pleasure your letter gave me, I mean a letter from you. Your past silence was a great loss to me, but no wrong. *Damnum sine injuria*. I hope that by official occasions, if not by other means, we may have a chance for some little correspondence and communication with each other, and to avoid the greater task of a dispatch, that you may think a private letter a relief, which you before thought a labour. I am grateful for the exertions you have made in our

---

[1] Add. MSS. 37875 f. 5.

[2] England having assumed the protectorate of Corsica in June 1794, Sir Gilbert Elliot was appointed Governor. He made Pozzo di Borgo President of the Council of State, whereupon Paoli, who had aspired to that position, began to intrigue for the expulsion of the British, but wsa himself exiled by Elliot. Corsica was evacuated by the British in October 1796

favour by the three Foreign Corps for which you have
agreed. It is a proof that we are not indifferent to you,
and that you have a just sense of the urgency of our
situation. You will believe, of course, that I should have
preferr'd British troops and for one reason that would
be a good one if there was none other, I mean that if you
had taken measures to give us those, we should have been
sure of having them ; but the realization of the Foreign
Corps does not appear so certain. It is become of late
much more difficult to get French soldiers. I have the
officers of six companies now recruiting in Italy and Spain,
but I am not sanguine in my expectations. I believe
Spain to be the best ground, for the French have been
very miserable there. I allow £3 10s. per man levy money,
of which 10s. to the captain for expense of enlisting,
traveling, and risk by Desertion—and £3 to the recruit
including the necessaries which he is to be furnished with,
so that the recruit cannot touch above 30s. I am to
cloath and arm them. Your terms to Dillon and Dr.
Corn are much higher, altho' the Colonels are charged
with the cloathing and arming, so that my Refugee re-
cruiters will have no chance if Dillon arrives *in their beat*
before they have done their business. I shall be glad,
however, to have them either way, if not both.

You can hardly conceive what a crowding back to
France there has been for many weeks past, and it has
by no means abated. In the last month the expense of
the Toulonese Refugees in Corsica has diminished exactly
one half compared with the month preceding, and a great
diminution, tho' not so great, has taken place in all our
other Toulonese Colonies. The alarms to which Corsica has
been subject, and the extreme timidity of this class of
Frenchman has operated very powerfully in driving them
hence. The day on which the French fleet appear'd off
Cape Corse, I sign'd about 300 passports for Toulonese
only. Not one of them came to ask for a musquet, not
one out of near a thousand. Admiral Hotham's action

I T

on the 14th March,[1] together with the arrival of the *Blenheim* of 80 guns, and *Bombay Castle* of 74 from England, has made a favourable change in our affairs. The advantage on the whole is not so great, however, as was at first imagined, for we have lost the *Illustrious*, a fine 74 gun ship. She was dismasted in the action and afterwards driven on shore near Gulf of Spezzia. Everything was done to get her off, but without success and she was burnt after saving every thing of value on board. Her stores and ship's company will strengthen the remaining ships.

The loss of the *Berwick* was the most unfortunate thing in the world. She was to have sail'd several days before. She actually sail'd the night before from San Fiorenzo to join the Admiral at Leghorn and if she could have continued her course that night she would have been safe; but some accident of wind and weather forced her back to San Fiorenzo. She sail'd again next morning by daylight and drop'd into the jaws of the enemy at Cape Corse. Another misfortune was the loss of the Captain, a very brave and good officer. He was killed nearly by the first shot, and after his death all seems to have been in confusion. Little or no resistance seems to have been made afterwards.

The French can hardly be said to have lost by their cruise. They have lost two ships, of which we can make no use for want of hands and masts. We have lost two ships, one of which will be fitted out against us immediately. But the arrival of the two first ships from England gives us a clear advantage. We had 13 ships of the line including the *Neapolitan*, against 15—we have now 15 against 14; and although one of ours, the *Courageux*, is dismasted and is out of service for the present, the other 14 are much superior to the Enemy in number of guns and size of the ships, as well as in skill

[1] In this action Admiral Hotham captured two French ships, the *Ça Ira* and the *Censeur*

and discipline and, I hope, bravery. We have gained in point of honour by this action. Captain Freemantle's engaging the *Ça Ira*, one of the largest 80 gun ships, with a frigate was one of the most distinguish'd actions which has happen'd in the war ; and Captain Nelson's 64 gun ship which succeeded Freemantle in the attack, seem'd little more than a frigate by that great ship. The prisoners speak with great admiration of those two ships, I mean the *Inconstant*, and the *Agamemnon*. The *Illustrious* and *Courageux* both acquired much honour. The *Courageux*, Captain Montgomery, was three hours in close action, and came out of it a complete wreck. The main body of the French fleet certainly declined the battle, and in circumstances which seem to render that conduct unjustifiable ; but the two ships that were obliged to fight certainly made a noble battle of it. The captain, now a prisoner, says he should not have fought so long or sacrificed so many of his People if he had not expected his own fleet to come down and support him every minute. I invited the five principal officers to dine with me, on their way to Corse where they are to have their Parole. The Captain of the *Ça Ira* is an intelligent fellow and has something of the manners and language of a gentleman, tho' these qualities do not overflow even in him. The rest are such ragamuffins as have seldom been seen out of France. They are horribly ugly with a strong Banditti, or rather hangman, cast of countenance, and in manners and address are about the pitch of the mate of a guineaman. They have fought resolutely, however, and have thus extorted a sort of respect.

The arrival of the *Blenheim* and *Bombay Castle* was a providential thing. They came into San Fiorenzo while the French fleet was off Cape Corse, almost in sight. If the enemy had been a few leagues to the westward they must have been taken with a naval store ship, and 7 or 8 merchantmen under their convoy.

Now for grievances or ill fortune --These two ships

were detach'd by Lord Howe at Sea, without having suspected that they were to come here, having nothing on board for the Mediterranean, and being short of stores —while other ships along with Lord Howe which were full of many things much wanted here and intended for us, were retain'd. I flatter myself, however, that they may yet be coming on with the convoy. Another misfortune and a serious one is that of four naval store ships only one has arrived and it is that one which has the least material articles on board. The *Campbell* which had *masts*, the grave desiderata at present, has somehow or other been prevented from coming on, and there seems some uneasiness about her as well as the bulk of the Mediterranean convoy on account of a gale of wind which happened soon after the *Blenheim* left Lord Howe. I hope with all my heart Lord Hood is now on his passage with the remainder of the reinforcement; for in our present state another victory might undo us; and it must be remember'd that five ships are on the stocks at Toulon, of which we are assured that two will be launched this month. This article should by no means be neglected.

It is difficult to say with certainty what object the French fleet had in coming out. All the prisoners say positively that it was intended to fight Admiral Hotham and make a decisive day of it. I believe, however, they thought our fleet dispersed and crippled by their former tempestuous cruise, and when they saw 14 sail of the line ready to act, they possibly altered their plan. It was objected to the Captain of the *Ça Ira*, when he said their object was to fight our fleet, that they would not in that case have embarked so many troops, field and battering artillery, &c. He accounted for these things by saying that the first intention had been to bring out the transports, with all the troops, for an expedition, together, and that there not being room in the transports for all the troops, they had embarked a considerable number on board the ships-of-war; that after that was done the plan was altered, and it was suddenly determined that the Fleet should first engage the English, and then return for the transports. In this manner they came out with the troops which had been put on board on a different Idea. I rather think this likely to be the truth. It is at least the most probable account of the matter. I cannot say positively what the intended expedition was to be. But as it is pretty certain that General Gentili, and the former municipality of Bastia were on board the fleet, it does seem likely that Corsica was the object—and it probably continues to be so.

Our Parliament goes on more smoothly than most Parliaments do. Paoli,[1] however, is playing the old rogue and the old fool most egregiously. But I must not enter on so wide a field at the end of a letter. Pray do not quote me, or at least only to persons of confidence, concerning Paoli.

P.S. We are all well. I am to be left alone, however, in the hot weather, as Lady Elliot is afraid to trust this climate with the children during the unhealthy season. She proposes to pass the summer at Lucca baths.

Notwithstanding the measures you have taken for assisting us with foreign troops, I cannot part with the hope that some British are intended for us, and may already be on their passage hither. Captain Barclay of the *Blenheim* conceived that the 29th and another Regiment were coming out with the convoy; but this report is too agreeable, and at the same time too vague, to be relied on. It is, nevertheless, undoubtedly true that the number of British now in Corsica is much too small, even on the supposition of Foreign corps being made effective in any reasonable time. The nature of the service does not admit of the Foreign troops being employ'd either wholly alone or with a very great superiority of numbers. The Emigrant mind has, indeed, of late been so much on the wheel, and at this moment has such a strong determina-

---

[1] Pasquale de Paoli (1726- 1807), Corsican patriot and general.

tion, as Physicians say, towards France, that in circumstances at all critical they are not to be much trusted;
especially in this country which is a recent conquest from
France, to which not one Frenchman that I have yet seen
can bring himself to subscribe. Our British numbers,
small as they are, must decrease dayly, if not supplied.
Besides the natural and constant causes of diminution in
all numbers, we have the climate to assist in reducing
us, and it is material to recollect that there are very few
of our soldiers who had not a few months ago had in-
termittent fevers, which leave a permanent debility and
render a relapse always likely; so that either by the
fatigue of service, if any should occur, or by the return
of the unhealthy season, which begins in July, we must
expect to dwindle to little short of nothing. Mr. Dundas
has given me hopes of 1000 men in February, and I therefore still hope. My grand reliance is, however, still on
Lord Hood and his naval reinforcement. He is,
indeed, much wanted here *himself—very much.* This
is for your very private and confidential ear. If
anything should prevent Lord Hood from coming out,
measures should be taken to leave *Sir Hyde Parker*[1] in
the command. He is, in that profession, in the *very first
form,* and perfectly master of this business, having been
Captain of the fleet under Lord Hood last year, and commanding a division of the fleet ever since. These things
are amazingly material, and the choice of men for difficult
and important situations is, by the course of business,
and the invincible stream of human habits and affairs,
too often left to chance. Admirals Hotham and Goodall
are now before Sir Hyde Parker in the Mediterranean, but
without disparagement to either of them, it would be a
very great point gain'd in the war to get over that difficulty. Admiral Hotham is a gentlemanlike man, and
would, I am persuaded, do his duty in a day of battle.

[1] Admiral Sir Hyde Parker (1739 1807), subsequently Commander-
in-Chief at Jamaica 1796 18 .

But he is past the time of life for action ; his soul has got down to his *belly* and never mounts higher now, and in all business he is a piece of perfectly inert formality. It is, in short, the sort of thing that *palsies*, as the French say, all the force you could give him. Goodall is a spirited lively old man ; but should not deprive us of one of the first, if not the first, admiral in the Navy. I write now as a *very private* friend, and the matter is so delicate as to have a doubt of its being quite justifiable even from me to you. It seems hard, however, on the world that delicacy should stand in the way of its interests or safety, and that it should be impossible for any one to say a useful or necessary thing.[1]

WILLIAM WINDHAM *to* THE HON. THOMAS PELHAM

Hill Street : April 21, 1795

. . . The state of general politicks, though as bad as can be in some respects, I mean in the resistance of the King of Prussia (at least, so there is all reason to believe) is in others altogether as good. Every account from the Interior parts of France confirms the opinion that a change there is operating very fast ; and that if the combined powers would only remain firm, though resting on their arms, the re-establishment of Monarchy would hardly fail to be brought about. The surrender of Charette[2] is rather to be considered as a peace dictated by an independent and superior power. What you have seen in the papers in that respect by no means exceeds the truth, if it even comes up to it. Upon the whole, if no violent change is made by this intolerable baseness of the King of Prussia, and you can keep that mischief from Ireland, I am in tolerable good spirits as to the event.[3]

[1] Add. MSS. 37852 f. 226.
[2] François-Athanase Charette de la Contrie, Vendean Royalist (1763–1796).
[3] Add. MSS. 33101 f. 179.

DR. SAMUEL PARR [1] *to* WILLIAM WINDHAM

Hatton : May 8, 1795

You will excuse me for trespassing so far upon your remembrance of past events, as to believe that you will not refuse what I am going to ask to one who has never been disposed to refuse you greater things.—Yesterday I was struck down with horror and dismay upon hearing that an order for going on shipboard had been suddenly given to Mr. Joseph Gerrald,[2] a Scholar of mine, whom Mr. Pitt, furnished as he is with inferior learning, endow'd with talents certainly not superior, and actuated by a spirit more adapted to the coarseness of a Convention than to the gravity of a Parliament, has once, or more than once, called Gerrald. Though I most widely dissent from Mr. Gerrald's fantastic opinions, though I entirely disapprove of his impetuous behaviour, though I have often warned him of danger, and often endeavour'd to preserve him from guilt, yet I must in common with many wise and good men, reprobate his sentence as wholly unwarrantable by sound law, and ever shall I deplore that ungracious and most inauspicious policy which is now on the point of carrying that sentence into plenary execution.

From the relation which I bore to Mr. Gerrald in his happier, and better days, from the admiration which I feel for his mighty talents, from the opportunities which I have had for tracing many of his misfortunes and much of his misconduct to their earlier sources, I cannot think of his present or his future condition without the keenest anguish of pity mingled with indignation. To you, dear Sir, I say this without disguise, for you are a man of letters, and without apology, for you are a man of honour. Yes, with genius such as rarely is to be found at the Bar, or in the Senate, Mr. Gerrald, after a few hours' notice and

[1] Dr. Samuel Parr, divine and scholar (1747–1828).
[2] Joseph Gerrald (1763–1796), sentenced to fourteen years' transportation for sedition 1794.

DR. SAMUEL PARR

in the dreary silence of night, was hurried away from his prison in Scotland ; and now, scarcely with a change of apparel, and without books to console him amidst the sorrows he is doomed to suffer on a spot where solitude itself would be a blessing, he has been summon'd very suddenly from his confinement, and thrown into the transport.   The rapidity of the former measure may, for what I know, be justified by the circumstances of the moment ; but the severity of the latter is most wanton indeed.—What I have to request from you is, that you would prevent for a few days his being sent from England, 'till by the kindness of his Friends he is furnished with some clothes and a few books.[1]

EDMUND MALONE *to* WILLIAM WINDHAM

May 21, 1795

I have called two or three times at the War Office with the hope of meeting you there, but have been out of luck.

I think you said you regretted you had not bought some one picture at Sir J. Reynolds' Sale, as a Memento.

I purchased one on speculation for my brother, without being commissioned by him, and now find that it will not answer the purpose for which I intended it.   It is by an eminent Master, *Baroccio*, and cost 42 Guineas.   I have since got it new lined, which I suppose will cost about a Guinea.—Will you call any morning, and take a look at it ; as in case you should not think of having it, I will send it forthwith to some picture-dealer, if I can find one who will give me what it cost.

I suppose you know poor Boswell died on Tuesday Morning, without any pain.   I don't think he at any time of his illness, knew his danger.   I shall miss him more and more every day.   He was in the constant habit of calling upon me almost daily, and I used to grumble sometimes at his turbulence ; but now miss and

---

[1] Add. MSS. 37914 f. 149.

regret his noise and his hilarity and his perpetual good humour, which had no bounds. Poor fellow, he has somehow stolen away from us, without any notice, and without my being at all prepared for it. On Tuesday Morning, I went thro' the melancholy office of examining all his papers, in order to find a Will, but found none. His family imagine there is one in Scotland. I wish we could shew his memory some mark of regard, but there is no opportunity, for his body is to be carried to Auchinleck.[1]

EDMUND BURKE *to* WILLIAM WINDHAM

June 9, 1795

I have said so much, to so little purpose to our friend Elliot,[2] about the Scheme of the new Transportation of the unhappy fugitive Clergy of France, that I don't know how I can justify myself in troubling you again on the Subject. But I am so strongly impressed with the mischief of this new exile of the Reliquiæ Danaum that I cannot forebear once more to warn you against that measure, both on their account and on yours. At this moment the popular mind is in a very unsettled state, and I am as sure as I live, that a vast migration, thro' the heart of the Kingdom, of strangers, that will be considered no better than vagrants, Enemies, and rivals of the Poor in the Bounty of the Rich, will produce an ill effect, that no ordinary consideration of military convenience can possibly counterbalance. I say nothing on the economical part of the Question, though it is evident that it will cost twice as much to have these unfortunate people twice as ill off as they are at present—where they are fitted to the situation and the vicinage 'reconciled to them with all sort of good will and mutual accomodation. This is a publick Hospital, and applied to that use. I doubt as much the Justice, as the policy, of turning people out

---

[1] Add. MSS. 37854 f. 130.   [2] William Elliot, of Wells.

of your Hospital when you have once possessed them of it.   Charity has its own Justice, and its own rules, as well as any other part of human intercourse ; and if I give a Cottage to a poor man to live in I have no more right to turn him out of it than if I had let it to him for Rent.   There is nothing in these things voluntary but the beginning of them.   But be that as it may, where in the world can you arrange them ?   I hear of Bolsover Castle.   This is like the Duke of Portland's generosity. But is there at Bolsover (which, after all, will be a new exile to these wretches) the market of all kinds which exists at Winchester ?   Excuse me, my dear friend, this importunity.   I believe you will be the first to repent this Measure.

[P.S.] What the Devil are you all doing about the Prince ? [1] If you are not to consider him as a Prince, and keep him as such, by an honourable establishment of a Court—there is no reason why you should give him anything on his private and personal merits.   What is a Prince without people of distinction about him ?   If he were willing to give up this Establishment (and I am afraid he is but too ready to do it), he ought not to be permitted so to do.   Fatal ! fatal Measure !

Put the *animal*, if you will, to short allowance.   But, for God's sake, save the monarchy, if you can ; which; (neither in the possession, nor succession) can be anything but by its attendance.   The Duke of York may as well be commander-in-chief without a company of Soldiers, as a King or Prince of Wales what they are without a Court. It ought not to go beyond decorum—but that ought to be.   He is not, and cannot be, as Mr. Fox and Mr. Sheridan sometimes represent him—a Gentleman.   He is a prince or he is nothing.   If you Ministers are firm—the House of Commons may be brought to reason—and the Prince may, by suitable means, be put out of the reach of future Debts.   Why not put his Houses, Goods, etc. out of

---

[1] The Prince of Wales, who was very heavily in debt.

the reach of Executions ? They are purchased by the publick and are the publick property ; and no private man, no, not the Prince, ought to have a power of alienating them. Use,—as much as you please and even a little abuse—but no dominion. Why not make it an act of Bankruptcy in a Dealer—a misdemeanour in any other—to credit him, except by an order under his own hand, countersigned by his great officers ? For his private expenses, let him have an handsome privy purse. Abuse let there be ; but let there be limits to the abuse. These restraints are no humiliation. Just the contrary. They are a part, a necessary part, a noble part, of greatness. They are only the meanest beings in the Community whose Will is not worthy of a Rule. I really do not know what state these things are in. In my poor Judgement the plan first stated by Mr. Pitt was the best—if there was then a Majority sufficient to carry it. Now all seems at Sea again. Let the allowance be what it will a decent Establishment ought to be kept up. So far from being necessarily expensive it will lessen the general Charges.[1]

SIR GILBERT ELLIOT *to* WILLIAM WINDHAM

Bastia : August 2, 1795

For God's sake, attend immediately and seriously to the dispatch I send by Captain Moore of the Light Dragoons to the Duke of Portland, dated 31st July. Paoli is throwing off the mask, and we are in a most critical and difficult situation. The grand evil is the opinion, now universally prevalent here, that I am not supported at home, and that I am to be immediately recall'd. As I have determined to fight the battle, I really must be recall'd if that resolution should not be approved of. If it is, I desire nothing to ensure victory, but the proof in one way or other that all these reports of my disgrace are inventions of those who wish to mislead this People, and that I possess the present confidence and

_____
[1] Add. MSS. 37843 f. 71.

shall have the steady support of Government.   But pray
read my private letter to Mr. Dundas on this subject as
well as my dispatch to the Duke of Portland.   Col. Moore
is a true son of his father, and I believe related to the
father of all mischief.   But this is not official and is
between ourselves.

The last action between the fleets is a *sad* story.   But
you will probably hear enough of that from other quarters.
I did my duty *once* on that subject, with some hesitation,
as you know, but understanding that the evil is not likely
to last long I am almost sorry to say as much now as I
have done.   I certainly wish to speak in confidence still ;
for *I* cannot attempt to prove.   But pray enquire ; it is
of much moment.

I expect this August to be a stormy month ; but I am
now so practised in storms that it seems as natural to me
as fair weather.   I do hope, however, that you will abridge
this gale as much as you can.   If Government had
fortunately spoke out sooner concerning me, as I have
been entreating them in vain to do at least seven months,
this mischief could not have happened.   I understand
I am in the same favour and enjoy the same confidence
as ever, yet every body here believes my successor to be
already named ; and of course the setting sun has not so
many worshipers.

When this fight is over, I really wish to retire and
breathe a little.   I do entreat you all, to bring me home
as soon as you can without inconvenience to the Publick
or dishonour to myself.   My family is all well at Lucca
Baths and return to me in October, provided things
are quiet.[1]

WILLIAM WINDHAM *to* SIR GILBERT ELLIOT

London : August 28, 1795

The trial I have had of official life has not served to
reconcile me to it.   It is the period of my existence in

---
[1] Add. MSS. 37852 f. 252.

which, I think, I have had the least enjoyment ; but whether that proceeds from the nature of the situation or from my having come to a state in which the last period is likely to be the worst, I will not venture to pronounce. I go doggedly on, however, resolved that what good I can do shall not be lost for want of assiduity, and enjoying, in fact, the persuasion till lately that my determination in that respect had not been without effect. The failure of the expedition to Quiberon, produced by a blind confidence and want of military capacity on one side, and by the eternal operation of French Cabal on the other, joined to the event of the Spanish peace,[1] has brought things to a state in which that consolation will probably be denied me. As long, however, as war goes on—of which I hope the conclusion is still far distant, I mean on any terms short of the destruction of the present French system—there will be still something for me to do. Should peace ever be made with the Republic, I think England will be no longer a country to live in ; and in that case, as there will be no country free from the effects of their power and of their insolence, one may as well choose that which has in other respects the most recommendations, and with that view I think I shall be inclined to choose Italy. If one is to submit to humiliation it had better be anywhere else than in one's own country.[2]

EDMUND MALONE *to* WILLIAM WINDHAM

Cheltenham : August 31, 1795

I was rejoiced to find that you had not forgot Oxford ; and that there is some chance of your finding time for a short excursion there. I shall, I believe, leave this place, with my brother and his family, next Saturday, and we steer our course to Malvern, where at the end of about a week we shall part. I shall then trace back my steps to Oxford, and hope to be there on Monday the

---

[1] France had made peace with Spain, July 22.
[2] "Life of Lord Minto" ii. 332.

15th of September.   Just as I received your letter, I was meditating to send you a line on the subject of the unfortunate Royalists.   Poor Sombreuil's Letter appeared to me very affecting, and *our friend* Puisaye, if his statement be true, is no better than a poltroon.   I have no patience with the commonplace talkers here and elsewhere, who affect to be greatly concerned, as if these troops were sent to certain destruction.   I think, on the contrary, that their supineness in not attempting any thing before, is their greatest blemish ; and had I lost my friends and estate and country, as most of them have, should have bless'd you for enabling me to cut my way, at any hazard, to the door of the Convention, that I might have one grapple with those miscreants who had robbed me of all.[1]

SIR GILBERT ELLIOT *to* WILLIAM WINDHAM

Bastia : September 30, 1795

I cannot sufficiently thank you for your letter of the 28th August and Postscript of the 1st September, which I received on the 26th inst. by the Post.   I have never doubted of the part which you or any of the ministers would take on this occasion ; but while the earnestness with which you have taken the matter up, and the dispatch you was anxious to give to the business is peculiarly gratifying to me from a friend, it is also comfortable and encouraging in the affair itself, as it shews that you have a due sense of the urgency and importance of the occasion. You will think it odd that I have kept this letter, gratifying as it is, a profound secret, but as I propose to forbear from strong measures, till I can give to them the full weight of the King's declared authority and commands, and as *the Enemy* observes during this interval of expectation, the same reason that I do, professing, still, submission to the King, and boasting of his support, I think it best to let him keep the People in that Course, till I am ready to act.

[1] Add. MSS. 37854 f. 132

For if any interval were to pass after it was known with certainty that I shall be supported at home, he might be tempted perhaps to prepare his people for resistance even to the King, while there is, I hope, a chance of his throwing the game up, or being deserted in it, when the loss of their English support, and the attack that will be made on them in Corsica come upon them at the same moment.

I am in hourly expectation of the messenger you promised me, and I am not without hopes of terminating this disagreeable business within the month of October. But who can answer for the cause of Revolutions and insurrections? In the mean while Lady Elliot and my family are making their grand tour, and scouring Rome and Naples. I do not wish to have them here in the moment of *projection*, and they will have finish'd their journey by the time I shall be ready to receive them. It is somewhat tantalizing to have been two years in the Mediterranean, and breathing the spray of the *Mare Tyrrhenum* without having seen Rome. I shall be as long in getting to the Tiber as Æneas was; though I have as great a desire to go from Corsica to Rome as Seneca had, when he was in my present neighbourhood. The Tower which he inhabited exists still, and is about six or eight hours ride from hence.

My life at this moment would be intolerable if it were not for Frederick North. I cannot express how much comfort and relief I find in his company, or how much real assistance I derive from his abilities and application in business. His talents for business and his qualifications as a man of business are very much superior to what those friends who have known him only as an idle man may have allow'd him, and I really do not know any body whom I should name as better, or so well, fitted for the foreign line. I say this with perfect sincerity and you may trust me in it, notwithstanding my private regard for him. Considering you as no less his friend, it may not be amiss to tell you now that the great and perhaps extreme object of his ambition and wishes is a Mission to one of the Italian courts—Tuscany, *Rome* or Naples.   I believe he would prefer Rome to every thing else, but that hangs on so many doubts and considerations that he puts it out of the question, and then Naples is the thing, if it should fall in his time—and Florence; though not best, would be consider'd by him as excellent.

As for myself I wish most earnestly to be amongst you again.   I have already said that while there is any thing like danger or difficulty here nothing shall induce me to go, but being turn'd out, or an opinion that somebody else might be more useful than myself.   But I really *cannot* pass another summer here.   If I did I must again be separated from my family, whom I must send to England for the sake of my boys, and whom I cannot expose again to another Italian summer even if it were not high time to have them at school.   I shall have been out of England two years and a half, go when I may, having expected an absence only of some months.   I never liked foreign life, though the peculiarity of my present situation, with the views I had and have of its probable influence on the happiness of our Country and prosperity of another; made it highly gratifying to me.   But having performed my task here, as I reckon that I have, my views and wishes whether publick or private all point strongly homewards and I think myself now entitled to be relieved.

I have told the Duke of Portland that if Paoli's present mischief is defeated and things are settled as I trust they will very soon, my *wish* is to have leave to go to Italy at *Christmas* or *the New Year*, make my tour, of about two months, and then return to England in the Spring.   My successor might come in Spring, and North in the mean while would carry on the business here perfectly well.   This, in a private view, would be the best for me.   But if a fit man is ready, let him come; and I will resign my vice-crown the moment he arrives.   Only, for God's sake, let the choice be good for this one turn.

May I beg you to communicate all this confidentially to Mr. Dundas on whose friendship as well as on that, I hope, of Mr. Pitt, I may rely for complying with my very earnest wishes, by preparing my return at the time I have mention'd. It is proper to observe at the same time that this matter should be as private as possible, as any notion of my approaching departure might do harm at this moment.

You cannot imagine how valuable any thing you can now and then snatch a moment to drop on the affairs and events near you is here. I felt the Quiberon disaster severely before I supposed that you was particularly connected with it. But seeing the causes of that failure; which belong only to peculiar circumstances in the execution, and not to the plan or principle, I hope you are sturdy enough to be consoled, so far as your own feelings are concern'd, by having been the first to push into practice that great principle of giving support to the Vendée, which I think remains as unimpeach'd as before that accident had disappointed the first attempt of that nature.

Things are at this moment in a situation as yet untried. We have heard of the Convention's having left Paris and taken refuge with the army; but this is all we know of the matter; and the wind; by detaining our packets; has kept us some days in suspence concerning the cause; the extent or the tendency of this revolution. The situation is new and may, therefore, produce new consequences. I think it must do good, in some degree or other. But as all will be known before you read any speculations we can make here on this event, I may as well spare you the trouble of stale conjectures. I beg you to remember me most kindly to the Legges. I must not think of such persons, or of such comforts as their names bring to one's mind, till you tell me that I have a prospect of enjoying them.[1]

[1] Add MSS. 37052 f. 254.

WILLIAM WINDHAM *to* LORD GRENVILLE

October 11, 1795

It becomes very urgent as well as important to come to some determination as to the supply of stores and money, when we can give nothing else to the unfortunate Royalists ; who are still contending with zeal and energy, unconscious of the changes that are taking place, and still supposing that they have a country behind ready to support their efforts at least by feeding their wants : and to prevent, for a long while to come, the powers of the Convention from being wholly turned to their destruction. We shall really risk something more than injury to a cause which includes all other causes, if, as long as we maintain the war, and till we formally apprize the Royalists that they must no longer count upon our support (a notification, by the way, which our former declarations hardly leave us the liberty to make), we do not continue to afford them all such assistance as we cannot show to be actually out of our power. As it stands at present, orders are preparing to a large amount, and with reasonable dispatch, for clothing and other necessaries of that sort ; powder is sent, or on its way, to the amount of more than 1000 barrels (eight or nine thousand would not be too much, supposing the thing to go on) and authority is given to send by opportunities, as they occur, such additional quantities as the stores at Portsmouth may furnish, and the demands of other service can spare. Arms will be supplied, not in large quantities, but in such as the numbers manufactured and the demand for other service can admit ; and, lastly, 50,000*l.* has been sent out with General Doyle,[1] exclusive I believe of 10,000*l.* intended for the payment of his own army, and which is now in great part expended ; and 50,000*l.* more has lately been sent out by the *Robusta.* This is the whole, I believe, of what has hitherto been

---

[1] General (afterwards Sir John) Doyle (1750 ?–1834).

done; and this, for the present moment, and for Charette's army, may be sufficient; though certainly it is at this moment that that army may be most pressed, and when a large sum of money ready to be instantly applied might produce an effect, either of obtaining good or averting evil, which could not be hoped from tenfold such sums at a later period. But we must recollect that Charette's army is only a part of the Royalist force; and of that force which even his success and safety requires to be maintained. There is the whole of the force under Puisaye, including Scepeau's army, which has now elected him as their chief. There is a large district under M. de la Vieuville, whose conduct has been in the highest degree meritorious; and another still larger district, and under the direction of a person equally meritorious, M. de Frotté. Neither of these three armies can well receive assistance directly from *Monsieur*,[1] nor with 100,000*l.*; pressed as he is likely to be, could he well spare any. I would, if my own judgment were to direct, send without a moment's delay a sum of money to each of these. A very moderate or inconsiderable one would be sufficient; 20,000*l.* to Puisaye, and 10,000*l.* to each of the others; or even 10,000*l.* to Puisaye, and 5000*l.* to the other two. Nor would there be any difficulty of finding agents to whom I should feel no hesitation of trusting. To Puisaye, indeed, it should be conveyed from Quiberon. To M. de Frotté means might be found of conveying it from St. Marcout [Marcouf] quarters. With M. de la Vieuville a constant communication is kept up, as you may have observed, from Jersey. To none of these should I feel the least scruple of confiding sums to a much larger amount, with a full confidence of their being fairly applied to their proper purpose. M. Frotté is a man strongly recommended, and who has shown himself perfectly devoted to the general cause. M. Vieuville, with the same proofs

[1] Charles Philippe, Comte d'Artois, Charles X (1757–1836). *See* vol. i, p. 191 *note* 1.

from conduct, is the heir of property in Brittany to a great amount. Of Puisaye, though I have often had reason to complain of rather too great magnificence in the expenditure of public money, I have never had the smallest reason to doubt of the integrity and correctness as to all views of private emolument, or of idea of appropriating any part to himself.

Money is now almost the only means by which we can assist them; for arms in great abundance we have not to send, besides the difficulty of conveying them into the country. They all agree that with money a great deal is to be done in gaining both arms and powder from the Republicans; as well as in gaining the Republicans themselves.

Without such assistance, all those who are here; Allègre, Boisberthelot (the two persons that went into France previous to Puisaye's expedition) and Préigent, who, though of inferior condition, has merited by his services, that some attention, should be given to his opinion, all agree that the cause in that quarter must die away. Puisaye, in his letters since his landing, speaks with great confidence of the force and spirit still remaining in the country, and of the means which he has of co-operating with Charette, but strongly enforces, in order to give effect to them, the necessity of pecuniary aid. The utility indeed of this seems to be clear. It cannot but do good as far as it goes; and what is the comparison between the value of 50 or 100 thousand more in the expenses of this war, and the chance even of the effect that may be produced by it ? [1]

WILLIAM WINDHAM *to* WILLIAM PITT

October 16; 1795

Though I have long seen and lamented the little disposition that there is to give to the Royalist cause the sort of support which I should think necessary: of which I cannot but consider the late decision of the Cabinet as a new and unfortunate proof: yet there is one species of

[1] Fortescue MSS. iii. 137'9

resistance which I thought it was agreed to continue without abatement during the continuance of the War,— I mean that of arms, ammunition and money. Are we, however, doing any such thing? Independent of the decision, which I have just been regretting, and which will have the effect, I fear, of lessening in an inverse proportion the facility of our communication with Charette; there are no less than seven large enrolments of people, that may not be improperly called armies, the lowest being 8000, and the highest 20 or 25 thousand, some of which are in a situation to be supplied from the money sent from Monsieur, even if Monsieur should find the means of landing, and of taking that money with him. These have long represented their capacity and disposition to act, and to make important diversions, in favour of Charette, if they could be assisted by means, and those not very considerable ones, of assembling and putting their people in motion. The greatest part of these are under the conduct of people, perfectly well known to us; and on whom entire reliance can be placed for a due application of any sums entrusted to them. Some of these persons are here; and for the others are agents ready, on whom an equal reliance might be placed.

It becomes absolutely necessary to come to some resolution on this point. For, as it is, these persons are acting under a persuasion that no assistance which this country can give them of the sort above described, and of which it would be sure of the application, would be withheld. To say the truth, I feel myself in a very unpleasant situation : for, having uniformly contributed to give this persuasion in some instances more directly, in others less so, if a contrary determination is taken, or if this is not certain of being acted upon, I must of necessity take the earliest steps to undeceive them. But I may not be instrumental in leading them into an error so fatal as that of expecting that which they are not likely to receive. My own case, however, in this respect is little different from that of any member of the Government ; except inasmuch as I may have had with many of the parties more personal communication : for nothing that I have conveyed to them differs from that which is to be found in effect in various publick instruments, both written and printed. We are all, therefore, interested in coming to some explicit determination upon the subject : and interested likewise; that this should be done speedily, in order that no more precious time should be lost, of which there has been already a great deal, if the intention has been to give to the force still subsisting in Brittany all the effect of which I think it to be capable. I am the more anxious to understand distinctly what is intended with respect to these supplies, as, from a letter of Mr. Dundas of which an account was given me yesterday, I am apprehensive that some idea is entertained of stopping in degree even this article of supply. Perhaps indeed that alone, seeing the great difficulty of conveying arms into the country, will do very little ; and that if other means are not employed; that alone is hardly worth continuing.

Though the whole of the measure of evacuating differs so much from my ideas of what is expedient, so far as I am at present advised, that I am not very good counsel upon it, yet I cannot help suggesting that even with the order for bringing away the Troops; it may be very necessary to send out considerable supplies of forage, of fuel, and even of temporary buildings, as the wind may very possibly be such as to make a long interval before the embarkation, during which the troops for the want of these articles, may be grievously distressed, and yet communication with the shore not be so completely cut off as not to admit the articles being landed. With this review, whatever is so sent out should be put as much as possible on board of small vessels.

I trouble you with this long letter; not knowing how soon you are to be back.[1]

---

[1] Add. MSS. 37844 f. 104.

WILLIAM PITT *to* WILLIAM WINDHAM
Walmer Castle : October 18, 1795

I received your Letter this morning, and tho' I cannot but feel the impossibility under the present circumstances of risking any further operations with our own Troops on the Coast of France, I entirely agree with you in the Expediency of sending liberal supplies of Money, where-ever we have reasonable ground to hope that they will not be misapplied. I have accordingly given directions for procuring as expeditiously as possible a further sum of 100,000*l.* in dollars.

The Precaution you suggest of sending Stores, &c.; for our own Troops with a view to their possible detention, is certainly highly proper ; and directions have been sent for providing the most necessary articles. I shall certainly be in Town on Tuesday.[1]

EARL SPENCER *to* WILLIAM WINDHAM
Admiralty : November 10, 1795

Though you desire me not to answer your Letter of yesterday, I feel it so impossible to let the matter rest in the light in which you appear to view it, that I take the first moment which the breaking up of the House of Lords gives me, to say a few words in my own justification on the charge of a want of disposition to oblige or serve you in any respect, or upon any occasion, a point which I do assure you is very far indeed from being unimportant to my feelings.

Had I not thought you fully apprized of the true state of this matter, I should long ago have taken an opportunity of clearing it up. I have in truth been very desirous ever since I have been in Office of doing service to your Nephew,[2] and of bringing him forward. Though he was

---

[1] Add. MSS. 37844 f. 106.   [2] Captain Lukin.

obliged from the necessity of the Moment in the respect
to men to wait a good while before his Sloop was manned,
I took the earliest opportunity possible of directing that
object to be forwarded, and intended immediately to
have placed him on some of the most desirable Stations, if
at the Period when he was ordered to St. Helena, there had
been one other vessel of the same kind that could have
been appropriated to that Service, which was very pressing
and unexpectedly called for.   This unlucky circumstance
has been the Cause of the disappointment hitherto, for
had he remained in any home Station he would have
been promoted long since, but I did not think that you
could wish him to receive another Step before he had
been a single Cruize as a Master and Commander.   As to
the Instances you mention, Captains Bagot and Garnier
were attached to the Princess's Escort before I came to the
Board, and were to be promoted as a thing of Course on
their Return ; and Captain Herbert was appreciated on
the never-ceasing importunities and remonstrances of
Lord Carnarvon, who made such an outcry about his Son's
disappointments that I thought it absolutely necessary in
a political view only to gratify him ; not thinking it could
be possible that you could for a moment imagine I meant
thereby to show that Lord Carnarvon's Claims either on
the ground of Friendship or on any other ground could be
held by me in as high an estimate as yours.

I have gone into the detail because I cannot help feeling
a good deal hurt at the tenor of your letter.   God knows
I cannot avoid feeling so, if I am to conclude from it, that
any thing I have done or omitted to do has in the smallest
degree diminished your confidence in the sincerity and real
warmth of my friendship for you.   I trust however that
this explanation may be satisfactory and I shall feel the
greatest pleasure in being very soon enabled to put into
execution the Intention I had formed of promoting
Lukin immediately after his return.

If I should still have the Misfortune to appear to you

to have been deficient in what you had a Right to expect of me; I can only say that I shall look upon this as a very severe addition to the many painful circumstances which have attended the Situation into which I suffered myself to be drawn in a great degree contrary to my own judgment; and entirely against my Inclination and from my Entrance into which to this moment I have experienced little but a continued Series of Vexation and Anxiety unaccompanied by the consolation which I flattered myself would have counterbalanced them, the satisfaction of its producing considerable publick benefit.[1]

EDMUND MALONE *to* WILLIAM WINDHAM

Oxford : November 18; 1795

I ought to have thank'd you long ago for your kind letter, but you know the barrenness of Oxford, and *I* know how little time you have to spare. Notwithstanding this, however, I am tempted at present to trespass on you for five minutes, in consequence of the debates that have been lately, in your House.[2] I never, I think, before felt a strong desire to be a publick man :—not that I could do anything, if I were one, unless zeal would make up for all other defects. But I am quite out of patience at the manner in which your side of the House argue the momentous topicks now before them, and particularly with the long speech on Monday of this *cold* Attorney General with his wife and his children and his own character, &c. I cannot but think that you are all too much on the *defensive*, and that it would be infinitely better to carry the War into the Enemies' Quarters ; and to mark them out plainly and directly as men, who, if they do not conspire and intend to overturn the Constitution, *act* as if such were their intentions, and give all the counten-

---

[1] Add. MSS. 37845 f. 136.
[2] The debate on the Treasonable Practices Bill. Windham spoke on November 16.

ance they can to those who professedly have that object in view.

We have no right to argue on the motives or intentions of men, but certainly we have on their *actions ;* and we may fairly say, that those who meant the worst, could pursue no other conduct than they are pursuing.   Then why should you suffer yourselves to be *pinn'd* down to *prove* that the attempt on the King grew out of the meeting at Copenhagen House ? or out of any other specific meeting ?   I say it grew out of that and twenty other meetings ; it grew out of all the libels and seditious practices of these *three years* past ; it grew out of the French Revolution; out of French Philosophy and French Impiety ; and it grew out of the eulogiums pronounced by your opponents on all these, and the support and approbation they have uniformly given to those men; who at the very moment they were acquitted of High Treason, were convicted, in the opinion of every impartial man, of other enormous offences.

With respect to writing and seditious harrangues; Fox says, they never can produce rebellion or overthrow a constitution ; and the Civil War in the last Century and the consequent destruction of our government were occasioned by the arbitrary conduct of the King. Whatever the War was occasioned by, he must be very ill read indeed in our History, if he thinks this statement to be correct.   Did the continual attacks on the Church Establishment, which were made by the Puritans for ten years before 1644, when the Bishops were abolished, do nothing ?   Were Milton's and Goodwin's Treatises to shew that all the Ministers of the Church ought to be on a level, of no use ?   Was the Buffoon Hugh Peters,[1] who used frequently to preach on the subject of King-killing, and who, two days before King Charles was put to death, preached at St. Margaret's on the favourite text of that day—" And they bound their kings in fetters of iron," &c.,

[1] Hugh Peters (1599-1660), executed because he advocated regicide

was this of no use; to lead the minds of the misguided rabble to the point that Cromwell and the rest aimed at ? What tho' Cromwell, who was at Church that day, was observed to laugh at the buffoonery and tricks that Peters exhibited in the Pulpit; (as Fox and Sheridan may now do at Thelwall), was the mischief therefore the less ? It is of little consequence whether the constitution be overthrown by a religious fanatic in a pulpit, or a political fanatick in a Lecture Room or a Field.

As for Sheridan; and his idle babble of the Ministry having hired persons to print the treasonable handbills that are circulated, &c.; I should only apply to him what Henry the Fifth says to Falstaff, when he dismisses him :— " Reply not to me with a fool-born jest."

There never, I think, was a finer subject for speaking on, than you will have on Monday. I conjure you to give it two or three days' quiet thinking, that you may do what I know you *can do* with it.

I wish you would run your eye over, a tract written by Mr. Hobbes,[1] entitled " Considerations on the repu- tation, loyalty, manners, and religion of Thomas Hobbes; written by himself ; " and published in his tracts, 8vo., 1680. There are some good topicks in it. Lest you should not find it, I will transcribe a little from it, very applicable to the present times.—It is a Letter from Hobbes to *Dr. Wallis* (the decypherer, &c.), vindicating his own loyalty; and proving Wallis to have been the very reverse of loyal :—

" Further he [Hobbes] may say, and truly; that you were guilty of all the treasons; murders; and spoil, com- mitted by Oliver, or by any upon Oliver's or the parlia- ment's authority : for during the late troubles; who made both Oliver and the people mad, but *the preachers of your principles ?* But besides the wickedness; see the folly of it. You thought to make them mad but just to such a degree as should serve your own turn ; that is to say,

[1] Thomas Hobbes, of Malmesbury, philosopher (1588-1679).

RICHARD BRINSLEY SHERIDAN

mad and yet just as wise as yourselves. Were you not very imprudent to think to govern madness ? Paul they knew, but who were you ? Who were they that put the army into Oliver's hands (who before; as mad as he was, was too weak and too obscure to do any great mischief), with which army he executed upon such as you, both here and in Scotland, that which the Justice of God required ?

" Therefore of all the crimes (the great crime not excepted) that were done in that Rebellion; you were guilty ; you, I say, Doctor (how little force or wit soever you contributed), for your *good will* to the cause. The King was hunted as a partridge in the mountains ; and though the hounds have been hang'd, yet the hunters were as guilty as they, and deserved no less punishment.— Perhaps you would not have had the prey killed, but rather have kept it tame. And yet who can tell ? I have read of few kings deprived of their power by their own subjects, that have lived any long time after it, for reasons that every man is able to conjecture." This was written in 1662, when the old fellow was seventy four. Is it not very spirited ?

Excuse these hasty suggestions; which have probably all occurred to you again and again.[1]

EDMUND MALONE *to* WILLIAM WINDHAM

Oxford : November 29; 1795

I sit down to write you a few lines by candlelight; however ungrateful to my eyes. Some things that have lately passed in your House and some assertions that have been uncontradicted, have so provoked me, that I can't refrain—*Facit Indignatio*—and I know you will excuse my commonplace suggestions for the goodness of the intention.

If ever there has existed a Catiline since the days of

---

[1] Add. MSS. 37854 f. 134.

Cicero, it is Sheridan. A more black and determined conspirator, I am confident, never existed.—I know you have an old leaning towards him,—but no matter. He is not, indeed, noble, nor at the head of a band of profligate and ruin'd nobles, but at the head of a troop of miserable ruffians.—What would Catiline have done, had he lived now ? Would he not have begun with an unlimited approbation of the French Revolution in all its parts ? Would he not have uniformly persevered in his eulogium on it, through every stage, and through all its iniquity, carnage and atrocity, though every day's experience shewed the fallacy of all his prognostications on the subject ? Would he not shut his eyes to all the danger arising to this country from the wild doctrines grounded here upon it, and affect to treat them as mere surmises, while in fact he endeavoured to the utmost of his power to realise and bring them into effect. And finally, when his vile doctrine of equality had not spread to his mind, and tho' every sober man must be apprehensive that the common people cannot for ever withstand it, yet when he finds that it actually has *not* gained much footing, would he not, in order to give it currency cry out, that the rich set themselves against the poor, and that *they themselves* are making those distractions, which they must know can only lead to their own destruction.— Should not then this man be shewn in colours tenfold stronger than I am able to paint him ? On some part of the arts used by him and others, should there not be an appeal to the common sense of mankind ?—If Jonas Hanway or Sir Joseph Andrews, or any other man, that has devoted himself to publick charities and publick works, is for ever introducing the subject of the *Poor* then we give him credit, and it is consistent with all the rest of his character: but without saying anything invidious of S[heridan] or others, their private lives do not denote any such complete *devotion* to the interest of the distressed and wretched, and therefore these piteous complaints, it is manifest, have no other object than to set the poor against the rich, and to *put arms* in their hands for the destruction of all above themselves; and that in a country where there is such a gentle gradation of rank that there is hardly any man but what places himself in a better class than what strictly he is entitled to.

Then, for the business immediately before you. This atrocious and treasonable attack, *he* calls an *accidental outrage*, words that a scholar should be ashamed to use; but they sufficiently denote the heart and mind of the man. An outrage, *in vi primo*, cannot, like a shower of rain or fall of a stack of chimneys, be ACCIDENTAL: it necessarily denotes something premeditated, and growing out of the heart and mind of the person committing it. When Sir Charles Sedley and his friends stripped themselves stark naked, and walked thro' the Park, it was an *outrage* against decency and good manners; but can any one say that it was accidental? Did they pull off their cloaths by *accident*, and step out of the tavern in Covent Garden by *accident?* But this is metaphorical, and without resorting to it, it is manifest that this was a *traitorous* outrage, and that whoever does not consider it as such, is himself a traitor.

Another position that has pass'd current and on which this same person is most clamorous, is, that all names appended to any petition are of equal value. The object of this absurd assertion, of which it is hard to say whether the folly or wickedness be greater, is, if it be uncontradicted, to flatter the omnipotence of his friends the mob; and if it be refuted, to make the refutors unpopular.—What, on a great question of polity, if all the principal landowners in the kingdom, meeting in their respective counties, and all the principal merchants of London, call for a certain measure to repress sedition and to save the constitution from subversion, all these names are to have no more weight, than a similar or I will say double the number of such wretches as Mr. Thelwall or Horne Tooke may assemble to debate or to petition on the same measure in St. George's Fields! If it be so, then let wisdom and gravity, and education and learning, go for nothing; let all the judges, and all the Nobles, and all the wise men of the land, burn all their books, and throw all their title deeds into the fire, and each *man die by lottery*. At this rate five hundred men of the city of *York* signing a petition, from evidently self-interested views grounded on the cloathing trade suffering by war, are to be considered with as much attention and as much weight given to their advice, as if it were perfectly disinterested, and grounded upon views embracing the general interest of the whole kingdom : to state which is sufficient to shew the absurdity of it.

I am astonished at that flimzy lawyer E——'s assertion, relative to the verdict of Juries, passing uncontradicted. In my mind, it should be refuted, when ever it is mentioned. What, says he, the Verdict against Mr. York is to be final and conclusive, but not so for the persons who were tried at the Old Bailey for treason? Now, here is the merest paralogism, as I think, the Logicians call it, that can be conceived. The assertion of *acquitted felons*, which is true, and from which I never would depart, is not grounded upon the *verdict* of the Jury, but upon credible *evidence* before that jury; which, tho' in their minds, it did not convict the prisoners of High Treason, convicted them (probably in the minds of the Jury, but certainly in the minds of all the impartial part of mankind,) of other atrocious crimes, short of treason. And so in York's case *non constat*, but on his trial it appeared that the very day that he was guilty of a seditious misdemeanour, he was also guilty of a rape or of homicide or of twenty other offences, none of which are noticed in the verdict, so *vice versa* in the other case.

I know not what to say of the *wickedness* of introducing the times of Charles the First on the present occasion; —the purport of it is obvious enough but the baseness and malignity of F[ox] in introducing it, surely should not be pass'd by. What, *these* times compared,—when our constitution is completely settled by that Revolution of which we hear so much on every occasion, and when we are the envy of the world for the *perfection* of our system ? But Charles was brought to the block by the mal-administration of his *Ministers :* and all the tumult in England at present and all the danger of an *immediate revolution* (for so we are threatened) is from the present unpopular and wicked administration.—Now there is not a single part of this proposition that is not false. To begin with the last. It certainly is not true that the present Administration is unpopular. When you were with F[ox], tho' I wished the Opposition most cordially to *be* popular, I never could find, that it was generally so ; and it was the *only* Opposition I ever remember, (I mean from 1784) that was not so. But for this *remnant* of *factious traitors,* almost conspiring with France to subvert their country and to deluge it with blood, for *them* to talk of their popularity, is insufferable. Now it is equally false that Charles the First suffered by the mal-administration of his Ministers. He fell by his own vain attempt to do without parliaments for 12 years, from 1628 to 1640, and from a preconcerted scheme of the Puritans to overturn the Constitution, which was begun in the reign of King James or rather of Elizabeth. Any one that knows anything of history knows that the Puritans in that time never ceased in their attempts to destroy the *Hierarchy,* and if that be a part of the Constitution, to destroy the Constitution also. In doing this, they struggled for and established a few rights of the people ; but with no regard for Monarchy, no true notions of our present excellent mixed constitution ; for, the moment that they got any power, not contenting themselves with demolishing the bishops, the inutility of whom they and all the herd of proselytes from the schools of Geneva had been enforcing for twenty years before the Civil War, they claimed the

I   λ *power of the Army* and forced the King to make them *perpetual* by giving up his power of dissolving them; two acts which were more flagrant and pernicious violations of the constitution than any done by any English King from the days of William the Conqueror to this hour. And the Dissenters of this day, the immediate descendants of the Puritans, are not a whit better, and indubitably are equally bent on overturning the present establishment as their predecessors were. Of this there needs no other proof than their joining on all occasions with those they hate most, the Papists, to effect their purpose.—Witness Ireland lately.

Does not the personal attack on you about *leaving them*, call for a marked answer : two or three sentences that would be remembered and might be carried away ? The leaving of Traitors is a curious charge. But be assured these perpetual attacks, unless constantly repelled, undermine. And in the Vindication, might not something be said of Burke, a man whose name and memory will be respected, when those of Lauderdale, M. A. Taylor, Curwen, and all the barkers against him, are sunk in the whirlpool of Oblivion.

Pray excuse all this Rhapsody—I have written, as you may observe, and as I fear all that I have stated shews too clearly, without any deliberation ;—but I am *hearted* to the cause. I shall barely save the post.[1]

WILLIAM WINDHAM *to* MRS. CREWE

December 7, 1795

Thank you for your information relative to the poor soldiers, which shall not fail to be attended to,—though I doubt if anything can be done. Whatever sum shall be given them, there is no providing against their spending it before the time for which it was calculated, or saying, at least, that they have done so. We are going on here

[1] Add. MSS. 37854 f. 137.

in a bad way, not perhaps according to general opinion, but very much so according to mine. All the gentleman-like spirit of the country being fled, it seems to me, that a descent into Jacobinism, easy and gradual perhaps, but perfectly certain, is at this moment commenced. Fare-well! Were I twenty years younger, I would pack up my books, and retire to some corner of the world, where I might hope to enjoy the use of them unmolested, and leave the world to settle its affairs its own way. There seem to be but two modes of life to be followed with any satisfaction, military and literary. The Management of civil affairs, depending, as they do, on the consent of others, is liable to be thwarted at every step by their sordidness and folly, and is the most thankless employ-ment of all. I am sick of the world, and dissatisfied; though not for anything that I have done in the way of publick conduct.[1]

WILLIAM WINDHAM to MRS. CREWE

December 27, 1795

The world is undone by shabbiness, at least in this country, and by this sacrifice of the right to the ex-pedient. To a certain degree, it must be made; and it may be the fault of Mr. Burke, that he does not make it enough; but I am sure that, by a habit of erring on the other side, as great mischiefs are done, though more gradual and silent, and that the counsels and character of a country become insensibly debased and impoverished, as is eminently the case of ours at present. By this continual yielding, the higher nature becomes at last subjected wholly to the lower, and we are, accordingly, not governed by Mr. Pitt and others, that we naturally should be, but by Mr. Wilberforce and Mr. This-and-t'other that I could name, and who have not only low and narrow notions of things, but their own private interest

---

[1] The Crewe Papers: Windham Section, p. 29 ("Miscellanies" of the Philobiblon Society, vol ix.).

to serve. There are one or two of our friends that have minds of a more plebeian cast than I had been willing to hope. I am not in this number including Pelham, whose views of the war are, according to my conception, perfectly just, and who is not chargeable, at least as I have all reason to feel persuaded, with any mistaken conception, which I must think Grenville's to be, upon the subject of the bills. I am not inclined, however, to blame Grenville, with his opinions, for having staid away, instead of coming down to vote against them, according to a notion not always judiciously applied, that upon measures of importance you are bound in all cases to take a decided part one way or the other. Farewell ! I am for a moment in better spirits than I was, though it may very possibly be for a moment only. It is from this feeling, perhaps, as well as from what I have at all times, that I have been tempted to take up the pen and write to you more than I ought. I must now go down to some Frenchmen that I have waiting for me in different apartments, and by means of whom I hope to improve the temporary gleam of comfort that has lately come across me.[1]

WILLIAM WINDHAM *to* LORD GRENVILLE

December 16, 1795

It will be very desirable that at M. de Moustier's[2] return from Portsmouth, whither he is set off this morning, we should be prepared with such instructions, as it may be thought proper to give him ; and above all that we should make up our minds, as to the Degree, to which we will in point of fact follow up our Professions of assisting the Royalists ; supposing that they should be still desirous, as I conceive they will, of receiving our assistance.

---

[1] The Crewe Papers : Windham Section, p. 31 ("Miscellanies" of the Philobiblon Society, vol. ix.).

[2] Clément Edouard, Marquis de Moustier (born 1779), French Royalist. In 1796 he was Aide-de-camp of Louis de Frotté, chief of the Royali + ir Brittany, and later came to England.

I urge this latter point of consideration ; because I certainly do not think, that we have acted hitherto, like persons really intent on giving their assistance, which still, whenever the subject has been mentioned, we have professed to make part of our Plan.

In the Instance of the Expedition to Quiberon; every thing was done, in respect of supply, that the circumstances admitted or required : but I cannot say the same of the Period either preceding or following. For these last six weeks, stores have been lying at Portsmouth; that had been prepared for that very purpose, and were of little value for any other ; Arms have been lying there, that are not of a quality and Calibre to be employed in our service, yet I have never yet been able to obtain an order for these being put on board a ship, to take the chance of such opportunities of being landed, as we have Reason to think have actually happened, and as we have too much Reason to apprehend, are not likely to happen again.

If the Royalists of Brittany should at this moment have received any supply, the Importance of which it is impossible to calculate, they owe it to causes, from which I am afraid we can take no credit. At all Events, there is Reason to suppose, that if the Stores now lying at Portsmouth; had been sent out in time they might have received them into the Bargain; and so many more men have added to their force as there would have been muskets included in the supply. All this might have been effected without the least Interference with any other service : For I am afraid the service in Question is not sufficiently popular to hope for any attention; as long as any of the others shall remain unsatisfied in any of their least considerable wants. It is the Cinderella of the fable, which is sacrificed in every Instance to her more favoured sisters ; but which may prove like her, in the End; the only one really deserving of favor and affection.

It is very important if M. de Moustier is to go at all, that he should go as speedily as possible. It is necessary too, that a reasonable Degree of attention should be paid to his Safety; and for this Reason; as Admiral Harvey is coming away, that He should go in a frigate. On board this frigate it is very desireable, that an opportunity should be taken of sending as many arms as she can conveniently dispose of, or perhaps that a Transport or two should be sent with her. We know how long such preparations often are in being carried into Effect. It is necessary therefore, if they are to be made, that they should early be determined on.

I trouble you with the suggestion; first with a view to the paper to be prepared for M. de Moustier; and the conversation which you may wish to have with him; and then for the purpose of accelerating any meeting, which on other accounts You may wish soon to be held.[1]

WILLIAM LUKIN *to* WILLIAM WINDHAM

Boston : December 21; 1795

I have had several opportunities lately of conversing with a Naval Officer about the Quiberon expedition; who was employed in an active situation on that Service. It does in a great measure confirm the idea I had of M. Puisaye's character and conduct : the arguments and representations of this officer to me who am but ill informed are unanswerable : there is no head to be made against them if he speaks the truth; and I am sure he is quite unbiass'd and without the knowledge that his account stood the least chance of being communicated to anybody in power. He goes so far as to say; that nothing short of the most vile and base treachery could have lost the place; once in our possession; and that it must have been sold. This Man had great opportunity of seeing the different transactions; as far as they could be from

---

[1] Add. MSS. 37846 f. 12.

sea, as he commanded the *Leda's* Launch, behaved with great gallantry, and absolutely took from the beach in his boat twenty Royalists, tho' under the fire of the Enemy's guns, and with a boat sunk quite near him.

He imputes the failure (as far I mean as he could have an opportunity of judging) to two things, In the first instance to the amazing supineness of M. P[uisaye] and in the second to the disagreement and variance subsisting between him and M. Sombreuil,[1] arising, I understand, from the latter feeling a great repugnance at being commanded by a man who was not bred a soldier, and whose integrity he had reason to doubt. He adduces as proofs of the first position, that they took little or no care to throw up any works or mount any cannon upon their first landing, that the place, tho' naturally the strongest in the world next to Gibraltar, was put in no state of defence more than nature has given it, and that M. P[uisaye] threw constant obstacles in the way of those men who wished to do well, even so far as to withhold ammunition, and that the advanced Guard (at Fort [*illegible*], I think) were positively without cartridges when they were attacked, that Sombreuil who was evidently the fittest man to be placed in the situation requiring the greatest skill and gallantry was shamefully kept back in that part of the Peninsular farthest from the Isthmus ; and that, lastly, M. P[uisaye] took himself so timely to flight with his money that he was asleep in Sir J. Warren's Cabin in the height of the Massacre. He next went on to explain of what vast use the [*illegible*] Captain Ogilvie was, in taking off the Troops as she completely turned the front of the republicans, and obliged them to desist in their pursuit. The rest one is so sorry was not put in execution that I shall forbear to mention it except

---

[1] Charles Virot de Sombreuil, royalist, served in the army of the King of Prussia and afterwards under the Prince of Condé. He was sent by the British Government to superintend the debarkation of the Royalists at Quiberon Bay, but arrived twenty-four hours after the attack and was taken prisoner. As he held no military commission, he was shot.

that if they had fled to the extreme point their reembarkation might have been almost completely cover'd by the *Venus*. I am aware that I am giving you a bad account of transactions, of which you must have had the best, and that the subject, from the unlucky turn it took, may be unpleasant. Then You'll say I had little to induce me to say anything about it, but I felt that you would not be angry, and that I might by chance throw some new light upon the affair and tend to convince you that M. Puisaye is not the best man in the World, which you seem'd to doubt. It may, to be sure, be possible, that, from the possession you have of his instructions and his motive you may be able in a great measure to exculpate him. My relation of the facts are the best I could gather from a person who was on the spot and who simply said, and took such of the things, as he had from hearsay, for granted, that the generality of men then did not choose to contradict. Is it true that M. P[uisaye] is killed by the Chouans ? No fair wind, and I am quite tir'd of being here.[1]

WILLIAM WINDHAM *to* LORD GRENVILLE

December 22, 1795

Upon this occasion, and with a view to the prospects that are every day opening in that country, I cannot but lament what seems to be the determination of the Cabinet that no derangement is to be made, however inconsiderable, of the general naval service for the sake of keeping possession of Quiberon. The fleet once withdrawn, it is perfectly possible that the enemy will take possession of it, and, by stationing a few ships in proper places, and assisting them with gun-boats and batteries on shore, make it impossible for us ever afterwards to have any use of that station. How far this will be advantageous for the mere naval service may well be a question ; but I am sure if the consequence must be, as it must, the total

<hr>

[1] Add. MSS. 37912 f. 186

interception of all means of communicating with and aiding the Royalists, the general loss to the interests of the war will be such as no naval advantages, were they ten times greater than they can be hoped to be, will ever compensate. Unless it shall be the opinion of naval officers, which the accounts that I have received formerly from French naval officers does not lead me to expect, that the enemy may always be dislodged from there, I, for one, must protest strongly against that station being given up. Should the enemy, upon Admiral Harvey's coming away, slip in a few ships of the line from Orient, there is an end of all hopes of landing M. de Moustier, and much more, any of the stores which it will be desirable to send with him. There will be an end, too, if they cannot be displaced, of any further effectual support to be given to the enemies of the Republic in that quarter.[1]

LORD GRENVILLE *to* WILLIAM WINDHAM
Dropmore : December 29, 1795

I have this evening received your letter of this date, and with it a letter from M. de Moustier, which I inclose to you, as he does not seem in that paper to abandon the idea of going. He rests a great deal too much upon the reaconings he draws from his supposed employment by this Government. You know that the idea of his being sent originated with the French themselves, on receiving the account of Puisaye's arrest. They proposed as questions for our advice three alternatives, of which the best appeared to me to be (out of all question) that of sending a person of confidence to that Country with such powers as Monsieur could or would delegate to him. They made the choice, and having made it applied for a frigate to carry M. de Moustier over. It was then that the idea occurred of taking that opportunity to convey arms and stores into the Country. He now seems disposed

---

[1] Fortescue MSS iii. 21

I

to make the condition of his going, to be our keeping a squadron of large ships stationary at Quiberon.   This may or may not be a wise measure for us to adopt in the general view of a Naval Campaign, but I am most clearly of opinion that it would be utterly unfit for me to bind ourselves to him, or to the Royalists, on that subject, especially after the specimen which the passage I have marked in his paper gives us of his manner of interpreting promises.

As to the rest, I agree with you entirely and completely that Moustier's going or not going should not alter our wish to throw stores or arms into the Country, and I every day feel more strongly the absolute necessity of some communication with the Royalists to the effect stated in the note to the Duc D'Harcourt which Moustier was to have carried over.   Lord Spencer can best judge of the most convenient and expeditious mode of answering these two objects which I am earnestly desirous of forwarding by any means in my power.

What I mentioned the other day about the difficulty of throwing in supplies related rather to the question of doing it by temporary and occasional attempts without the possession of the Bay than to what might be done in favourable weather if the general services of our navy should admit of our occupying that station permanently.[1]

[1] Add. MSS. 37846 f. 16.

END OF VOLUME I

Lightning Source UK Ltd.
Milton Keynes UK
UKHW051406210319
339599UK00005B/313/P